P9-BVM-384

WITHDRAWN

PATHWAYS THROUGH ADOLESCENCE

Individual Development in
Relation to Social Contexts

 # The Penn State Series On Child & Adolescent Development

Series Editors:
David S. Palermo and Richard M. Lerner

PATHWAYS THROUGH ADOLESCENCE

Individual Development in
Relation to Social Contexts

Edited by
Lisa J. Crockett
Ann C. Crouter
The Pennsylvania State University

LEA LAWRENCE ERLBAUM ASSOCIATES, PUBLISHERS
1995 Mahwah, New Jersey

Copyright © 1995 by Lawrence Erlbaum Associates, Inc.
All rights reserved. No part of the book may be reproduced in
any form, by photostat, microform, retrieval system, or any other
means, without the prior written permission of the publisher.

Lawrence Erlbaum Associates, Inc., Publishers
10 Industrial Avenue
Mahwah, New Jersey 07430

Library of Congress Cataloging-in-Publication Data

Pathways through adolescence : individual development in relation to
social contexts / edited by Lisa J. Crockett, Ann C. Crouter.
    p.   cm.
Includes bibliographical references and indexes.
ISBN 0-8058-1500-7
    1. Adolescence—Congresses. 2. Teenagers—Social networks—
Congresses. I. Crockett, Lisa J. II. Crouter, Ann C.
HQ796.P332 1994
305.23'5—dc20   95-29514
                                                                      CIP

Books published by Lawrence Erlbaum Associates are printed on acid-free paper,
and their bindings are chosen for strength and durability.

Printed in the United States of America
10 9 8 7 6 5 4 3 2 1

Contents

RESILIENCE IN CONTEXT

6   The Knowledge Base on Resilience in
    African-American Adolescents   87
    Linda F. Winfield

7   Social Context and Adolescence: Perspectives on
    Development Among Inner-City African-American Teens   119
    Linda M. Burton, Kevin W. Allison, & Dawn Obeidallah

8   Lessons About Adolescent Development From the
    Study of African-American Youth: Commentary   139
    Susan M. McHale

PART III: INTERRELATIONS AMONG SOCIAL CONTEXTS

9   Examining Parenting Practices in Different Peer
    Contexts: Implications for Adolescent Trajectories   151
    B. Bradford Brown & Bih-Hui Huang

10 Trajectory and Forms of Institutional Participation   175
    Penelope Eckert

11 How Parenting Styles and Crowd Contexts Interact in
    Actualizing Potentials for Development: Commentary   197
    Rainer K. Silbereisen

PART IV: APPROACHES TO INTERVENTION

12 Enhancing Contexts of Adolescent Development:
    The Role of Community-Based Action Research   211
    Stephen A. Small

13 Community-Based Action Research and Adolescent
    Development: Commentary   235
    Aaron T. Ebata

PART V: FUTURE DIRECTIONS

14 Commentary: On Developmental Pathways and
    Social Contexts in Adolescence   245
    Laurence Steinberg

    Author Index   255

    Subject Index   263

Foreword

Anne C. Petersen
University of Minnesota

This volume documents the rapid growth of adolescence research. Like young adolescents when they experience their growth spurt, the field has quickly begun to examine identified gaps. This volume presents initial models and theories, as well as some results on the nature of social contexts, and their effects on adolescent development, thus providing an important start to understanding how contexts interact with individuals in shaping development. Similarly, models, theories, and results about influences on continuity and change presented in the volume advance our understanding of how developmental processes work. The volume thereby leads the field into important frontiers, with some of the contributors breaking new, exciting ground.

A continuing challenge to the field is that presented by the PRIDE effort at Penn State and stimulated by the Carnegie Corporation of New York. As we develop scientific agendas, it is important to also consider societal needs. Adolescence has become more risky for some young people in current developed societies. Although youth in these countries are less likely to die of starvation or disease than in earlier times, relative societal affluence has not protected them from such ravages as drugs, violence, or hopelessness. It is important to understand the effects of contexts and the processes of development. Doing so will improve the contexts and developmental pathways through them, increasing the likelihood that young people reach adulthood as healthy human beings who are effective in adult roles such as citizen, worker, and parent. Will at least some of our research provide information useful to policymakers and program developers interested in these goals? This is the question we should regularly pose.

This volume breaks new ground scientifically; it also poses questions about scientific relevance and pursues policy and practice implications. It establishes an important model for research–policy–practice discussions that merits further development. Thus, it is important both for the information it imparts and the approach it represents.

Preface

Young adolescents face significant turning points. For many youth 10 to 15 years old, early adolescence offers opportunities to choose a path toward a productive and fulfilling life. For many others, it represents their last best chance to avoid a diminished future.
—Carnegie Council on Adolescent Development (1989, p. 8)

The choices that adolescents make about peer relations, risky behavior, investment in school, and income-producing activities set the stage for subsequent development in later adolescence and into adulthood. Moreover, at the aggregate level, these choices have tremendous implications for the quality of life in such key social contexts as families, schools, neighborhoods, and communities. Thus, the pathways that young people follow through adolescence and beyond affect us all. Adolescents' choices, however, are not made in a vacuum; these social contexts provide opportunities—or obstacles—that influence the probability that adolescents will choose certain pathways and not others. Therefore, understanding these critical choices, and the ways in which they affect and are affected by social contexts, is of great importance both for developmental research and scholarship and for the creation of effective programs and policies focused on youth.

In October 1992, an interdisciplinary group of scholars convened at the Pennsylvania State University to discuss these issues, share findings and methodological approaches, and consider the implications of the various findings for programs and policies. Entitled "The Impact of Social Contexts on Adolescent Trajectories," the conference was organized to address two cutting-edge issues in the field of adolescence: (a) the emergence and crystallization in early adolescence of behavioral trajectories that, if maintained, could affect development throughout adolescence and into adulthood; and (b) the role of the adolescent's social contexts in establishing and maintaining these trajectories. Recognizing that adolescents participate in an array of social contexts on a daily basis, we were especially interested in how the interrelations among these contexts might influence adolescents' behavioral trajectories, or pathways. Because some of the behaviors in which adolescents engage (e.g., substance use, delinquency, sexual activity, academic involvement, prosocial behavior) can have an important impact on their future lives, we saw early adolescence as a key developmental transition—a time in which pathways begin to take shape. Ultimately, our goal was to integrate emerging perspectives on trajectories with information on adolescents' social contexts in order to explore the processes underlying healthy and less healthy pathways of development. In addition, we were interested in identifying the implications of these issues for policies and programs focused on youth.

ACKNOWLEDGMENTS

Both the conference and the development of this volume were funded by the Carnegie Corporation of New York as part of the Penn State PRIDE Project, an acronym meaning "Policy, Research, and Intervention for Development in Early Adolescence." Initiated in 1990 by Dr. Anne C. Petersen, then dean of Penn State's College of Health and Human Development, the PRIDE Project sought to create linkages among researchers from diverse disciplines, program providers, and policymakers—with the overall aim of promoting healthy development in early adolescence. In 1992, leadership of PRIDE passed to Susan McHale, Katherine Fennelly, and Ann Crouter, who organized a new wave of PRIDE activities focused on university–community collaborations to enhance youth development.

Many people contributed to making this volume a reality. First and foremost, we thank the authors of the chapters and commentaries for their excellent ideas, their openness to feedback, and the enthusiasm with which they responded to the conference discussion. We are also indebted to Bea Mandel, who handled all the logistics of the conference smoothly and professionally. Without her skillful facilitation, the conference would not have been the stimulating and enjoyable session that it was. In addition, we have benefited greatly from the skillful clerical assistance of Linda Greenawalt, Sandy Fenush, and Donna Ballock.

We appreciate the generous support of the Carnegie Corporation of New York, and of the perspectives of David Hamburg, Elena Nightingale, Vivien Stewart, and Ruby Takanishi from the Carnegie Corporation, who, in their response to the proposal for the PRIDE Project, helped push our thinking about early adolescence. We also thank Anne Petersen, Susan McHale, and Kathy Fennelly for their leadership on the PRIDE Project and their support of the conference and the creation of this volume. Finally, we thank each other, our families, and our friends—all of whom have been sources of intellectual ideas and social support during the preparation of this volume.

—L. J. Crockett
—A. C. Crouter

CHAPTER ONE

Pathways Through Adolescence: An Overview

Lisa J. Crockett
Ann C. Crouter
The Pennsylvania State University

Adolescence is commonly viewed as a period of preparation for adulthood. During adolescence, young people reach physical maturity, develop a more sophisticated understanding of roles and relationships, and acquire and refine skills needed for successfully performing adult work and family roles. The developmental tasks of this period—coping with physical changes and emerging sexuality, developing interpersonal skills for opposite-sex relationships, acquiring education and training for adult work roles, becoming emotionally and behaviorally autonomous, resolving identity issues, and acquiring a set of values (e.g., Havighurst, 1972)—are all tied to successful functioning in adulthood in one way or another.

The movement toward adulthood colors our expectations of adolescents, and hence our treatment of them. We expect adolescents to move away from the adult-directed activities of childhood toward the emotional autonomy, responsibility, and self-direction that are characteristic of adulthood. Consistent with these expectations, adolescents are granted increased freedom of choice: To varying degrees, adolescents select their academic courses; choose their friends and activities; and make plans concerning post-high-school education, employment, and family life.

Many of these decisions have important implications for young people's subsequent life course. Educational decisions, such as whether to attend college or not, affect future career opportunities and vocational development (Klaczynski & Reese, 1991; Osipow, 1983). Similarly, becoming an adolescent parent often limits educational attainment and employment opportunities

(Hayes, 1987). Such choices commit young people to certain courses of action, thus affecting the social environments they enter and the influences they encounter (Nurmi, 1993). Even short-term decisions can have serious consequences: Adolescents who go out with friends rather than study for an important test, who engage in unprotected intercourse or experiment with a new drug, or who ride home with an intoxicated driver may unknowingly affect the direction of their future lives. Moreover, short-term choices may evolve into regular patterns of behavior or lifestyles, which, in turn, influence future development (Elliott, 1993). Thus, the choices that adolescents make and the developmental course they define can profoundly shape their later lives.

Therefore, the adolescent's movement toward autonomy entails both growth and risk (Crockett & Petersen, 1993). On the one hand, adolescents need to experience greater freedom of choice so they can begin to exercise self-direction. On the other hand, their increased freedom presents risks: Empowered to make critical life decisions, adolescents may make choices that jeopardize their subsequent development. As a number of scholars have suggested (e.g., Carnegie Council on Adolescent Development, 1989; Hamburg, 1993), the risk of detrimental choices is particularly high today because adolescents' exposure to potentially dangerous behaviors has increased, while guidance in the form of consistent behavioral norms has decreased. Although many adolescents will make wise decisions despite these obstacles, some will make choices that severely limit their future opportunities. Of even greater concern is the possibility that some adolescents will develop lifestyles involving drug abuse, unprotected sexual intercourse, or violence, putting them at risk for serious long-term problems (Elliott, 1993).

Given the connection between adolescent behavior and future well-being, it is important to understand the choices that adolescents make and how patterns of behavior evolve and are maintained during this period. The premise of this volume is that we can describe the behavior patterns young people develop in adolescence, and piece together the decisions that shape their paths through adolescence and into adulthood. Moreover, we can begin to identify the dynamic processes that affect adolescents' life choices, the emergence of behavior patterns, and the development of lifestyles.

This volume seeks to address three questions. How can developmental pathways in adolescence be most usefully conceptualized? What sets of influences combine to shape adolescents' pathways? What implications do our answers to these two questions have for research and policy?

In this introductory chapter, we provide a brief overview of adolescence as a formative phase in the life course. We then offer an initial conceptualization of developmental paths in adolescence, and describe the contributions of "person" and "context" in shaping them. These observations set the stage for the chapters that follow.

ADOLESCENCE AS A TURNING POINT

Adolescence stands out as a time of significant change in multiple life domains (Crockett & Petersen, 1993; Petersen, 1987). For example, adolescents
experience the physical and hormonal changes of puberty, reach physical
maturity, and become capable of reproduction (Brooks-Gunn & Reiter, 1990).
They also mature cognitively, developing more sophisticated ways of thinking about themselves and others (Keating, 1990). On a social level, they
enter new institutional settings such as secondary schools, and they assume
new roles connected with school and jobs. These changes in biological
functioning, cognition, and social environments, in turn, precipitate transformations in interpersonal relationships and self-conceptions (Harter, 1990;
Savin-Williams & Berndt, 1990; Steinberg, 1990). The plethora of changes
presents avenues for growth in new directions, making adolescence—and
especially the early part of it—a period rich in the potential for novel behavior
and positive change (Carnegie Council on Adolescent Development, 1989;
Hamburg, 1993).

Despite the potential for plasticity, adolescence is also a period when
existing behavioral orientations have an opportunity to solidify into enduring
lifestyles (Elliott, 1993). Two processes that foster continuity in behavior—the
selection of environments and the production of environments (Bandura,
1982)—may contribute to the crystallization of behavior patterns during this
period. First, the greater autonomy granted to adolescents increases their
capacity to select companions and social settings compatible with their own
interests and proclivities. In addition, adolescents may have a greater capacity
to influence their social environments by virtue of their increased cognitive,
social, and physical maturity (Lerner, 1987; Lerner & Busch-Rossnagel, 1981).
Under these circumstances, initial behavioral dispositions can be reinforced.
Thus, although adolescence affords opportunities for change in positive
directions, it is also a time when behavior patterns may become entrenched,
increasing subsequent continuity. For these reasons, early adolescence is
considered a window of opportunity for intervention: Interventions launched
at this point in life may prevent detrimental choices and redirect young
people so that they develop healthy lifestyles with lasting benefits (Carnegie
Council on Adolescent Development, 1989; Hamburg, 1993).

PATHWAYS THROUGH ADOLESCENCE

The preceding discussion suggests that the developmental course that an
individual sets in adolescence will evince some continuity and will, in important ways, set the parameters of his or her later development. This raises
two questions driving the present volume. How might we best conceptualize

the developmental path or course an individual follows in adolescence? What set of forces shapes the path an individual takes through adolescence and into adulthood?

Defining Developmental Paths

How best to conceptualize (and operationalize) developmental paths is a matter of continuing debate (e.g., Hogan & Astone, 1986). Kagan, Kearsley, and Zelazo (1978) offered the metaphor of a *tree*. The branching of the tree represents turning points or forks in the developmental path. Normative age-graded changes such as school entry or puberty, non-normative life events such as a personal illness or parental divorce, or even chance encounters (Bandura, 1982) may precipitate a turning point. Moreover, the direction taken at each turning point affects later development. According to Kagan et al. (1978), "Each developmental journey contains many points of choice where the individual can move in any one of several directions. After each choice the probability of some final outcome is changed a wee bit" (p. 20).

Thus, in the course of development, an individual encounters numerous decision points and makes numerous "choices" (consciously or unconsciously), each having some impact on future development. The sequence of these decisions describes the individual's developmental path. Moreover, the impact of these decisions is cumulative, progressively constraining the array of subsequent options and likely developmental outcomes (Caspi, Bem, & Elder, 1989). Of course, new events and choices can always lead to redirection; and because some of the events are unforeseeable "chance encounters," prediction of outcomes is not possible except at a general level. Nonetheless, the accumulation of decisions should make certain outcomes increasingly unlikely. It is highly unlikely that a high school dropout will earn a PhD and become a university professor; similarly, barring some bizarre accident, it is highly unlikely that a university professor will become a janitor. Such outcomes are possible, but become increasingly improbable with time.

Although turning points occur throughout life, they may be concentrated in particular developmental periods. As suggested earlier, adolescence holds a number of potentially critical decision points concerning lifestyle and future roles; thus, the branching of the developmental path appears to be particularly dense during this period. Moreover, adolescents have a greater capacity than younger children to select the direction they follow at each fork in the road, and the choices they make have a greater influence on the subsequent life course than those of earlier periods. For these reasons, the path defined in adolescence has significant implications for later development. As Clausen (1986) suggested, "the sorting processes that go on in adolescence—self-sorting and social sorting—tend to determine potentialities for the rest of the life course" (p. 85).

In the present volume, we are interested in the sequence of choices that an adolescent makes, consciously or unconsciously, which together define a path and which progressively increase the likelihood of particular outcomes while reducing the likelihood of others. We see adolescence as a period of self-sorting and institutional sorting, in which the range of probable adult outcomes is progressively narrowed and a likely future life course begins to coalesce. The first goal of the volume, then, is to find ways to conceptualize an adolescent's developmental path.

Determinants of Developmental Paths

The second goal of the present volume is to identify influences that shape the specific choices an adolescent makes at key decision points and, more broadly, the path he or she follows. More precisely, the task is to identify factors that give rise to decision points, as well as processes that affect an adolescent's responses at these points and his or her subsequent behavior. To do this, we need to consider the two primary forces that jointly influence development: personal characteristics and the social environment.

Personal Characteristics. Personal characteristics affect the ways in which individuals engage their environment and, consequently, the experiences they accrue. According to Block (1981), "how experience registers, how environments are selected or modified, and how the stages of life are negotiated depend, importantly and coherently, on what the individual brings to these encounters—the resources, the premises, the intentions, the awareness, the fears and hopes, the forethoughts and afterthoughts that are subsumed by what we call personality" (pp. 40–41).

The personal characteristics of interest here are those that determine the nature and timing of the turning points that a particular adolescent confronts, those that affect the array of options available at key decision points, and those that influence the adolescent's responses or "choices." One perspective on these individual factors comes from the literature on stress and coping. Garmezy (1983) and Rutter (1983) identified several personal characteristics that affect individuals' responses to challenge. These include temperament, biological predispositions to specific types of stressors, intelligence, coping style, and social skills. Each of these characteristics may affect young people's responses to the challenges they confront in adolescence and their choices at key decision points. For example, an adolescent who responds to changes in setting and routine with intense negative emotion (difficult temperament) can expect to have more trouble coping with the normative changes of the adolescent period than one who responds to novelty with enthusiasm and a tendency to approach.

Speaking more broadly, Bronfenbrenner (1989) identified four types of "developmentally instigative" characteristics that condition young people's responses to their experiences. The first involves "personal stimulus qualities" that affect the ways in which an individual is likely to be responded to by others. These include temperament and physical attractiveness, but probably also gender and ethnicity. Three other types of characteristics affect how the individual responds to and manipulates the environment. *Selective responsivity* refers to preferences for and selection of activities and stimuli, *structuring proclivities* refers to tendencies to elaborate and restructure the environment, and *directive beliefs* reflect the individual's conception of his or her own power to reach life goals.

Many personal characteristics, such as gender, race, and intelligence, show considerable continuity from childhood through adolescence (Sameroff, Seifer, Baldwin, & Baldwin, 1993). Others, such as personality, interactional style, and characteristic ways of interpreting experience, take shape during childhood and are carried forward into adolescence—to be modified by new experiences. Some also undergo significant change during this period, particularly in early adolescence. For example, during puberty, adolescents develop secondary sex characteristics and experience a growth spurt. The changes in body size and sexual attractiveness affect the way the adolescent is treated by others. In addition, increasing cognitive sophistication is likely to affect adolescents' perceptions of both themselves and others, and hence the processes of selective responsivity, structuring proclivities, and directive beliefs. Again, these developmental changes suggest the potential for modifications in person–environment interactions, and hence in the direction taken at developmental turning points.

Contextual Influences on Adolescent Pathways. The paths that young people take through adolescence and into young adulthood also depend on the nature of the environment in which they are developing. Key contexts such as the family, school, peer group, and local neighborhood help shape the actual (and perceived) opportunities available to developing adolescents, as well as the risks to which they are exposed. These settings are embedded, in turn, in broad social, cultural, and historical contexts that shape, in part, the resources and opportunities available in those more proximal settings.

The multiple contexts that an adolescent experiences also affect development through the activities they encourage and the norms they promote. The influence of particular contexts may be synergistic, as when the child of highly educated parents attends a competitive high school with an academically oriented group of friends, or discordant, as when the academic values of the school conflict with the attitudes of parents or friends. It is not the influence of a particular context that may have the greatest impact on an adolescent's emerging path, but the pattern of influences arising from the constellation of settings (Ianni, 1989).

Contexts are dynamic; the possibility of minor and major changes in the environment is always present. However, some features of the context are likely to be more continuous than others. For example, for young adolescents, the general socioeconomic position of their family is likely to be similar across childhood and into adolescence. Taking a comprehensive approach, Sameroff and his colleagues (Sameroff et al., 1993) documented considerable stability in social and family risk factors for children followed from ages 4 to 13. Of the 10 risk factors examined, maternal education and family size were the most stable, whereas family support (i.e., presence of father) and maternal mental health demonstrated the least stability over time.

Against a backdrop of some contextual continuity, however, important contextual changes are experienced by many young people, especially in early adolescence. For example, the transition to secondary school signals both a shift in physical location and a movement from a small, often intimate setting—in which one teacher handles most of the educational content for a given group—to a large setting—in which the student moves from class to class with new teachers and, frequently, different classmates (Eccles et al., 1993; Simmons & Blyth, 1987). A change in school may lead to new friendships and new peer groups—relationships that grow in influence in adolescence (Brown, 1989). In addition, with increasing autonomy from parents, adolescents may spend more of their free time away from home, "hanging out" with friends in community settings such as malls, streets, and parks, potentially increasing the influence of neighborhood conditions on development.

Notably, the relations among key contexts, and the resulting patterns of influence, may also undergo important shifts during adolescence. For example, parents may not be able to exert as much influence over their adolescents' activities and choice of friends as they were able to exercise in early and middle childhood. Similarly, parents may find it more difficult to establish lines of communication with teachers, because adolescents are exposed to multiple teachers, each of whom teaches one subject to many students.

Non-normative events constitute another source of contextual change. These unexpected events include family moves, parental divorce and re-marriage, serious illness, and changes in parents' employment situations. Although non-normative events can occur at any point in the life span, their effects may be particularly pronounced in adolescence because they co-occur with other developmental and contextual transitions experienced during that period (Petersen, 1987; Simmons, Burgeson, Carlton-Ford, & Blyth, 1987). A non-normative event may alter structural aspects of the family environment, and it also may change key processes operating in the environment, such as parenting practices (see Crouter & McHale, 1993).

Person–Environment Interactions and Adolescent Paths. Under-standing the decisions that adolescents make, which shape their pathways into adulthood, thus requires attention to the environment and opportunities (and obstacles) it presents, as well as to the characteristics of the individual that might predispose him or her to make some choices and not others. The roles of person and environment in this process have been conceptualized in several ways. Ecologically oriented researchers have taken an interactional perspective, emphasizing that development is the product of the joint con-tribution of "person" and "context." For example, Bronfenbrenner (1979) argued that, in ecological research, main effects are likely to be interac-tions—meaning that people respond differentially to the effects of context as a function of their personal characteristics. These ideas are woven through the growing literature on "risk and resilience." Research studies indicate that, under stressful life conditions such as poverty or family dissolution, children and adolescents are "protected" by certain personal characteristics (e.g., intelligence) or certain features of the immediate environment (e.g., a close, committed relationship with an adult; Maccoby, 1983; Masten & Garmezy, 1985; Rutter & Quinton, 1984; Werner & Smith, 1982). Similarly, personal characteristics can further jeopardize the well-being of adolescents in stressful circumstances. For example, Elder and his colleagues reported that physically unattractive girls were most "at risk" to experience paternal irritability and negative parenting when fathers experienced economic deprivation during the Great Depression (Elder, van Nguyen, & Caspi, 1985).

Behavior geneticists have identified several specific ways in which the person may engage the environment (Scarr & McCartney, 1983). One process is an "evocative" one, in which the child elicits certain responses from the environment. Personal characteristics that evoke responses from others in-clude intelligence, physical attractiveness, and temperament—all qualities that have a genetic component. A second process involves the child's actively selecting activities and relationships and actively attending to and processing his or her experiences; people "niche pick" on the basis of predispositions, skills, and experiences. According to Scarr and McCartney, both processes become stronger as the child becomes more autonomous. These two proc-esses are not unlike the processes of environment selection and production discussed by Bandura (1982), or those of "personal stimulus qualities" and "selective responsivity" discussed by Bronfenbrenner (1989). However, be-havior geneticists raise two additional points: They see the processes as reflecting the child's genotype, and they note that these and other processes cause person characteristics and environment to be correlated, making it difficult to disentangle "person" and "environment" effects. This creates con-ceptual and methodological problems for analyzing the "causes" of adoles-cents' choices and their resulting developmental paths. In thinking about pathways through adolescence, we must be mindful that such routes are often selected, not randomly assigned, and that adolescents choose their routes through adolescence and into adulthood on the basis of both their personal characteristics and the forces emanating from their environments. In conclusion, an individual's path through adolescence and into adulthood depends on the history of interactions between person and environment occurring both in daily life and at critical turning points. Developmental turning points and the pathways they define are thus constrained by characteristics of the person, by resources and opportunities in the social environment, and by the patterns of interaction, or "co-action" (Gottlieb, 1991), that develop between person and context over time. Although there is widespread agreement among developmental researchers that both personal and environmental influences play an important role in shaping pathways across adolescence and into adulthood, less is known about the complex mechanisms involved. Research on this issue requires attention both to individual development and to the multiple contexts in which the individual participates. It also requires a longitudinal design, with an extended temporal canvas long enough to chart decision points and to examine their sequelae. Ideally, such studies would be comparative as well, charting how adolescents construct their pathways through adolescence in settings that differ dramatically in terms of resources, opportunities, and definitions of both adolescent and adult "success." Currently, we know little about how distinct populations of adolescents undertake the process of moving through adolescence and into adulthood. This volume is an attempt to pull together a diverse set of researchers who have demonstrated their interest in parts of the complex array of issues outlined here.

ORGANIZATION OF THE VOLUME

The volume is organized around the three questions identified at the outset, as well as related themes. The first section is devoted to charting pathways through adolescence and identifying the processes that maintain continuity (or produce discontinuity) in behavior. The chapter by Huizinga (chap. 2) charts pathways in one particular domain—delinquent behavior. Huizinga examines several types of delinquency and the factors associated with transitions from one type to another. The chapters by Cairns, Leung, and Cairns (chap. 3), and Caspi (chap. 4) point to interactions between person and environment that promote behavioral continuity and the differentiation of developmental pathways. Cairns et al. discuss adolescents' social groups, identifying processes of peer-group selection that may support continuity in antisocial behavior despite changes in peer-group membership. Caspi focuses on the impact of school context on girls' delinquency, and finds that the effect of a mixed-sex environment depends on personal characteristics of the girls. The commentary chapter by Crockett (chap. 5) discusses conceptual models of developmental pathways, as well as the role of the social context in shaping pathways and promoting continuity in behavior. The second section focuses on the impact of social contexts on the lives of African-American adolescents. Winfield (chap. 6) addresses the issue of resilience, focusing on the potential role of the school and community in fostering healthy development among African-American adolescents. Burton, Allison, and Obeidallah (chap. 7) address the role of poverty in shaping the developmental paths of inner-city youth. The commentary by McHale (chap. 8) examines the implications of research findings on African-American youth for developmental theory and interventions.

The third section of the volume examines the interrelations among key social contexts (family, peers, and school), and how they influence adolescents' behavior, choices, and preparation for adulthood. Brown and Huang (chap. 9) discuss the capacity of the peer group to moderate the effects of parenting style on adolescent behavior. Eckert (chap. 10) illustrates how the "fit" between the institutional goals of the high school and the values of different peer groups create divergent high school experiences among youth and shape their orientations toward social institutions in general. The commentary by Silbereisen (chap. 11) presents alternative interpretations of some of the data on peer groups presented in these chapters.

The fourth section focuses on community-based approaches to research and interventions with adolescents. Small (chap. 12) presents a collaborative model, in which researchers and communities cooperate to implement research on youth and to develop interventions to facilitate positive outcomes. The commentary by Ebata (chap. 13) focuses on key issues raised by Small's "community-based action-research" model, and points to gaps in the current research base. In the final chapter and section, Steinberg (chap. 14) offers an overall commentary on the volume and the field of adolescent development. He chronicles the sequence of conceptual models of adolescent development, compares this to the current volume's focus on pathways and social contexts, and suggests some directions for future research and policy initiatives.

REFERENCES

Bandura, A. (1982). The psychology of chance encounters and life paths. *American Psychologist, 37*, 747–755.

Block, J. (1981). Some enduring and consequential structures of personality. In A. I. Rabin, J. Aronoff, A. Barclay, & R. Zucker (Eds.), *Further explorations in personality* (pp. 27–43). New York: Wiley.

Bronfenbrenner, U. (1979). *The ecology of human development: Experiments by nature and design.* Cambridge, MA: Harvard University Press.

Bronfenbrenner, U. (1989, April). *The developing ecology of human development: Paradigm lost or paradigm regained?* Paper presented at the biennial meeting of the Society for Research on Child Development, Kansas City, MO.

Brooks-Gunn, J., & Reiter, E. O. (1990). The role of pubertal processes. In S. S. Feldman & G. R. Elliott (Eds.), *At the threshold: The developing adolescent* (pp. 16–53). Cambridge, MA: Harvard University Press.

Brown, B. B. (1989). The role of peer groups in adolescents' adjustment to secondary school. In T. J. Berndt & G. W. Ladd (Eds.), *Peer relationships in child development* (pp. 188–215). New York: Wiley.

Carnegie Council on Adolescent Development. (1989). *Turning points: Preparing youth for the 21st century.* Washington, DC: Author.

Caspi, A., Bem, D. J., & Elder, G. H., Jr. (1989). Continuities and consequences of interactional styles across the life course. *Journal of Personality, 57,* 375–406.

Clausen, J. (1986), *The life course: A sociological perspective.* Englewood Cliffs, NJ: Prentice-Hall.

Crockett, L. J., & Petersen, A. C. (1993). Adolescent development: Health risks and opportunities for health promotion. In S. G. Millstein, A. C. Petersen, & E. O. Nightingale (Eds.), *Promoting the health of adolescents: New directions for the twenty-first century* (pp. 13–37). New York: Oxford University Press.

Crouter, A. C., & McHale, S. M. (1993). Familial economic circumstances: Implications for adjustment and development in early adolescence. In R. M. Lerner (Ed.), *Early adolescence: Perspectives on research, policy, and intervention* (pp. 71–91). Hillsdale, NJ: Lawrence Erlbaum Associates.

Eccles, J. S., Midgley, C., Wigfield, A., Buchanan, C. M., Reuman, D., Flanagan, C., & MacIver, D. (1993). Development during adolescence: The impact of stage-environment fit on young adolescents' experiences in schools and in families. *American Psychologist, 48,* 90–101.

Elder, G. H., van Nguyen, T., & Caspi, A. (1985). Linking family hardship to children's lives. *Child Development, 56,* 361–375.

Elliott, D. S. (1993). Health-enhancing and health-compromising lifestyles. In S. G. Millstein, A. C. Petersen, & E. O. Nightingale (Eds.), *Promoting the health of adolescents: New directions for the twenty-first century* (pp. 119–145). New York: Oxford University Press.

Garmezy, N. (1983). Stressors of childhood. In N. Garmezy & M. Rutter (Eds.), *Stress, coping, and development in children* (pp. 43–84). New York: McGraw-Hill.

Gottlieb, G. (1991). Experiential canalization of behavioral development: Theory. *Developmental Psychology, 27,* 4–13.

Hamburg, D. A. (1993). The opportunities of early adolescence. *Teachers College Record, 94,* 466–471.

Harter, S. (1990). Self and identity development. In S. S. Feldman & G. R. Elliott (Eds.), *At the threshold: The developing adolescent* (pp. 352–387). Cambridge, MA: Harvard University Press.

Havighurst, R. J. (1972). *Developmental tasks and education* (3rd ed.). New York: McKay.

Hayes, C. D. (Ed.). (1987). *Risking the future: Adolescent sexuality, pregnancy, and childbearing* (Vol. 1). Washington, DC: National Academy Press.

Hogan, D., & Astone, N. (1986). The transition to adulthood. *Annual Review of Sociology, 12,* 109–130.

Ianni, F. A. J. (1989). *The search for structure: A report on American youth today.* New York: Free Press.

Kagan, J., Kearsley, R. B., & Zelazo, P. R. (1978). *Infancy: Its place in human development.* Cambridge, MA: Harvard University Press.

Keating, D. P. (1990). Adolescent thinking. In S. S. Feldman & G. R. Elliott (Eds.), *At the threshold: The developing adolescent* (pp. 54–89). Cambridge, MA: Harvard University Press.

Klaczynski, P. A., & Reese, H. W. (1991). Educational trajectory and "action orientation": Grade and track differences. *Journal of Youth and Adolescence, 20,* 441–462.

Lerner, R. M. (1987). A life-span perspective for early adolescence. In R. M. Lerner & T. T. Foch (Eds.), *Biological-psychosocial interactions in early adolescence* (pp. 9–34). Hillsdale, NJ: Lawrence Erlbaum Associates.

Lerner, R. M., & Busch-Rossnagel, N. A. (1981). Individuals as producers of their development: Conceptual and empirical bases. In R. M. Lerner & N. A. Busch-Rossnagel (Eds.), *Individuals as producers of their development: A life-span perspective* (pp. 1–36). San Diego, CA: Academic Press.

Maccoby, E. E. (1983). Social-emotional development and response to stressors. In N. Garmezy & M. Rutter (Eds.), *Stress, coping, and development in children* (pp. 217–234). New York: McGraw-Hill.

Masten, A. S., & Garmezy, N. (1985). Risk, vulnerability, and protective factors in developmental psychopathology. In B. B. Lahey & A. E. Kazdin (Eds.), *Advances in clinical child psychology* (Vol. 8, pp. 1–51). New York: Plenum.

Nurmi, J. E. (1993). Adolescent development in an age-graded context: The role of personal beliefs, goals, and strategies in the tackling of developmental tasks and standards. *International Journal of Behavioral Development, 16,* 169–189.

Osipow, S. H. (1983). *Theories of career development.* Englewood Cliffs, NJ: Prentice-Hall.

Petersen, A. C. (1987). The nature of biological-psychosocial interactions: The sample case of early adolescence. In R. M. Lerner & T. T. Foch (Eds.), *Biological-psychosocial interactions in early adolescence* (pp. 35–61). Hillsdale, NJ: Lawrence Erlbaum Associates.

Rutter, M. (1983). Stress, coping, and development: Some issues and some questions. In N. Garmezy & M. Rutter (Eds.), *Stress, coping, and development in children* (pp. 1–41). New York: McGraw-Hill.

Rutter, M., & Quinton, D. (1984). Long-term follow-up of women institutionalized in childhood: Factors promoting good functioning in adult life. *British Journal of Developmental Psychology, 2,* 191–204.

Sameroff, A. J., Seifer, R., Baldwin, A., & Baldwin, C. (1993). Stability of intelligence from preschool to adolescence: The influence of social and family risk factors. *Child Development, 64,* 80–97.

Savin-Williams, R. C., & Berndt, T. J. (1990). Friendship and peer relations. In S. S. Feldman & G. R. Elliott (Eds.), *At the threshold: The developing adolescent* (pp. 277–307). Cambridge, MA: Harvard University Press.

Scarr, S., & McCartney, K. (1983). How people make their own environments: A theory of genotype-environment effects. *Child Development, 54,* 424–435.

Simmons, R. G., & Blyth, D. A. (1987). *Moving into adolescence: The impact of pubertal change and school context.* Hawthorne, NY: Aldine.

Simmons, R. G., Burgeson, R., Carlton-Ford, S., & Blyth, D. A. (1987). The impact of cumulative change in early adolescence. *Child Development, 58,* 1220–1234.

Steinberg, L. (1990). Autonomy, conflict, and harmony in the family relationship. In S. S. Feldman & G. R. Elliott (Eds.), *At the threshold: The developing adolescent* (pp. 255–276). Cambridge, MA: Harvard University Press.

Werner, E. E., & Smith, R. (1982). *Vulnerable but invincible: A longitudinal study of resilient children and youth.* New York: McGraw-Hill.

PART ONE

DEVELOPMENTAL TRAJECTORIES
IN ADOLESCENCE

CHAPTER TWO

Developmental Sequences in Delinquency: Dynamic Typologies

David Huizinga
University of Colorado

There has been recent interest in the notion of developmental sequences, pathways, or progressions in delinquent behavior (Farrington, Ohlin, & Wilson, 1986; Huizinga, Esbensen, & Weiher, 1991; Loeber & LeBlanc, 1990; Loeber et al., 1993), although it is not perfectly clear whether references to such sequences or pathways refer to growth curves of particular kinds of delinquent behavior, normative behavior patterns for specific ages, sequences of ages of initiation of different behaviors, or the movement between various types and levels of involvement in delinquent behavior. In addition, given a particular notion of a sequence or pathway, it is not clear what kinds of procedures can or should be used in identifying a specific pathway and the individuals who traverse it. Also, as Loeber et al. (1993) noted, there are only a few studies examining developmental sequences of delinquency, and even fewer prospective studies examining this issue. As a result, little is known about the paths taken in a delinquent or criminal career or the long-term adult outcome of child and/or adolescent delinquent involvement, although some findings and considerations about these issues can be found in Moffit (1993), Farrington (1986), and Elliott (1994).

In this chapter, a typological approach is used to provide some preliminary examination of developmental sequences in delinquent behavior over the child to adolescent years. Thus, the focus is on the through-time movement of individuals through various types or combinations of delinquent behavior, rather than on the through-time changes or relationship of particular variables. In this sense, a pathway represents a particular sequence of behaviors

15

traversed by some group of individuals that is different from the sequences of behaviors followed by others. The importance of focusing on persons and types of persons, rather than variables, in developmental research has been recently emphasized by Bergman and Magnusson (1992). Analyses that relate variables to each other do not generally allow identification of groups having different developmental behavioral patterns.

In some previous work (Huizinga et al., 1991; Huizinga, Esbensen, & Weiher, 1993), the use of both empirical typologies derived through cluster analysis and conceptual typologies based on a priori definitions have been illustrated. However, because delinquent behavior is not a uniform domain, but rather a heterogenous collection of problem behaviors (whose unifying theme is that they are problematic and proscribed by law), exactly what kinds of delinquency and levels of involvement should be included in an examination of developmental progressions in delinquency is not obvious. Distinctions in frequency, seriousness, and "kind" of behavior are all possible. In this chapter, the work of Loeber (1988) and Loeber et al. (1993) is followed by conceptually identifying overt or aggressive behaviors and covert or concealing behaviors, and classifying individuals on the basis of their involvement in one or both of these kinds of behaviors. In addition, a status offense–public disorder set of offenses is used to identify individuals engaged in these behaviors. This conceptual framework allows the separation of aggression (a factor of some current concern) from other forms of delinquent behavior, so that the developmental relationship of other kinds of behavior to aggression can be examined.

The ability to identify transitions between behavioral patterns in a longitudinal typology also affords the opportunity to examine etiological factors that influence these transitions. A preliminary examination of some explanatory factors that describe adolescents who move to an aggressive status, who terminate involvement in this behavior, or who are not involved in aggression over a several-year period is also provided to illustrate this potential.

SOME COMMENTS ON A PERSON-CENTERED DEVELOPMENTAL TYPOLOGY

Given the use of a person-oriented typological approach in this chapter, it is perhaps appropriate to further specify the variable-oriented versus person-oriented distinction, and to provide some further details of the use of a typological approach in obtaining a developmental perspective (although only some concepts of such an approach are illustrated in later sections of this chapter). In focusing on the relationship between variables, the goal is often to understand how one, or several, variables affect other variables. Frequently this involves the use of omnibus models, with the supposition that the variables have the same relationship or "work the same way" for everyone (i.e, for all elements of some population), and to eliminate individual differences by considering such differences as "error" that hides true underlying multivariate relationships. In contrast, a person-oriented typological approach assumes that there may be types or patterns of person/individual characteristics that give rise to various subgroups, and within each subgroup the variable relationships "work in different" ways. The use of such a typological approach clearly presumes that the over-time configurations of individual situations and characteristics are not the same for everyone, but that these personal configurations are not so unique that they prevent the identification of groups with similar developmental stages or processes.

In addition, the developmental typological approach often focuses on state-to-state or type-to-type changes, thus providing descriptions of evolving stages of individual characteristics and behavior patterns. Thus, the approach provides probabilities for an array of qualitatively, as well as quantitatively, different outcomes; provides probabilities for particular sequences or paths that relate initial to outcome states; and provides for a variety of person–situation configurations (Runyon, 1980). The use of person-centered developmental typologies to obtain descriptions of changing behavioral configurations or types over time helps answer the question, "Given a particular behavioral history, what behavior patterns are likely to come next?" These typologies are also useful in examining the influence of etiological variables on behavioral transitions and thus explain why some individuals with a common behavioral history move to a particular behavioral pattern, while similar individuals move to another.

The use of a person-oriented typological approach to provide a developmental perspective is not particularly new (e.g., Carter, Morris, & Blashfield, 1982; Huizinga, 1979; Rice & Mattson, 1966; Runyan, 1980). But the emphasis on the importance of this approach in providing an appropriate developmental perspective appears more recent (Bergman & Magnusson, 1992; Cairns, 1986; Cairns, Cairns, & Neckerman, 1989; Magnusson & Bergman, 1990). There are, however, a number of methodological issues that arise in the construction of such typologies. How are the types to be identified? How are the transitions between types to be described? How is the influence of etiological variables to be examined? There are a number of answers to each of these questions, but for none is there one generally accepted procedure, nor is there a fully developed, generally available package that attempts to integrate the pieces of a full person-oriented developmental, typological analysis. That is, current analytic strategies are not designed to search for and identify types of individuals with different developmental sequences, nor are they equipped to identify covariance matrices with nonlinear interactions for different unspecified and unknown subgroups.

To identify the developmental types in a developmental dataset, in which there are measures taken on the same subjects at a number of time points, a simple procedure is to conceptually divide measurement variables into distinct parts (e.g., high, medium, low), and then at each time point to cross-classify individuals by their position on each of the variables. Alternatively, numerical taxonomy or cluster-analytic methods could be used at each time point to identify "clusters" or types of persons in the time-ordered multivariate space. These procedures are generally available as part of standard statistical computer packages.[1] Given a set of types at each time point, the developmental or longitudinal types can then be formed by grouping those who belong to the same sequence of types across time, and the resulting developmental types might be considered a set of multivariate developmental profiles.[2] If there are measures from several domains at a given time point, all the measures could be used simultaneously in the classification process, or separate classifications could be created for each domain and the final types constructed by cross-classifying the distinct partitions formed within each domain. Additionally, it should be noted that there is no requirement that the measures or domains of measurement used in a developmental typology remain constant over time.

Once the types have been identified, descriptions of the types at each time point are relatively straightforward. However, descriptions of the movement between types across time often become more cumbersome, and frequently face a "plethora of types" problem. Some options include simple description of type-to-type transitions, tree diagrams, listings of sequences of time-ordered types, and the use of transition matrices, which provide the probabilities that an individual in a given type at one point in time will move to another type at the next point in time. In addition, the concepts of absorbing states, occupation and passage times, and recurrent versus transient states can be usefully borrowed from Markov chain analysis (see, e.g., Parzen, 1962), although it seems unlikely that the transition matrices of developmental processes would satisfy the Markov property (i.e., that the movement from one state to the next is only dependent on the current state and not on prior history).

In examining etiological or predictive variables, at least three options for examining the ability to predict certain state-to-state transitions, sequences of state-to-state transitions, or final-outcome states can be identified. First, the explanatory or predictive variables can be included in the formation of the original types or classification. Descriptive relationships between levels of explanatory variables and particular stages of the developmental types may

[1]It should be noted that simply executing a cluster-analytic procedure does not guarantee that the clusters returned are particularly distinct entities. Thus, careful evaluation of the distinctness and separation of the derived clusters is necessary.

[2]A different approach to the construction of developmental types is also possible, in which all variables across all time points are considered simultaneously (e.g., in a cluster analysis). Given several measurement variables at several time points, however, the quality of the derived clusters often becomes questionable, and therefore this method is not pursued in this chapter.

then become clear as a description of the developmental typology is constructed. Second, separate classifications based on the explanatory variables could be created at particular time points, and the resulting partition of individuals cross-classified with the original developmental typology or at specific time points of the typology, thus specifying conditional transition probabilities that depend on levels and interactions of postulated explanatory variables. Third, the transition probabilities could be expressed as functions of the explanatory variables. Except for Markov models (see, e.g., Tuma & Hannan, 1984), however, the statistical machinery for obtaining estimates of these functions is not available, hence in general, this is currently not a viable option.

With this overview of the construction of a person-centered developmental typology, the remainder of this chapter returns to the relatively simple example of such a typology that employs data from a study of delinquency.

METHODS

Sample

The data used in this chapter come from the Denver Youth Survey (DYS),[3] an ongoing longitudinal study of the development of prosocial or conventional behavior and of the development of delinquency, drug use, and other problem behavior. The overall design of the study is based on an accelerated longitudinal survey. That is, the sample includes multiple birth cohorts with overlapping age ranges during the survey years, so that a wide age range can be examined in only a few years. The survey involves annual personal interviews with a probability sample of five birth cohorts and their parents, selected from areas of Denver, Colorado that have a high risk for delinquency. The subjects include 807 boys and 721 girls. At the point of the first annual survey, covering the 1987 period, the child and adolescent subjects were 7, 9, 11, 13, and 15 years of age. To date, five annual surveys have been completed; of the 1,528 Year 1 respondents, over 91% have completed interviews in each of the second through fifth years, and over 90% have participated in at least 4 of the 5 years. This chapter uses data from the first 4 years of the survey.

Selection of survey respondents entailed a three-stage process. First, neighborhoods were selected based on their "high-risk" status. Risk was determined by a social-ecology (factor and cluster) analysis that identified

---

[3]The Denver Youth Survey is part of a larger collaborative research effort known as the Program of Research on the Causes and Correlates of Delinquency; it involves the University of Colorado, the University of Pittsburgh, and the State University of New York at Albany. Some recent comparative findings across the sites of this program are available in Huizinga, Loeber, and Thornberry (1993, 1994).

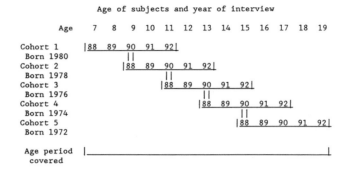

FIG. 2.1. Research design of the Denver Youth Survey. Five birth cohorts, ages 7, 9, 11, 13, and 15 in 1987, interviewed annually in 1988, 1989, 1990, 1991, and 1992.

"socially disorganized" areas (based on socioeconomic status [SES], family structure, housing characteristics, mobility, ethnicity, and age composition), and by official crime rates.[4] Second, all households in these communities were enumerated. Third, interviewers were sent in person to a random sample of these addresses. This last stage required interviewers to speak with an adult and determine the ages of household members in approximately 20,000 households. All eligible children and youth in the selected households became the subjects for the study, thus eligible siblings were included. Over 92% of the selected households were successfully screened for the presence of eligible youth, and over 85% of identified eligible children and youth—and one of their parents—participated in the study.

The design of the study and demographic characteristics of the sample are given in Fig. 2.1 and Table 2.1. As can be seen in the figure, after the first 3 years of the study, the cohorts begin to overlap at ages 9, 11, 13, and 15; at the fifth year, the cohorts cover the 7- to 19-year-old age period. The sample consists largely of minority youth, with only 10% of the sample identifying themselves as White. At the point of the first survey, 42% of the child and youth respondents lived in single-parent households, 38% lived with both natural parents, 10% lived with a natural parent and a stepparent, and 10% were in other living arrangements.

Measures

Although the DYS involves measurement of a wide range of behaviors and etiological variables, the focus here is on delinquent behavior and a few explanatory factors. As part of the annual surveys of the DYS, child and youth

---

[4]For recent reviews of social ecology and social disorganization, and their relationship to crime and delinquency, see Bursik and Grasmick (1992) or Sampson and Lauritsen (1992).

TABLE 2.1
Sample Characteristics of the Denver Youth Survey

Characteristics	Sample (N)	%
Sex		
Male	807	53
Female	721	47
Total	1,528	—
Race		
White	152	10
African American	505	33
Hispanic	685	45
Other	185	12
Age		
7	346	23
9	309	20
11	301	20
13	303	20
15	269	18
Family Structure		
Natural parents	581	38
One natural, one stepparent	149	10
Single parent	647	42
Other	148	10

respondents are asked how many times in the past year they have engaged in each of a variety of delinquent acts. The delinquency measures used in this chapter are based on a subset of these items. The included items were grouped into overt-aggressive behaviors, covert-theft behaviors and status–disorder behaviors. The items included in these categories are listed in Table 2.2.

Based on these categories of behavior, a typology was developed that emphasized the role of aggression and theft behaviors (i.e., involvement in these behaviors superseded involvement in status and other offenses as a type definition) and that required more than a single exploratory involvement in each type of behavior. The following types were defined:

Nondelinquent (or exploratory): No more than one offense of each category (aggressive, theft, status–disorder).

Status: At least two status–disorder offenses, and only one or zero from each other category.

Theft: At least two theft offenses, only one or zero aggressive offenses, and any number of status–disorder offenses.

Aggression: At least two aggressive offenses, but only one or fewer theft offenses, and any number of status–disorder offenses.

TABLE 2.2
Delinquency Measures of Denver Youth Study

Measure	Youth (Ages 11–19)	Child (Ages 7–10)
Overt-Aggressive	Aggravated assault	Physical fighting other kids
	Robbery	Physical fighting siblings
	Gang fights	Hitting adults
	Rape	Throw objects to injure
	Hit to injure	Purse snatch
	Throw objects to injure	Carried hidden weapon
	Purse snatch	
	Carried hidden weapon	
Covert-Theft	Burglary	Burglary
	Theft less than $5	Stolen at school
	Theft $5–$50	Stolen bike
	Theft $50–$100	Theft from car
	Theft more than $100	Taken money at home
	Joyriding	Avoided payment
	Auto theft	Arson
	Fencing	
	Illegal credit card use	
	Other fraud	
	Avoided payment (sneaking in, etc.)	
	Arson	
Status–Disorder	Runaway	Runaway
	Skip school	Skip school
	Vandalism	Vandalism
	Public disorder	Public disorder
	Prostitution	
	Drug sales	

Both: Two or more aggressive offenses, two or more theft offenses, and any number of status–disorder offenses.

In some prior research, we have found evidence that individuals engaged in particular delinquency offenses do not necessarily engage in these behaviors in consecutive years, even though they have extended multiple-year involvement (Elliott, Huizinga, & Morse, 1987; Huizinga et al., 1993). Because of this, individuals were classified by their most "serious" type in adjacent years, with the intent that, by examining 2-year intervals, the through-time types might be more stable. For example, for the ages of 7 and 8, and using the previous typology, individuals were classified as nonoffenders if they were nonoffenders at both of these ages, as theft offenders if they fit the theft classification in at least one of these years, as aggressive offenders if they fit the aggressive classification in at least one of these years, or as "both" if they met the criteria for both theft and aggressive types during the 2-year period.

To examine some potential explanatory factors related to aggression, variables found to relate to delinquency in previous studies from the family, school, peer, personal, and neighborhood contexts were used. Theoretical rationales for most of these variables can be found in Elliott, Huizinga, and Ageton (1985) and Elliott, Huizinga, and Menard (1989). Included are: parental monitoring and youth involvement in family activities; involvement in other conventional activities (school, community, religious); attachment to school and school grades; personal attitudes and characteristics of (a) attitudes about the wrongness of delinquent behavior; (b) neutralization or moral disengagement, (c) guilt associated with engaging in delinquent acts, (d) empathy, and (e) self-esteem; and the delinquent behavior of the respondent's friends. Further descriptions of these measures are included in the appendix.

Identifying and Examining Longitudinal Types

As noted earlier, to identify patterns of type-to-type transitions over time, several options are available. For example, these "developmental pathways" or "longitudinal typologies" could be displayed by listing all possible type-to-type transitions and examining their characteristics and correlates. Alternatively, hierarchical tree structures, or dendograms, could be constructed with earlier stages combining to form later stages and leading to some final outcome state. If there is a good deal of movement between types, however, these approaches identify a large number of longitudinal types, often too many for reasonable presentation. An alternative, and the one used in this chapter, is to examine transition matrices of the type-to-type changes over time. This not only provides summaries of type-to-type transitions, but also allows determination of the probability of moving from initial states to later states through matrix multiplication.

RESULTS

Distribution of Delinquent Behavior Patterns

The distribution of the previously described delinquency types by sex and age is given in Table 2.3. Because the design of the study involves multiple overlapping cohorts, the information from each of the cohorts that overlap at given ages has been combined to provide an estimate for these ages. Although this ignores potential cohort differences, given the relatively short time interval involved, it is assumed that such variations reflect sampling differences in cohorts and not systematic cohort or period effects, so that the combined estimate is not unreasonable.

As seen in the table, for both females and males with increasing age, there is a general increase in the proportion of youth who become substantially

TABLE 2.3
Distribution of Delinquency Types by Age and Sex

Age	Nondelinquent	Status–Disorder	Theft	Aggression	Both
		Males			
7–8	66.7	5.2	6.1	17.2	4.8
9–10	56.7	5.3	5.5	22.6	9.9
11–12	53.0	11.1	6.6	15.8	14.7
13–14	32.5	19.5	9.1	16.6	22.4
15–16	19.5	30.3	13.4	13.9	23.0
17–18	17.6	34.2	14.6	12.0	21.6
		Females			
7–8	73.1	4.6	6.7	13.1	2.5
9–10	71.1	5.3	6.7	13.5	3.5
11–12	68.3	11.7	7.9	7.6	4.6
13–14	33.7	32.9	7.5	14.1	11.9
15–16	23.6	85.4	12.4	11.2	10.3
17–18	24.5	49.0	9.9	10.6	6.1

involved in delinquency. For both sexes, there is a sizable jump in the prevalence of delinquency at ages 13–14, with only about one third of each sex being classified as nondelinquent at this age. Interestingly, at the younger ages, the most prevalent form of delinquency is involvement in only aggressive behavior, whereas at the older ages involvement in only status–disorder offenses is the most prevalent. Again, this holds for both sexes.

With increasing age, there is also a general increase in the prevalence of individuals engaged only in theft (more pronounced for boys than girls), but a general decrease in the prevalence of individuals engaged only in aggression, and a general increase in the prevalence of individuals involved in both behaviors. Although during the teen years the largest percentage of males involved in the more "serious" theft and aggressive behaviors are involved in both kinds of behavior, a substantial proportion are involved in only theft or only aggressive behaviors. This fact suggests specialization in either covert or overt behaviors by some individuals during at least some part of their lives. For females, specialization appears to be more prevalent than engaging in both kinds of behavior at all ages.

Longitudinal Sequences in Types of Delinquent Behavior

Although normative data by age are of interest, they do not provide information about developmental type-to-type transitions with increasing age. As noted earlier, for this purpose transition matrices for the age-to-age transitions were constructed. These matrices are displayed for males and females in Tables 2.4 and 2.5. It should be recalled that these matrices reflect data over a 4-year period, with initial states covering a 2-year period and outcome states covering a 2-year period as described earlier. In somewhat standard notation, the rows of each matrix reflect the status of individuals at earlier ages (or input status), and the columns reflect the status at later ages (or output status). The total row and column percentages are also provided to indicate the relative size of each type at each age. For example, Table 2.4 reveals that for the 66.7% of the 7- to 8-year-old age group that are nondelinquent, 73% remained nondelinquent at ages 9–10, whereas 3.3% of this type became status–disorder offenders, 4.1% became theft offenders, 17.8% were involved in aggression only, and 1.9% were involved in both theft and aggression.

Given the design of the study, each of these matrices reflects the experience of a particular cohort, so that each is based on the same sample of individuals. If it were assumed that there was equivalence across cohorts, so that the set of matrices could be considered a "synthetic cohort," the transitions across the full age range of 7–18 could be examined by multiplying the appropriate transition matrices. This is a rather large and unfounded assumption to make, however. Hence, except for some general observations, this possibility will not be pursued in any detail.

As these matrices illustrate, for both boys and girls, even allowing 2-year periods for type identification, the delinquency typology is rather unstable at any age. In general, one half or less (and often substantially less) of each type maintains the same delinquency classification in the next time period. Also, although there are more frequent longitudinal type-to-type transitions, in general the data do not suggest an invariant pattern of developmental stages or types of delinquent behavior that is applicable to a majority of youth.

There are some clear age and sex differences in the type-to-type transitions. For males at younger ages (7–10), the most likely transition from a nondelinquent status is to a status involving only aggressive behavior, although at the next age period the largest proportion of these early aggressive individuals reverts to a nondelinquent status. In contrast, for male teenagers and females at most ages, the most likely transition is from a nondelinquent status to a status–disorder offender type. However, movement out of the status–disorder type includes movement to all of the other types, and rates of movement appear to vary with age. Thus, a large number of "pathways" through types or sequences of delinquent behavior occur.

In general, there appears to be a consistent ordering of the stability (i.e., the probability of maintaining a particular classification over time) of the more serious delinquency types across ages (at least across ages 7–16). Being involved in both theft and aggression is more stable (30%–50%) than being

TABLE 2.4
Transition Matrices of Delinquency Types for Males by Age

		Ages 9–10				
		Non	Stat	Thft	Aggr	Both
		65.7	4.0	5.9	17.4	7.0
	Non	73.0	3.3	4.1	17.8	1.9	66.7
Ages 7–8	Stat	76.1	10.4	0.0	0.0	13.5	5.2
	Thft	50.0	11.6	11.6	8.9	17.9	6.1
	Aggr	45.9	3.2	11.4	29.1	10.4	17.2
	Both	45.0	0.0	11.3	0.0	43.7	4.8

		Ages 11–12				
		Non	Stat	Thft	Aggr	Both
		57.1	9.5	5.9	17.3	10.1
	Non	75.8	7.0	3.7	11.1	2.5	47.6
Ages 9–10	Stat	70.5	11.6	8.9	0.0	8.9	6.6
	Thft	38.4	38.4	11.6	11.6	0.0	5.1
	Aggr	42.1	7.0	4.3	29.3	17.4	27.8
	Both	21.2	12.0	13.9	25.8	27.2	12.8

		Ages 13–14				
		Non	Stat	Thft	Aggr	Both
		33.7	23.3	8.5	13.2	20.9
	Non	47.3	31.1	8.2	9.4	4.1	46.8
Ages 11–12	Stat	28.5	27.2	19.8	13.9	10.6	12.6
	Thft	18.4	16.0	8.0	8.0	49.5	7.2
	Aggr	21.6	8.2	9.4	29.8	31.0	14.2
	Both	18.9	15.9	3.0	11.7	50.4	19.3

		Ages 15–16				
		Non	Stat	Thft	Aggr	Both
		21.3	30.5	10.1	15.9	22.2
	Non	41.8	36.8	4.3	12.8	4.3	31.2
Ages 13–14	Stat	7.4	36.2	23.4	0.0	33.0	15.6
	Thft	26.5	20.4	6.2	0.0	46.9	9.4
	Aggr	19.1	33.2	0.0	28.6	19.1	20.0
	Both	3.2	20.3	19.3	25.9	31.5	23.8

		Ages 17–18				
		Non	Stat	Thft	Aggr	Both
		17.6	34.2	14.6	12.0	21.6
	Non	31.5	41.1	10.3	12.0	5.2	17.7
Ages 15–16	Stat	23.9	35.4	11.5	11.5	17.8	30.1
	Thft	4.2	43.0	18.2	4.2	30.3	16.7
	Aggr	19.6	47.0	7.7	0.0	25.6	11.8
	Both	7.7	14.9	22.6	24.4	30.4	23.7

26

TABLE 2.5

Transition Matrices of Delinquency Types for Females by Age

Ages 9–10

		Non	Stat	Thft	Aggr	Both	
		77.5	5.5	3.8	9.7	3.4	
Ages 7–8	Non	81.2	6.8	2.9	7.3	1.8	73.1
	Stat	83.6	0.0	0.0	16.1	0.0	4.6
	Thft	80.0	0.0	0.0	11.3	8.7	6.7
	Aggr	53.2	4.5	8.9	21.8	11.6	13.1
	Both	76.7	0.0	23.3	0.0	0.0	2.5

Ages 11–12

		Non	Stat	Thft	Aggr	Both	
		64.5	17.8	7.0	5.8	5.0	
Ages 9–10	Non	73.1	14.3	4.5	5.7	2.2	64.6
	Stat	56.1	43.9	0.0	0.0	0.0	5.1
	Thft	49.6	13.3	15.2	0.0	21.9	9.5
	Aggr	47.4	25.0	15.4	7.3	4.7	17.3
	Both	41.1	17.9	0.0	23.2	17.9	3.5

Ages 13–14

		Non	Stat	Thft	Aggr	Both	
		37.9	31.4	8.0	12.5	10.1	
Ages 11–12	Non	42.6	35.3	5.9	11.3	4.9	72.1
	Stat	27.7	24.1	12.1	24.1	12.1	5.6
	Thft	25.2	19.8	17.6	7.7	29.7	8.8
	Aggr	14.5	16.7	16.7	26.1	26.1	9.3
	Both	47.7	31.8	0.0	0.0	20.6	4.2

Ages 15–16

		Non	Stat	Thft	Aggr	Both	
		27.9	43.8	12.2	9.9	6.3	
Ages 13–14	Non	46.8	32.8	10.2	10.2	0.0	29.5
	Stat	22.7	53.4	6.9	11.2	5.7	34.3
	Thft	9.4	40.6	40.6	9.4	0.0	6.9
	Aggr	22.1	43.7	9.6	15.0	9.6	15.7
	Both	15.9	44.8	18.7	0.0	20.7	13.6

Ages 17–18

		Non	Stat	Thft	Aggr	Both	
		24.5	49.0	9.9	10.6	6.1	
Ages 15–16	Non	55.2	13.3	13.3	13.3	4.8	19.3
	Stat	21.2	64.1	1.7	10.7	2.2	41.6
	Thft	5.7	50.8	18.9	5.7	18.9	12.5
	Aggr	15.0	50.9	15.0	11.6	7.5	12.4
	Both	16.7	50.0	16.7	10.1	6.5	14.2

involved only in aggression (29%–30%), and being involved in only aggression is more stable than being involved in only theft (6%–18%). Thus, there is indication that involvement in multiple forms of delinquency results in a more enduring involvement.

There are numerous patterns of transitions that can be described, and further explorations of these transition matrices are left for interested readers. It can be seen, however, that although involvement in aggressive behavior is not highly stable, it is the most stable of the more serious delinquent behaviors (especially when the *aggressive only* and *both* categories are combined). In the following, the experience of a particular cohort is used to explore some factors thought to relate to the maintenance and termination of this behavior.

**Factors Affecting Transitions
to and From Aggressive Behavior**

To examine differences between individuals that remain nondelinquent and those who move to an aggressive status, and between those aggressive individuals that maintain this behavior and those who terminate aggressive involvement (at least over a 2-year period), the previous typology was collapsed into two types—a nonaggressive type consisting of the nondelinquent and those involved only in status–disorder or theft offenses, and an aggressive type that combines the two types involved in aggression. Across the age ranges used earlier, transition probabilities for aggression to aggression in the next period vary from .41 to .53 for males and from .17 to .28 for females. This confirms the earlier observation that aggression is not particularly stable, at least over the 4-year intervals across the 7- to 18-year-old age range used here.

The mean scores on various family, school, personal, and peer variables across the nonaggressive to nonaggressive, nonaggressive to aggressive, aggressive to nonaggressive, and aggressive to aggressive groups for the 1974 birth cohort are listed in Table 2.6. In that table, the longitudinal types are labeled Non → Non, Non → Agg, Agg → Non, and Agg → Agg, respectively. For all exploratory variables, tests for heteroscedasticity across the groups were all nonsignificant, and an analyses of variance (ANOVA) was conducted to test for statistically different means. Post hoc tests were used to explore individual group differences when significant differences at the .05 level were found. These results are also outlined in the table.

As seen in Table 2.6, for both boys and girls, involvement with delinquent peers appears to be the variable that most clearly distinguishes the four groups. The nonaggressive youths who become aggressive have a substantially greater number of delinquent friends. Similarly, the aggressive youths who maintain their aggressive behavior have a substantially greater number of delinquent friends than do their age mates who "terminate" this behavior over the next 2

TABLE 2.6
Mean Scores of Groups With Different Aggression Transitions

Category	Sex	Non → Non	Non → Agg	Agg → Non	Agg-Agg		P
Monitoring	M	10.1	9.2	9.6	9.2		.054
	F	10.8	10.0	10.4	10.1		.159
Family isolation	M	9.5	10.9	10.3	10.1		.164
	F	9.5	12.3	11.2	11.0	1 > 0	.004
Conventional involvement	M	7.3	6.3	5.4	6.1		.096
	F	6.8	6.8	6.4	5.3		.715
School grades	M	3.4	3.1	3.5	4.0	2 > 3	.010
	F	3.6	3.5	3.4	3.5		.782
Attachment to school	M	27.9	24.1	27.7	25.4	2 > 1	.000
	F	28.1	28.5	27.0	25.4	0 > 1,3	.100
Attitudes to delinquency	M	43.4	39.4	41.5	36.7	2 > 3	.000
	F	43.5	42.4	42.0	36.2	0 > 3	.000

(Continued)

29

TABLE 2.6
(Continued)

Category	Sex	Non → Non	Non → Agg	Agg → Non	Agg-Agg	P
Neutralization	M	30.9	36.8	33.0	37.2	.000
	F	29.6	33.5	32.6	35.1	1 > 0 3 > 0,2 .003
Guilt	M	2.5	2.2	2.3	2.0	No group diff. .000
	F	2.6	2.3	2.4	2.2	0 > 2 2 > 3 .001 0 > 3
Empathy	M	12.9	12.1	12.3	11.8	.050
	F	14.3	14.1	14.3	13.6	No group diff. .569
Self-esteem	M	40.9	39.9	43.3	42.1	.032
	F	41.4	42.2	42.0	40.3	No group diff. .804
Peer delinquency	M	20.8	30.6	23.0	28.8	.000 3 > 0,2
	F	18.3	23.7	20.4	25.5	1 > 0,2 .000 1 > 0 3 > 0,2

years. Also, for both sexes, the aggressive groups differ in their attitudes about delinquency (beliefs about how wrong delinquent behavior is). Those who stop their aggressive behavior have stronger beliefs that delinquency is wrong than do those who continue this behavior over time.

There are also some group differences unique to specific sexes. For males, there is less attachment to school and greater neutralization (willingness to use excuses for engaging in delinquent acts) for those nonaggressive youth who become aggressive. Differences in neutralization are also seen between the aggressive youth who maintain their aggression over time and those who stop their involvement. Also, there is a statistical difference in levels of guilt associated with engaging in delinquent behavior between those who terminate their aggressive behavior and those who do not. However, the actual difference in this variable between these two groups is quite small.

For girls, the only variable—in addition to delinquent peers and attitudes toward delinquency—that is significantly different between the groups is family isolation, which distinguishes those who become aggressive from those who remain nonaggressive.

Some variables thought to be associated with aggression—parental monitoring, involvement in conventional activities, empathy, and self-esteem—do not differ significantly across the four groups. Although this is not a predictive analysis, the important role of peers in both "initiating" and continuing aggression appears once again to be indicated.

Discussion

The purpose of this chapter was to illustrate one procedure for identifying sequences or pathways over time, and the context in which such pathways develop. The procedure takes a typological approach and examines transitions or movement between types over a developmental period. Following the type-to-type changes permits identification of "pathways" to various intermediate and outcome states. Because of a "plethora of types" often encountered in this approach, transition matrices were used to describe type-to-type transitions. The data used do not allow a full exposition of this approach because they are based on several overlapping cohorts. Additional data to construct a "synthetic cohort" or sufficient data to follow single cohorts over longer periods are needed. Nevertheless, some of the basic concepts could be illustrated.

A brief look at some contextual variables that indicated the important role of peers was also provided. An alternative strategy for examining the influence of these variables might involve the development of a contextual typology that is cross-classified with the behavioral typology to better explore developmental processes in both explanatory and behavioral stages and their interrelationship.

The instability of the delinquency types also underscores the need for multiwave longitudinal data that are collected over several contiguous time periods to study delinquency (and perhaps other behavior problems). Classification of individuals into types on the basis of cross-sectional data is likely to misclassify the nature of many individuals, and the identification and strength of risk or protective factors derived from such data may be in error. Similarly, longitudinal designs involving a single early measure and a measure much later in life may also suffer similar problems (unless infallible memories are presumed, and the intermediate data are obtained).

Finally, it should be noted that the process presented here is largely descriptive in nature and not based on complex statistical models. On the one hand, this is a very real limitation—the statistical procedures developed and being developed for longitudinal data are not being utilized. On the other hand, interest in typological approaches also appears to be increasing once again, and an emphasis on longitudinal taxonomic description may provide valuable insights, thus following Cattell's (1965) dictum that "nosology precedes etiology."

APPENDIX: BRIEF DESCRIPTION OF EXPLANATORY MEASURES USED IN THIS CHAPTER

Parental monitoring. This is a measure of parents' knowledge of a child's whereabouts during the day, fixed times to be home, and knowledge of child's friends. (Alpha inappropriate, and test–retest correlation not available.)

Youth involvement in various activities. This measure indicates the amount of time a youth spends in various activities, such as school activities or religious activities. (Alpha inappropriate, and test–retest reliability not available.)

Attitudes toward delinquency. This is a 12-item measure that indicates how wrong a respondent believes it is to engage in different delinquent acts. ($\alpha = .91$)

Neutralization. This 11-item measure indicates the willingness of a respondent to use a variety of excuses for engaging in delinquent behavior. ($\alpha = .83$)

Guilt. This is a 7-item measure that indicates how bad or guilty a respondent would feel if he or she engaged in a variety of delinquent behaviors. ($\alpha = .85$)

Empathy. This is an 11-item measure developed by Eysenck and Eysenck (1978) to measure empathetic responses in a number of situations. ($\alpha = .67$)

Self-esteem. Rosenberg (1965) self-esteem measure. (α = .78)

Peer delinquency. Respondent's perception of the proportion of his or her friends who are engaged in each of a variety of delinquent acts. (Alpha inappropriate, and test–retest not available.)

REFERENCES

Bergman, L. R., & Magnusson, D. (1992). Stability and change in patterns of extrinsic adjustment problems. In D. Magnusson, L. R. Bergman, G. Rudinger, & B. Torrestad (Eds.), *Problems and methods in longitudinal research: Stability and change* (pp. 323–346). New York: Cambridge University Press.

Bursik, R., & Grasmiek, H. (1992). *Neighborhoods and crime: The dimensions of effective community control.* New York: Lexington Books.

Cairns, R. B. (1986). Phenomena lost: Issues in the study of development. In J. Valsiner (Ed.), *The individual subject and scientific psychology* (pp. 97–112). New York: Plenum.

Cairns, R. B., Cairns, B. D., & Neckerman, H. J. (1989). Early school dropout: Configurations and determinants. *Child Development, 60,* 1437–1452.

Carter, R. L., Morris, R., & Blashfield, R. K. (1982). *Clustering two dimensional profiles: A comparative study.* Gainesville, FL: J. Hillis Miller Mental Health Center.

Cattell, R. (1965). Factor analysis: An introduction to the essentials. *Biometrics, 21,* 405.

Elliott, D. S. (1994). Serious violent offenders: Onset, developmental course and termination. *Criminology, 32*(1), 1–22.

Elliott, D. S., Huizinga, D., & Ageton, S. S. (1985). *Explaining delinquency and drug use.* Beverly Hills, CA: Sage.

Elliott, D. S., Huizinga, D., & Menard, S. (1989). *Multiple problem youth: Delinquency, drugs and mental health problems.* New York: Springer.

Elliott, D. S., & Huizinga, D., & Morse, B. (1987). Self-reported violent offending: A descriptive analysis of juvenile violent offenders and their offending careers. *Journal of Interpersonal Violence, 1*(4), 472–514.

Eysenck, S. B. G., & Eysenck, H. J. (1978). Impulsiveness and venturesomeness: Their position in a dimensional system of personality description. *Psychological Reports, 43,* 1247–1255.

Farrington, D. P. (1986). Stepping stones to adult criminal careers. In D. Olweus, J. Block, & M. R. Yarrow (Eds.), *Development of antisocial and prosocial behavior* (pp. 359–384). New York: Academic Press.

Farrington, D. P., Ohlin, L. O., & Wilson, J. Q. (1986). *Understanding and controlling crime: Toward a new research strategy.* New York: Springer-Verlag.

Huizinga, D. (1979, April). *Longitudinal typologies: A means of exploring multivariate longitudinal data.* Paper presented at the 10th annual meeting of the Classification Society, Gainesville, FL.

Huizinga, D., Esbensen, F., & Weiher, A. (1991). Are there multiple paths to delinquency? *Journal of Criminal Law and Criminology, 82,* 83–118.

Huizinga, D., Esbensen, F., & Weiher, A. (1993). Examining developmental trajectories in delinquency using accelerated longitudinal designs. In H-J Kerner & E. G. M. Weitekamp (Eds.), *Cross-national longitudinal research on human development and criminal behavior* (pp.). New York: Kluwer.

Huizinga, D., Loeber, R., & Thornberry, T. (1994). *Urban delinquency and substance abuse: Initial findings.* Washington, DC: U.S. Department of Justice.

Huizinga, D., Loeber, R., & Thornberry, T. (1993, September). Delinquency, drugs, sex and pregnancy. *Public Health Reports* (108), 90–96.

Loeber, R. (1988). The natural histories of juvenile conduct problems, substance use and delinquency: Evidence for developmental progressions. In B. B. Lahey & A. E. Kazdin (Eds.), *Advances in clinical child psychology* (Vol. 11, pp. 73–124). New York: Plenum.

Loeber, R., & Le Blanc, M. (1990). Toward a developmental criminology. In M. Tonry & N. Morris (Eds.), *Crime and justice, an annual review* (Vol. 12, pp. 375–473). Chicago: University of Chicago Press.

Loeber, R., Wung, P., Keenan, K., Giroux, B., Stouthamer-Loeber, M., van Kammen, W., & Maughan, B. (1993). Developmental pathways in disruptive child behavior. *Development and Psychopathology, 5*, 111–133.

Magnusson, D., & Bergman, L. R. (1990). A pattern approach to the study of pathways from early childhood to adulthood. In L. Robbins & M. Butler (Eds.), *Straight and devious pathways from childhood to adulthood* (pp. 101–115). New York: Cambridge University Press.

Moffit, T. E. (1993). Adolescence limited and live course persistent antisocial behavior: A developmental taxonomy. *Psychological Review, 100*(4), 674–701.

Parzen, E. (1962). *Stochastic processes*. San Francisco: Holden-Day Inc.

Rice, C. E., & Mattson, N. B. (1966). Types based on repeated measurement. In M. Lorr (Ed.), *Explorations in typing psychotics* (pp. 151–191). Oxford, England: Pergamon.

Rosenberg, M. (1965). *Society and adolescent self-image*. Princeton, NJ: Princeton University Press.

Runyon, W. M. (1980). A stage state analysis of the life course. *Journal of Personality and Social Psychology, 38*(6), 951–962.

Sampson, R. J., & Lauritsen, J. (1992). Violent victimization and offending: Individual, situational, and community-level risk factors. In A. J. Reiss & J. Roth (Eds.), *The understanding and control of violent behavior*. Washington, DC: National Academy Press.

Tuma, N., & Hannan, M. T. (1984). *Social dynamics: Models and methods*. New York: Academic Press.

CHAPTER THREE

Social Networks Over Time and Space in Adolescence

Robert B. Cairns
Man-Chi Leung
Beverley D. Cairns
University of North Carolina at Chapel Hill

Peer influence and peer-group membership have long been implicated by sociologists as factors in antisocial and delinquent behaviors (e.g., A. K. Cohen, 1955). Peer effects continue to be seen in accounts of juvenile crime. A recent report of the National Youth Study concludes that deviant peer-group bonding is the primary factor in adolescent delinquency (Elliott, Huizinga, & Menard, 1989). However, focus on peer social networks has not been historically mirrored by research in developmental psychology. In this regard, Hartup (1983) concluded that only modest attention had been given to social-group affiliations beyond the dyad in childhood and adolescence.

That state of affairs in developmental research appears to be in the process of change, thanks to the efforts of several researchers in adolescence. Beginning in the early 1980s, exploratory efforts have been made to address diverse phenomena of social development from the perspective of social networks. A sampling of these new proposals includes the following.

Self-Cconcepts and Identity. Following the pioneering work of Youniss (1980), there has been explicit recognition of the role of social groups and peer friendships in the establishment and maintenance of social perceptions and social values, including ideas about the self and the attributions of others (Cairns & Cairns, 1988, 1995; Youniss & Smollar, 1985). This constitutes a fresh line of inquiry into an old issue, and it calls for the critical reexamination of the broadly held, but rarely tested, proposal that "each of us is in part someone else, even in his own thought of himself"

35

(Baldwin, 1897, p. 3). It also requires examination of the linkage between the development of self-identity and the contributions of peers and parents (Youniss, 1980).

Sex Role. Maccoby (1988, 1990) proposed that the dynamic function of social networks is to establish and maintain appropriate sex roles across development. Peer networks are typically sex segregated throughout childhood and adolescence. Maccoby argued that these peer influences constantly update age-appropriate sex behaviors, attitudes, and values (see also Cairns & Kroll, 1994).

Biosocial Development. One of the more inventive interpretations of the linkage between biosocial development and social-network affiliations has been offered by Magnusson and his colleagues (Magnusson, 1988; Stattin & Magnusson, 1990). These investigators discovered that very early-maturing girls showed higher levels of deviance than late-maturing girls on measures of school, social, and sexual behaviors. These authors propose that the effects of early pubertal maturation are mediated by differential social-group involvement, such that early-maturing girls become more affiliated with older peer groups than late-maturing girls. Such differential association based on pubertal maturation may promote, in turn, behaviors and attitudes that are more in synchrony with maturational age, rather than chronological age. Hence, a "developmental advance" in social affiliation among early-maturing girls may support the adoption of behaviors and attitudes deemed normative for older adolescents, but deviant for younger adolescents. This finding of maturation-differential association has been partly extended by Caspi and Moffitt (1991) in their longitudinal studies of New Zealand schools.

Developmental Psychopathology: Suicide, Aggression, and Depression. Other applications of social-network concepts to psychopathology have been less broadly recognized. The higher rates of suicide attempts among highly aggressive adolescents relative to nonaggressive adolescents has been speculatively linked to differences in social support and social alienation (Cairns, Peterson, & Neckerman, 1988). A broader argument could be made that age-related changes in social structure are directly associated with sex-related and age-related differences in depressive ideation and antisocial behavior.

Consider acting-out behavior, for example. To the extent that peer-group involvement supports antisocial and delinquent actions in males, a decrease in involvement with those social groups at early maturity should be linked to an age-related decrease in aggressive and criminal behavior. That is, "desistance" from crime and antisocial behavior may be linked to the decrease in social involvement with same-age, same-sex males. The interactional proposal is that aggression and antisocial behavior are linked to the social actions of deviant peers. Reductions in direct social interaction with aggressive and deviant male peers should, in turn, decrease the probability of aggressive and deviant acts in young adult males.

In addition, differential age- and sex-related changes in peer relations may be linked to higher levels in depressive disorders among women. To the extent that the social networks of young adult females become highly constricted—relative to adolescent girls and young adult males—increasing levels of social isolation would be experienced by these women. With the reduction in social support and intimate communication, young women might become more vulnerable to psychological stress and stress-related disorders.

Intergenerational Transfer. To limit the discussion of peer networks to adolescence belies the role of social influences that may operate over generations. In this regard, the focus of psychological theory on the role of peers in adolescent development has drawn attention away from the role of contemporaries and peer groups and toward parenting and socialization in young adults. The networks of young adults may differ in quantity and quality. To the extent that peer networks exist for females, it would seem reasonable to expect that they would be concerned with the tasks of that phase of development, including socialization and childrearing. Beliefs, values, and attitudes toward children and childrearing could be influenced, in large measure, by the beliefs, values, and attitudes of peers in similar circumstances. The indirect effects of adult social networks could be reflected in the children of adult peers.

Evaluations of these propositions on social networks have been handicapped by methodological shortcomings in the assessment of peer networks, on the one hand, and incomplete theoretical accounts of the development of social networks and processes, on the other hand. Further advances will hinge on the solution of both. Accordingly, the two objectives of this chapter are to (a) offer a framework on development to guide research on social networks, and (b) describe a method for the objective analysis of social networks. The concluding section of the chapter illustrates how a developmental–interactional perspective may clarify some puzzling issues on continuity and change of social networks in adolescence.

THE ONTOGENY OF SOCIAL NETWORKS

There have been few attempts to offer a coherent and integrated statement on the ontogeny of peer-group structures and dynamics from infancy to maturity. Of the systematic theorists who have covered the territory, the early contribu-

tions of Harry Stack Sullivan, Eric Erickson, and Lev Vygotsky have been highly
influential, as are the more recent models of James Youniss, Dexter Dunphy,
and Robert Selman. Sullivan and Vygotsky, like James Mark Baldwin, are
distinctive in their attempts to address the development of social-group
influences from infancy to early childhood and middle childhood. For instance, Sullivan focuses on the role of "chums" and small groups prior to
adolescence. Building on these early efforts, which were formulated in the
absence of systematic information on the nature of peer relations, a contem-
poraneous outline of the ontogeny of social structures can be depicted.

THE ONTOGENY OF SOCIAL STRUCTURES

We now have enough information to provide a sketch of the development
of peer groups from birth to maturity, and how it may recycle into the next
generation. A preliminary outline of this information, derived from multiple
sources over the past 30 years, is depicted in Fig. 3.1. Although the chronological ages corresponding to the five phases of development were inten-
tionally omitted, they refer roughly to infancy, preschool, school age,
adolescence, and early maturity. The breakdown within the levels refers to
an equally rough assignment of differences over time.

    Figure 3.1 presupposes that the normative development of social rela-
tionships and structures in humans follows a specifiable general course. It
is not a rigid structure, however, and there is ample room for individual,
subgroup, and cultural differences, given the adaptable nature of social
relations. Also implicit in the representations of Fig. 3.1 are five developmental concepts that should be made explicit: Level 1, the contextual em-
beddedness of relationships and structures; Level 2, the inevitability of developmental novelty; Level 3, developmental accumulation and integration;
Level 4, action context and the relativity of age and sex; and Level 5, intergenerational continuity.

Contextual Relativity and Influences Beyond Peers

The salient group influences and linkages depicted in the foreground of Fig.
3.1 provide only part of the picture. The contextual background is equally
important. The supportive role of context is depicted in the background
frame of each panel, and these frames differ according to subgroup and
cultural considerations. It is a happy myth that children exclusively determine
membership in their own peer groups. Although parental influences are not
explicitly depicted beyond Level 1, there is potentially an "invisible hand"
of parents in all groups of early childhood. This influence can be direct or
indirect, potentially heavy at times. So the usual distinction between "parent

Level III: Peer Clusters

Natural Clusters

Pre-Groups

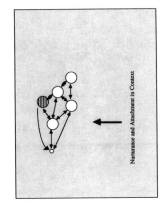

Level V: Intergenerational Cycle

Nurturance and Attachment in Context

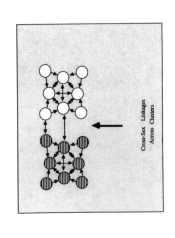

Level IV: Adolescent Transitions

Cross-Sex Linkages
Across Clusters

Level II: Early Peer Relations

Mixed Dyads

Reciprocal Dyads

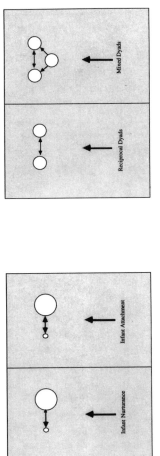

Level I: Adult-Infant Relations

Infant Attachment

Infant Nurturance

FIG. 3.1. Levels of social organization.

39

effects" and "peer effects" becomes an illusion. It may be proposed that, in most cases, these influences are correlated and represent different aspects of a similar configuration of influences over time. The same kinds of background effects occur in schools and classrooms, where teachers help regulate and direct the kinds of relationships and groups that are formed, both directly through the arrangement of space and indirectly through the establishment of attitudes (Hallinan, 1979; Hallinan & Smith, 1989).

A study conducted by Brown, Mounts, Lamborn, and Steinberg (1993) shows that parents still maintain a notable influence on their children's peer relationships during adolesence. Specific parenting practices, such as parent monitoring and joint decision making, were significantly associated with grade point average (GPA), drug use, and self-reliance of their children, which in turn were significant predictors of membership in common adolescent crowds.

Consider, as well, the nature of social structures during late adolescence and early adulthood, shown as Level 5. Studies of the social structures and social dynamics of persons in this age group have relied heavily on the findings obtained from college students. Extrapolation beyond the university is hazardous; college students typically have significantly different social interaction opportunities, living conditions, and family and financial responsibilities than same-age persons in the community. In this regard, college students live in a protected environment, with significant numbers of same-age peers with whom to affiliate. This setting provides opportunities to be involved in social clusters, much as they had been in earlier school years, thus maintaining a type of extended adolescence. Quite a different picture might be drawn for the social networks of the "forgotten half" of young people who are living on their own initiative.

Developmental Novelty

Not all features of mature social organization are available in infancy and early childhood. Some appear fresh in childhood, and some appear in adolescence. For example, the ability to simultaneously synchronize one's acts with three or more disparate persons does not appear in infancy; it is a process that emerges in early childhood.

Developmental Accumulation

A third assumption is that landmark social processes are not lost during ontogeny. For example, the ability to form close emotional attachments is not just a property of infancy: it recurs throughout ontogeny into maturity. It is an error to assume that these processes are distinctive to the earliest stages of development because they are, in fact, replicated throughout life.

They simply appear more salient in the early stages. They may be found with equal force in early adolescence and early adulthood. The tendency to form peer groups and cliques is not just a characteristic of adolescence—it persists into maturity. More generally, the processes of social interchange in individuals and groups do not get erased over development. Ontogeny provides for the accumulation of social and group competencies.

Action Context and the Relativity of Age and Sex

One reason precise chronological ages cannot be assigned to the various levels of social organization is that there is a relativity between the nature of actions and the level of social organization that may be observed. The point at which reciprocities and group coordination occurs is not merely a function of age, but of the activity and the other participants. With more competent partners and more salient, readily performed actions, coordination and reciprocation can occur at younger and younger ages. Although Fig. 3.1 depicts the normative occurrence of group relations in many activities of everyday life, the structure of groups at any one stage is strongly influenced by those acts in which members engage. In this regard, vigorous, salient actions provide a more primitive basis for social organization than quiet reciprocation. Mob actions are more readily synchronized than quiet play.

Sex roles constitute a special concern in accounts of group organization. To be sure, there are sex differences in normative activity and in patterns of exchange, and these differences contribute to sex-specific variations in group structure (Benenson, 1990; Berndt, 1982; Berndt & Hoyle, 1985; Eder & Hallinan, 1978; Waldrop & Halverson, 1975). On this count, Fig. 3.1 could be split into 3.1A and 3.1B, referring, respectively, to changes in social organization typical for females and males. Although this unisex depiction obscures sex differences, sufficient commonalities exist across males and females to justify emphasis on the main effects of development in social organization.

Intergenerational Transfer

The schema of Level 5 (on transgenerational structures and mother–infant interaction) points to the incompleteness of Level 1's schema (on early mother–infant relations). The Level 1 schema failed to take into account the network factors, in which both mothers and their infants are embedded. In brief, the depiction implies that the salient peer processes that appear in adolescence can be anticipated by events that occur earlier in ontogeny, and have consequences for social organization at maturity and into the next generation.

Although there are Hubble-like distortions throughout Fig. 3.1, it may prove useful in providing directions for further study. It suggests there may be greater continuity in social organization and peer processes than usually recognized in our theoretical models. The powerful effects that have been historically attributed to peer relationships in adolescence reflect processes that are active in earlier life and in later developmental stages. Some of the social structures depicted in Fig. 3.1 have been fully described, others have been studied in part, and still others remain in the exploratory stages of investigation. The outline also indicates that attention must be given to the mechanisms of transition and the social processes that link one form of social organization to other forms across time and space.

THE ONTOGENY OF SOCIAL PROCESSES

Because of the historical concern of sociology with the study of social structures, issues of social process and social change seem to be given only modest attention in sociological investigations of peer social networks. Although understandable in the light of the methods and emphases of the relevant disciplines, the short shrift given to understanding processes of change and transformation has led to some of the more stubborn controversies in the area. One ongoing debate concerns the origins of *homophily*—the ubiquitous finding of greater within-group similarities than between-group similarities in behavior (Berndt, 1982; J. M. Cohen, 1977). Is the similarity due to selective association (whereby similar persons are brought together by choice or default) or reciprocal socialization (whereby persons are made similar by their association and interaction)? Do birds of a feather flock together, or does flocking together help produce similar feathers? A focus on developmental processes may clarify and perhaps resolve the debate, albeit in nonintuitive ways.

Development implies change and reorganization in the individual and in the social institutions of which the individual is a part. In order for structural descriptions to be useful in developmental analysis, structural descriptions must be accompanied by explicit accounts of transition and change mechanisms. The processes of change—whether learning, maturational, or contextual—are the stuff of developmental psychology. Piaget (1954) specified the broad processes of assimilation and accommodation, and Bandura (1982) spoke of the social learning mechanisms of self-reinforcement, modeling, and self-efficacy. The trick is to clarify how these mechanisms are integrated over time in the establishment and change of social structures. Toward this end, Cairns and Cairns (1991) proposed that time cannot be ignored in the integration of processes because of the time-restricted nature of processes. They bring attention to both short-term interactional and long-term developmental processes of social change.

The first set of processes concerning interactional synchrony and interactional constraints has been derived from social learning–interaction theory.

Interactional synchrony refers to the family of short-term processes by which the acts of two or more individuals become synchronized and mutually supported or constrained. The details of this dyadic process begin with the symbolic interactionism of Cottrell (1942) and Sears (1951), and continue through the developmental interactionism of Cairns (1979) and Patterson (1982). These encompass a loose body of common propositions that constitute interactional theory.

One proposal of interactional theory that applies to social-network dynamics is the idea that individuals who directly interact necessarily have an impact on the behavioral actions and states of each other. This is because the actions of one person demand immediate accommodations in the actions of the other if an interaction is to be sustained. Such interactional sequences are highly responsive to learning, and sequences and patterns of responses can be readily established in particular relationships and specific contexts. This point has been emphasized in successive generations of social learning theorists (e.g., Bandura & Walters, 1959; Cairns, 1979; Patterson, Reid, & Dishion, 1992; Sears, Maccoby, & Levin, 1957). Whether the accommodation is one of reciprocity and increased similarity, or complementarily with increased difference, depends on the individuals, the roles, and the context of their interaction. In the case of peers and reasonable equality in roles, the usual accommodation to interaction is that of reciprocity. This means that an increased similarity in behavior, attitude, and mood is the rule. When this argument is extended beyond the dyad to cliques and groups, behavioral similarity has been called *homophily* (Kandel, 1978).

Entry into a social relationship—whether by choice, chance, or coercion—may serve multiple functions for the individual in the redirection of old actions and the support of new behaviors. It brings about a new context of development, for good or for ill. Acceptance into a social group is neutral insofar as the quality of the individual's current and future adjustment are concerned. The behaviors and attitudes supported by the group will determine whether the experience is ultimately beneficial or detrimental. Peer social clusters in adolescence may serve not only the prosocial functions of providing intimacy, but also are used to express hostility and to exercise control. They serve as "support groups" for insiders and as "attack groups" against outsiders. It is not necessarily the case that group involvement facilitates normal and healthy development. This depends on the values and behaviors of the groups with which individuals become affiliated and identified.

To illustrate, a teenager may be accepted into a peer group because of his or her status on a salient characteristic (e.g., smoking or high levels of aggression). Once a member, the person may come under social pressure to conform to the group's other correlated values, attitudes, and behaviors. These correlated characteristics, which extend beyond the conditions for initial membership, could involve sex, drugs, and attitudes toward school.

As long as the individual remains in the group, pressures toward conformity to the prevailing standards would persist, and they would ensure that correlations among behaviors are maintained.

One other social-interaction mechanism is often overlooked because of its ubiquity and commonplace operation. Physical propinquity—nearness in place and time—has long been recognized as a factor in the formation of social relationships and social groups. Homans (1950) observed that friendships form and groups become established by virtue of direct interactions fostered by close proximity. Similarly, Cairns (1966) argued that physical closeness promotes the establishment of robust infant–adult social attachments. In a series of experiments where nonhuman infants were randomly paired with caregivers, strong social attachments rapidly developed. The broader principle is that direct engagement—whether by choice or by constraint—tends to support joint behavioral organization and behavioral interdependency. This is because one's actions become organized by internal feedback loops, as well as the support provided through the actions of other individuals. The implication for social-group organization is that persons become embedded in a network of relationships provided by their recurrent interactions. As a consequence, propinquity is a major factor in social-group formation: Social structures and close social relations should be established among persons who recurrently interact with each other.

A second group of social-change processes involves slower acting, long-term mechanisms that have been implicated by developmental studies. These involve mechanisms of biosocial bias, age-developmental constraints, and biosocial–behavioral reorganization. These mechanisms, when taken in conjunction with social learning–interactive processes, help account for the normative structures and developmental changes in social organization.

Developmental and comparative studies indicate that there is a strong bias toward social synchrony at all developmental stages, even in the earliest stages of infancy. Mammalian infants do not have to learn to be social, although key characteristics are learnable. As outlined by Rosenblatt and Lehrman (1963) for nonhuman mammalian infants, and by Cairns (1979) for human infants, this early social bias is mediated by the synchrony of psychobiological processes in both the mother and the infant. Overt interactive behavior is supported and maintained by specifiable neurobiological and hormone-behavior features of the adult and the infant. The actions of the one help to maintain and support the biological conditions of the other in mutually adaptive pathways. Beyond infancy, the propensity of infants and young children to form reciprocal relationships is an inherent and normal feature of being human. Internal behavioral organization is supported and maintained by social interactions. This mutual dependency of internal and external states is replicated at several stages of development.

Social organization is also paced by age-related changes in the individual and in persons who are associated with the individual. As the person's needs and capabilities change, so should the social system that supports the behaviors of the person. These age-related constraints on action include changes in cognitive, emotional, and physical capabilities, on the one hand, and age-related changes in roles and expectations, on the other hand. Relationships within and between social units (dyads, families, clusters) inevitably shift over ontogeny due, in part, to developmental changes in persons and to dynamic forces within the unit. In the special case of family organization, for example, the social characteristics of the offspring show inexorable changes as a function of age—from infancy through childhood and adolescence to early adulthood. At each developmental level, changes are provoked in both the child's behavior and in the expectations of the family, including the roles and relationships among family members. Being a *daughter* or *son* has different meanings, depending on the age and developmental status of the offspring.

There is strong evidence for "correlated constraints," in that social characteristics occur in configurations, not as separate, isolated variables. The correlations among characteristics mean that many seemingly "separate" variables are mutually supportive, and it makes little sense to characterize persons or groups by a single, salient, independent variable. This principle may help clarify how deviant families or deviant peer groups extend their influence. There are norms for acceptance into peer dyads and clusters in order to promote personal integrity and maintain social synchrony.

Interpersonal and intragroup social synchrony is a commonplace, albeit remarkable, achievement. It is commonplace because it occurs across development, from early childhood through adulthood. It is remarkable because it requires the simultaneous integration of the internal states of individuals and their external actions with each other. When dysynchrony or disruption occurs—as inevitably happens—there are pressures for dissolution, independence, and breakdown of the social group. For example, there is inevitable dysynchrony in family groups when developmental changes in the offspring demand changes in parental behavior, expectations, and controls. However, there are significant barriers to premature family redefinition and change by children because of the financial, legal, and emotional ties within families.

Fewer barriers exist with respect to peer-group definition and change. A study of fluidity and dynamics of social-group processes is a necessary complement to the focus on structure if we are to understand how the relationships and networks of children and adolescents change over time and yet endure. We argue elsewhere that the fickleness of social groups and social relations is not without function (Cairns & Cairns, 1995). As individual needs and behaviors change, so might the social relationships that are best accommodated to the new conditions. The puzzle of development is how the stability and constancy of social organization can be achieved despite inevitable changes. This matter is particularly important for social organization, where the identity and nature of groups may change, along with changes in individual membership. To adumbrate our conclusions, we propose that there are powerful carry-over effects from membership in one group to membership in the next.

One striking finding to emerge from human studies concerns consistency and replicability in the ontogeny of social clusters and social organization. Social learning–interactional processes appear to be kept in line by synchrony with developmental processes. This combination produces predictable normative sequences in social organization and social outcomes. The development of attachment, reciprocity, and dyadic interchange in infancy and early childhood has been shown to follow consistent and predictable pathways; so has the emergence of same-sex clusters, and their reformation through mid-childhood and adolescence. Similarly, behavioral homophilies in adolescence have been repeatedly found in both behavioral deviance and conformity. Such consistencies in the normative course of group functions and structures point to the operation of correlated mechanisms in the interchanges, in the context, and within the interacting organisms. One of the challenges in the application of contemporary research will be to identify how these mechanisms operate together, and how to employ them in programs of prevention and intervention.

METHODS OF NETWORK ANALYSIS

With that goal in mind, one difficulty that remains in the investigation of social clusters is that few techniques are available to reliably identify social networks. Important shortcomings have been identified in several of the techniques that have been widely adopted. We briefly consider these issues in a concrete fashion by examining the major techniques now available. These include the traditional measures of sociometry, "ego" measures of peer influence, "sociometric status" measures of peer relations, social networks and the social–cognitive map.

Sociometry

The traditional methodology of sociometry involves the use of procedures introduced by Moreno (1934) to describe social organizations. Moreno's topographic diagrams provide a summary of information obtained from members of a network unit regarding persons who have been described by individual children as being "best friends" or "least liked." Early attempts were made to quantify this information and to determine its reliability and adequacy (e.g., Bronfenbrenner, 1944a, 1944b). These efforts led to the development of mathematical models for group structure in the work of Bavelas (1948) and Festinger (1949), among others. In sociology and anthropology, these contributions have been extended by investigators who have attempted to translate mathematical formulations of social networks into meaningful research programs (Berkowitz & Wellman, 1986; White, Boorman, & Breiger, 1976). The procedures have often relied on graph theory, and readily applicable software has been developed (e.g., Richards, 1986; Richards & Rice, 1981). In other instances, representations of social networks relied on multidimensional scaling techniques (MDS; see Burt, 1980; Burt & Minor, 1983; Levine, 1972; Marsden & Lin, 1982; Wellman, 1983).

Certain strengths and problems associated with sociometric procedures have been discussed elsewhere (e.g., Burt, 1980; Scott, 1988). In brief, modern computational algorithms (e.g., graph theory) permit the standardization of networks solutions, and thereby facilitate the use of sociometric procedures. These analyses permit the identification of separate clusters of individuals, and they preserve information about the relationships among persons within each cluster and between clusters.

Limitations in the research applications of modern sociometric procedures are of two types: restrictions on the datasets to which the analysis technique may be applied, and limitations in the information yielded about the social networks. In restrictions of the first type, available computational algorithms (a) often impose limits on the minimal size of the network (e.g., ≥ 20), (b) require a high proportion of the respondents in the network to participate in the data collection (e.g., $\geq 90\%$), and (c) require a minimum number of linkages to other persons by each individual in the network (i.e., three or more in some solutions). Beyond these practical limitations, which are nontrivial because they restrict the circumstances in which the procedures may be applied, the solutions typically ignore conventional notions of distance between persons (or things), and they are limited to two-dimensional representations of multidimensional clusters. (There are exceptions: MDS representations of networks, in contrast to graph theory solutions, preserve distance relations among objects that are clustered.)

The pragmatic shortcoming of sociometric procedures has been perhaps most troublesome for developmental researchers. Participation of virtually all individuals in a social structure is required to plot the social system. In current applications—where children and parents in a school must return active participation informed consent, or where only one individual of the social system is interviewed—this requirement for full participation is rarely met.

Ego Measures of Peer Influence

The previously stated problems in traditional sociometry have given rise to the broad use of "ego measures" of social networks, where an individual is asked to provide three kinds of information: (a) the peers in the individual's own social group, (b) the behaviors of the peers in this social group on some dimension (e.g., frequency of drug use, crime), and (c) the person's own behavior on these dimensions. The procedures have been broadly used in sociology (Elliott et al., 1989; Giordano, Cernkovich, & Pugh, 1986) and, to a lesser extent, in psychology (e.g., Feiring & Lewis, 1987). In brief, a single agent (the subject) provides information on the type and features of the social structure, on the other members in the social structure, and the agent's own behavior.

Such "ego-measures" methods of describing social networks and social influence unfortunately invite the confounding of information about the acts of the self, the structure of the social network, and the acts of peers. Consequently, many of the strong relationships between peer involvement and deviant behavior that have been cited in the criminological literature can be questioned on methodological grounds (see also Kandel, 1994). The problem is that subjects may provide self-enhancing responses at all three levels of inquiry. Leung (1993) recently showed that subjects tend to provide a self-enhancing picture of their social relationships by accentuating their affiliation with socially desirable peers and diminishing their affiliations with undesirable peers. Specifically, children in Hong Kong tend to name as friends and associates those persons who show high levels of academic performance and conventional virtues (e.g., hardworking, polite). In addition, subjects tend to provide self-enhancing reports in descriptions of their own behaviors on virtually all important social dimensions (Cairns & Cairns, 1988). Similarly, deviant behaviors—including drug use and delinquency—that youth attribute to their friends have a much stronger relationship to their own behavioral reports than to the behaviors reported by peers themselves.

All this suggests that the peer-group influence on the self, obtained by "ego measures" of group process, may be as much in the eyes and recall of the subject as in the behaviors of peers. Unambiguous interpretation of peer–subject behavioral associations seem to require independent information about the behavior of individuals, behavior of their peers, and the nature of the social organization. Ego reports of social groups, although undoubtedly important for learning about the subject's own self-perceptions and perceptions of peers, provide fallible guides for understanding peer-group influence—deviant or otherwise.

Sociometric Status

A third class of procedures relevant to social influence has recently evolved in psychology and education to identify the status of children relative to peers in the social network. Rather than focus on associations between persons, the procedure is concerned with "sociometric status," or acceptance by peers. This procedure involves the placement of children on a standardized dimension of *likability* or *unlikability* (e.g., Coie, Dodge, & Coppotelli, 1982; Peery, 1979), as well as a dimension of *social impact.* The information is employed to categorize children as *popular, rejected, average, neglected,* or *controversial* (Asher & Dodge, 1986; Coie & Dodge, 1983; Dodge, Schlundt, Schocken, & Delugach, 1983). Considerable research has been completed over the past decade on the social adaptations of children who have been so classified, with special attention given to the rejected children (see Asher & Coie, 1990, for an excellent summary).

The sociometric status technique is different from social-network procedures because it was designed to classify children in term of their popularity with peers, with special attention to those who are marginal in peer acceptance (i.e., those who are rejected, neglected, or controversial). The classifications are based on standard scores in order to have roughly the same meaning across contexts and social settings. Like the earlier sociometric procedures, a high rate of subject participation is required to establish reliable standard scores/classifications. Unlike most sociometric procedures, the sociometric status technique does not yield information about the relationships that are formed among specific children or groups of children, nor does it yield a picture of the social network as a unit (Asher & Coie, 1990; Cairns, 1983). The procedure is designed to classify children in terms of status, rather than to determine who their associates may or may not be, and the nature of the social networks in which they are embedded. For example, it is unclear whether children classified as *rejected* in this procedure are necessarily alone and shunned, or whether they may be central and dominant in the class. Moreover, social status measures are designed to provide individual-difference information on the reputation or likability of individuals, as opposed to social-network information about the nature of social linkages among persons.

Social Networks and the Social–Cognitive Map

Given these problems of methodology, we have explored some techniques for making the social groups of adolescence accessible for analysis and study over time. The pragmatic technique that has evolved is based on the proposition that children and adolescents carry about with them a "social map," whereby configurations of persons may be identified in terms of their relationships. Furthermore, these social maps appear to be readily accessed, and most children and teenagers are willing to share this knowledge. Although adolescents may distort their own role in the social world, they are reasonably good at describing the roles and relationships of others.

The method involves the construction of a composite social "map" by aggregating individual perceptions of the social network. Relative to other sociometric procedures, the requirements for research participation are liberalized because individuals provide information about social clusters beyond their own immediate set of friends and enemies. By way of definition, the term *social cluster* refers to subgroups of persons who selectively affiliate with each other. Depending on the age of the persons and the discipline of the investigator, such subgroups are usually called *cliques, coalitions,* or *gangs.* *Network unit* refers to the full set of individuals in a definable setting (e.g., classroom, club, platoon, department), typically consisting of one or more social clusters and persons who are not members of clusters. *Social network* is an inclusive term, referring to relationships among individuals within clusters and network units, as well as to relationships among network units (e.g., classrooms in school, clubs in a troop, living units in a summer camp). Following some introductory comments on modern sociometry, we describe the composite social map technique and review its merits and limitations.

The composite social–cognitive map (SCM) method rests on the simple observation that respondents are capable of describing—in free recall—much of the basic information about the social networks in which they participate. They know about and can easily report the social relationships of several persons—even those with whom they have no close affiliation. Individual children (or adolescents) are asked questions about the people in a definable network unit (e.g., class, school, neighborhood): Are there people who hang around together a lot? Who are they? On the basis of this probe, each respondent generates one or more separate groups or clusters of persons. This procedure permits the generation of different cognitive "social maps" for every respondent in the network unit. When asked the further question (Are there any people who don't hang around with a particular group?), respondents nominate persons whom they consider to be isolates. If respondents fail to nominate themselves in response to either probe, they are asked, What about yourself—do you hang around with any group? Taken as a whole, the procedure allows respondents to provide information about the entire network without being limited to describing their own personal circle of friends or enemies.

Given the free-recall nature of the task, respondents may forget, ignore, or otherwise neglect to mention individuals and clusters of individuals. Or respondents may be aware of all individuals or groups, but consider them to be unimportant to the network as a whole. Thus, "omissions" could reflect differences in the children's social knowledge, social attribution, or recall and memory. Despite these potential sources of error, high levels of similarity ordinarily appear in the social maps independently generated by this procedure.

This method has been used productively in several settings, including the study of leadership and social groups in summer camps (Edwards, 1990), social groups of children in residential treatment facilities (Farmer & Cairns, 1991), social behavior and social groups in private junior high schools (Cairns, Perrin, & Cairns, 1985), peer affiliations in aggressive youth (Cairns,

3. SOCIAL NETWORKS IN ADOLESCENCE

Cairns, Neckerman, Gest, & Gariépy, 1988), early school dropouts (Cairns, Cairns, & Neckerman, 1989), the stability of social groups in at-risk youth (Neckerman, 1992), and self-concepts and self-esteem in Chinese children and adolescents (Leung, 1993; Sun, 1992).

STABILITY, CHANGE, AND DEVELOPMENTAL PATHWAYS

One feature of social networks that can be illuminated by a developmental perspective concerns the consistency of peer-group influence despite the fickleness of social-group membership. In a recent study of fourth- and seventh-grade students, Cairns, Leung, Buchanan, and Cairns (in press) found that 90% of the social clusters can be reliably reidentified over a 3-week period. There is plenty of change in group membership. Approximately one fourth to one third of the children in the seventh grade shift groups over a 3-week period. When the time interval is stretched to 1 year (from the seventh to eighth grades), the proportion of peer groups that remained identifiable reverted to levels of near chance (Neckerman, 1992). Approximately 16% of the groups remained identifiable, even when a loose criterion was adopted. These results were puzzling until we looked at the reality of their lives.

Over a 1-year period, the families of adolescents may move or break up, or students may shift schools (Cairns & Cairns, 1995). Adolescents in U.S. public schools typically shift classes and social contexts. Because propinquity is a major constraint on peer-group formation, all of these factors that affect changes in propinquity may be translated into changes in relationships. The same forces lead to friendship changes as well, and all this occurs in the normal course of events. When these changes in social context are combined with developmental changes and changes in social dynamics, small wonder there is a sharp dropout in the survival of groups and friends. To be sure, some circumstances—such as the relative isolation produced in small private schools, schools in very small communities, or rigid tracking in large schools—can heighten the stability of groups and friendships.

In brief, social networks are more appropriately described as dynamic systems, rather than static structures. Over the 14 years that we have longitudinally tracked the flux and flow of adolescent social groups, we have rarely found social groups that remained identical and unchanged from year to year (Cairns & Cairns, 1995). The contexts in which youth are observed influence both short- and long-term relationship stabilities. For instance, new and intense group relationships may be rapidly established in summer camps (Edwards, 1990). The rapid establishment of these groups underscores the ease by which new structures may be formed and old ones modified. In addition, the social context may promote or diminish stability. Observations conducted over a year (seventh to eighth grade) in a small, self-contained, private middle school indicate higher network stabilities than those observed over a year in nearby public middle schools of a larger size (Cairns et al., 1985).

The fluidity of friendship strength and group membership reflects a dynamic process of social relationships. Why the fickleness of specific social relations, and why do any changes occur over a time period as short as 3 weeks? Although the fluidity of affiliations may seem, at first blush, to be a threat to personal integrity and social continuity, we may speculate that there are good reasons for affiliative change. Close relationships that were productive in one stage or one set of circumstances can diminish in relevance—or have maladaptive effects—if the stage shifts and/or the circumstances change. When new needs and contexts emerge, so should the strength and relevance of personal relationships.

Longitudinal data from the 14-year Carolina Longitudinal Study (CLS) also suggest that there are forces of influence constancy, despite changes (Cairns & Cairns, 1995). This outcome shows up in a variety of ways. One is the finding that, despite the fluidity of social relationships, there are relative constancies in the kinds of persons with whom a given adolescent will affiliate. This shows up in the year-to-year similarities in relationships, or behavioral homophilies. There are high levels of similarity in such characteristics as propinquity, sex role, social class, and age. For example, there is a strong tendency for adolescents to select and be selected for social-group affiliation by peers who are like themselves (i.e., school failure). Once these major demographic and age characteristics are taken into account, the field becomes rather narrow. Still, there are behavioral factors that figure into the equation. Every year, there are within-group similarities in characteristics that are labeled *deviant.*

Some recent findings on how this reshuffling process occurs have been revealing. In this regard, adolescents who grow up in relatively homogeneous sociocultural settings show, if anything, a greater tendency toward homophily than those in more diverse contexts. This factor may be important in the Stattin and Magnusson (1990) findings from Sweden, where the differences with respect to race and socioeconomic status (SES) are modest compared with the United States. This may help account for some of the discrepancies that appear between their data on the group-affiliation effects of puberty and those that have been emerging from more heterogeneous groups in the United States.

Neckerman (1992) showed that, in terms of deviant behaviors, adolescents tend to reshuffle themselves into new groups that are similar to the old ones. The continuity of influence can persist despite changes in persons and contexts. Deviant youth tend to reshuffle themselves into new groups with other deviant youth. Faces may change, but the peer influences remain similar over time.

More generally, as adolescents' needs and goals change, so should the relationships that are most likely to be productive for themselves and for others with whom they associate. On this count, changes in "best friends" may be, for many persons, adaptive in the course of growing up. The problem is that changes can be disruptive in the short term even if they are adaptive in the long term. From the reports of teenage subjects, there are few satisfying ways in which relationships may be broken up or modified without distress to one or both individuals (Cairns & Cairns, 1995). There are inevitable problems in disengagement with former best friends and pain from having been in love.

CONCLUDING COMMENT

Adolescent social groups and friendships are dynamic and fluid, yet they follow predictable developmental trajectories over time and space. The shifts do not occur willy-nilly, and they occur within a systematic framework. Moreover, the instability of friendships does not diminish their importance in personal development. The fickleness of peer relationships can ensure variability of influences and the evolution over adolescence of relationships consistent with the individual's preferences and life. In many adolescent experiences, it would appear that it is often more functional to switch than stay. Indeed, failure to switch friendships when interests, goals, and beliefs diverge may lead to chronic conflicts in the relationship and in the self as well.

It is often assumed that stability in friends and groups is good, and that social change is stressful. On this view, healthy adolescents are assumed to have stable friendships and social groups, and deviant or at-risk youth are assumed to have unstable friendships and groups. Such a perspective leaves little room for growth and change, particularly when change is called for. Not all relationships are healthy, and healthy relationships can sour. The fact that friendships and social-group affiliations shift may contribute to the meaning and significance of those relationships that remain. In the development of human personality, relationship stability must be continuously balanced with the dynamics of social change and individual growth.

REFERENCES

Asher, S. R., & Coie, J. D. (Eds.). (1990). *Peer rejection in childhood.* New York: Cambridge University Press.
Asher, S. R., & Dodge, K. A. (1986). Identifying children who are rejected by their peers. *Developmental Psychology, 22,* 444–449.

54 CAIRNS, LEUNG, CAIRNS

Baldwin, J. M. (1897). *Social and ethical interpretations in mental development: A study in social psychology*. New York: Macmillan.

Bandura, A. (1982). Self-efficacy mechanism in human agency. *American Psychologist, 37*, 122–147.

Bandura, A., & Walters, R. H. (1959). *Adolescent aggression*. New York: Ronald Press.

Bavelas, A. (1948). A mathematical model for group structure. *Applied Anthropology, 7*, 16–30.

Benenson, J. F. (1990). Gender differences in social networks. *Journal of Early Adolescence, 10*, 472–495.

Berkowitz, S. D., & Wellman, B. (Eds.). (1986). *Structural sociology*. London: Cambridge University Press.

Berndt, T. J. (1982). The features and effects of friendship in early adolescence. *Child Development, 53*, 1447–1460.

Berndt, T. J., & Hoyle, S. G. (1985). Stability and change in childhood and adolescent friendships. *Developmental Psychology, 21*, 1007–1015.

Bronfenbrenner, U. (1944a). A constant frame of reference for sociometric research. *Sociometry, 6*, 363–397.

Bronfenbrenner, U. (1944b). A constant frame of reference for sociometric research: Part II. Experiment and inference. *Sociometry, 7*, 40–75.

Brown, B. B., Mounts, N., Lamborn, S. D., & Steinberg, L. (1993). Parenting practices and peer group affiliation in adolescence. *Child Development, 64*, 467–482.

Burt, R. S. (1980). Models of network structure. *Annual Review of Sociology, 6*, 79–141. Palo Alto: Annual Reviews.

Burt, R. S., & Minor, M. M. (1983). *Applied network analysis: A methodological introduction*. Sage: Beverly Hills.

Cairns, R. B. (1966). Attachment behavior of mammals. *Psychological Review, 72*, 409–426.

Cairns, R. B. (1979). Social interactional methods: An introduction. In R. B. Cairns (Ed.), *The analysis of social interaction: Methods, issues, and illustrations*. Hillsdale, NJ: Lawrence Erlbaum Associates.

Cairns, R. B. (1983). Sociometry, psychometry, and social structure: A commentary on six recent studies of popular, rejected, and neglected children. *Merrill-Palmer Quarterly, 29*, 429–438.

Cairns, R. B., & Cairns, B. D. (1988). The sociogenesis of self concepts. In N. Bolger, A. Caspi, G. Downey, and M. Moorehouse (Eds.), *Persons in social context: Developmental processes* (pp. 181–202). New York: Cambridge University Press.

Cairns, R. B., & Cairns, B. D. (1991). Social cognition and social networks: A developmental perspective. In D. Pepler & K. H. Rubin (Eds.), *The development and treatment of childhood aggression* (pp. 249–278). Hillsdale, NJ: Lawrence Erlbaum Associates.

Cairns, R. B. & Cairns, B. D. (1995). *Lifelines and risks: Pathways of youth in our time*. New York: Cambridge University Press.

Cairns, R. B., Cairns, B. D., & Neckerman, H. J. (1989). Early school dropout: Configurations and determinants. *Child Development, 60*, 1437–1452.

Cairns, R. B., Cairns, B. D., Neckerman, H. J., Gest, S., & Gariépy, J.-L. (1988). Social networks and aggressive behavior: Peer support or peer rejection? *Developmental Psychology, 24*, 815–823.

Cairns, R. B., & Kroll, A. B. (1994). A developmental perspective on gender differences and similarities. In M. L. Rutter & D. F. Hay (Eds.), *Development through life: A handbook for clinicians* (pp. 350–372). Oxford, England: Blackwood Scientific Publications.

Cairns, R. B., Leung, M.-C., Buchanan, L., & Cairns, B. D. (in press). Friendships and social networks in childhood and early adolescence: Short-term stability and fluidity. *Child Development*.

Cairns, R. B., Perrin, J. E., & Cairns, B. D. (1985). Social structure and social cognition in early adolescence: Affiliative patterns. *Journal of Early Adolescence, 5*, 339–355.

Cairns, R. B., Peterson, G., & Neckerman, H. J. (1988). Suicidal behavior in aggressive adolescents. *Journal of Clinical Child Psychology, 17*, 298–309.

Caspi, A., & Moffitt, T. E. (1991, April). *Puberty and deviance in girls.* Symposium paper read at the biennial meeting of the Society for Research in Child Development, Seattle, WA.

Cohen, A. K. (1955). *Delinquent boys: The culture of the gang.* Glencoe, IL: The Free Press.

Cohen, J. M. (1977). Sources of peer group homogeneity. *Sociology of Education, 50*, 227–241.

Coie, J. D., & Dodge, K. A. (1983). Continuities and changes in children's social status: A five-year longitudinal study. *Merrill-Palmer Quarterly, 29*, 261–282.

Coie, J. D., Dodge, K. A., & Coppotelli, H. A. (1982). Dimensions and types of social status: A cross-age perspective. *Developmental Psychology, 18*, 557–569.

Cottrell, L. S. (1942). The analysis of situational fields in social psychology. *American Sociological Review, 7*, 370–382.

Dodge, K. A., Schlundt, D. C., Schocken, I., & Delugach, J. D. (1983). Social competence and children's sociometric status: The role of peer group entry strategies. *Merrill-Palmer Quarterly, 29*, 309–336.

Eder, D., & Hallinan, M. T. (1978). Sex differences in children's friendships. *American Sociological Review, 43*, 237–250.

Edwards, C. A. (1990). *Leadership, social networks, and personal attributes in school age girls.* Unpublished doctoral dissertation, University of North Carolina at Chapel Hill, Chapel Hill, NC.

Elliott, D. S., Huizinga, D., & Menard, S. (1989). *Multiple problem youth: Delinquency, substance use, and mental health problems.* New York: Springer-Verlag.

Farmer, T. W., & Cairns, R. B. (1991). Social networks and social status in emotionally disturbed children. *Behavioral Disorders, 16*, 288–298.

Feiring, C., & Lewis, M. (1987). The child's social network: Sex differences from three to six years. *Sex Roles: A Journal of Research, 17*, 621–636.

Festinger, L. (1949). The analysis of sociograms using matrix algebra. *Human Relations, 2*, 153–158.

Giordano, P. C., Cernkovich, S. A., & Pugh, M. D. (1986). Friendship and delinquency. *American Journal of Sociology, 91*, 1170–1201.

Hallinan, M. T. (1979). Structural effects on children's friendships and cliques. *Social Psychology Quarterly, 42*, 43–54.

Hallinan, M. T., & Smith, S. S. (1989). Classroom characteristics and student friendship cliques. *Social Forces, 67*, 898–919.

Hartup, W. W. (1983). Peer groups. In P. H. Mussen (Gen. Ed.) & M. Hetherington (Ed.), *Handbook of child psychology* (4th ed., Vol. 4, pp. 103–196). New York: Wiley.

Homans, G. C. (1950). *The human group.* New York: Harcourt Brace.

Kandel, D. B. (1978). Homophily, selection, and socialization in adolescent friendships. *American Journal of Sociology, 84*, 427–436.

Kandel, D. B. (1994, February). *The interpersonal context of adolescent deviance: What we know, what we need to know.* Open SRA Study Group paper read at the fifth biennial meetings of the Society for Research on Adolescence, San Diego, CA.

Leung, M.-C. (1993). *Social cognition and social networks of Chinese school children in Hong Kong.* Unpublished doctoral dissertation, University of North Carolina at Chapel Hill, Chapel Hill, NC.

Levine, J. H. (1972). Spheres of influence. *American Sociological Review, 37*, 14–27.

Maccoby, E. (1988). Gender as a social category. *Developmental Psychology, 24*, 735–765.

Maccoby, E. (1990). Gender and relationships—a developmental account. *American Psychologist, 46*, 513–520.

Magnusson, D. (1988). *Individual development from an interactional perspective.* Hillsdale, NJ: Lawrence Erlbaum Associates.

Marsden, P. V., & Lin, N. (1982). *Social structure and network analysis.* Beverly Hills, CA: Sage.

Moreno, J. L. (1934). *Who shall survive? A new approach to the problem of human interrelations.* Washington, DC: Nervous and Mental Disease Publishing Co.

Neckerman, H. J. (1992). *A longitudinal investigation of the stability and fluidity of social networks and peer relationships of children and adolescents.* Unpublished doctoral dissertation, University of North Carolina at Chapel Hill, Chapel Hill, NC.

Patterson, G. R. (1982). *Coercive family systems.* Eugene, OR: Castalia.

Patterson, G. R., Reid, J. B., & Dishion, T. J. (1992). *Antisocial boys.* Eugene, OR: Castalia.

Peery, J. C. (1979). Popular, amiable, isolated, rejected: A reconceptualization of sociometric status in preschool children. *Child Development, 50,* 1231–1234.

Piaget, J. (1954). *The construction of reality in the child.* New York: Basic Books.

Richards, W. D. (1986). *The NEGOPY network analysis program.* Burnaby, British Columbia, Canada: Simon Fraser University Press.

Richards, W. D., & Rice, R. E. (1981). The NEGOPY network analysis program. *Social Networks, 3,* 215–223.

Rosenblatt, J. S., & Lehrman, D. S. (1963). Maternal behavior of the laboratory rat. In H. L. Rheingold (Ed.), *Maternal behavior in mammals* (pp. 8–57). New York: Wiley.

Scott, J. (1988). Trend report: Social network analysis. *Sociology, 22,* 109–127.

Sears, R. R. (1951). A theoretical framework for personality and social behavior. *American Psychologist, 6,* 476–483.

Sears, R. R., Maccoby, E. E., & Levin, H. (1957). *Patterns of child rearing.* Evanston, IL: Row, Peterson.

Stattin, H., & Magnusson, D. (1990). *Pubertal-maturation in female development.* Hillsdale, NJ: Lawrence Erlbaum Associates.

Sun, S.-L. (1992, March). *Social relationships of children and adolescents in Taiwan.* Poster presented at meetings of Society of Research in Adolescence, Washington, DC.

Waldrop, M. F., & Halverson, C. F. (1975). Intensive and extensive peer behavior: Longitudinal and cross-sectional analyses. *Child Development, 46,* 19–26.

Wellman, B. (1983). Network analysis: Some basic principles. In R. Collins (Ed.), *Sociological theory* (pp. 144–200). San Francisco: Jossey-Bass.

White, H. C., Boorman, S. A., & Breiger, R. L. (1976). Social structure from multiple networks: I. Blockmodels of roles and positions. *American Journal of Sociology, 81,* 370–380.

Youniss, J. (1980). *Parents and peers in social development.* Chicago: University of Chicago Press.

Youniss, J., & Smollar, J. (1985). *Adolescent relations with mothers, fathers, and friends.* Chicago: University of Chicago Press.

CHAPTER FOUR

Puberty and the Gender Organization of Schools: How Biology and Social Context Shape the Adolescent Experience

Avshalom Caspi
University of Wisconsin

Where should I send my child to school? This question is now heard throughout the United States because "school choice" has become the rallying slogan for educational reformers of different political bents. But beyond political persuasion, parents wish to know the facts: What kind of school is best for my child?

Schools are important because they provide instruction. But they do more than that. Schools also provide youth with opportunities for social interaction. Indeed, what matters most about schools are their characteristics as cultural and social organizations—in particular, the values and norms to which they expose their pupils (Rutter, Maughan, Mortimore, & Ouston, 1979). Among the many characteristics along which schools can be evaluated, one characteristic stands out most clearly: gender composition.

The choice between coeducational (coed) and single-sex secondary schools is attracting a great deal of attention among feminists, leaders of different religious denominations, and students of education and socialization (Lee & Marks, 1992). Is coeducation at the secondary school level necessary to prepare adolescents to take their place in the natural world of men and women (Feather, 1974)? Or is coeducation harmful to adolescents because it subjects them to unnecessary heterosexual and social pressures and distracts them from academic pursuits (Coleman, 1961)? Studies that have compared the attitudes and attainments of students who attend coed versus single-sex schools provide radically diverging answers (e.g., Dale, 1974; Lee & Bryk, 1986; Marsh, 1989; Marsh, Owens, Myers, & Smith, 1989).

In fact, the extant evidence—containing many contradictory conclusions—
has been used to support widely differing policy recommendations.

Is the choice of coed versus single-sex secondary schools a straightforward
choice? Or does school choice depend on the type of child in question? If
the effect associated with attending different school types is simply a main
effect, advice can be dispensed with ease. But if the effect associated with
attending different school types depends on the type of child in question,
advice should be dispensed with caution.

In this chapter, I summarize some of what my colleagues and I have
learned about the effects of attending coed versus single-sex secondary
schools. The results from our studies are not definitive; they represent one
empirical contribution among other well-done studies. Our goal in conducting this work is twofold. We hope that our results will contribute information
to balanced debates about the effectiveness of different types of schools.
We also hope that our studies shed light on developmental pathways as
they unfold in relation to one of the most important social contexts of
adolescence: schools.

This chapter focuses on two adolescent outcomes: juvenile delinquency
and school attainment. I ask: What are the effects of attending coed versus
single-sex schools on participation in delinquent behavior and on scholastic
attainment? In this chapter, I limit my attention to girls. I do so because
much of the debate about school choice and the gender organization of
schools has been prompted by concern for the socialization and education
of young women.

METHODOLOGICAL PROBLEMS IN ESTIMATING
THE EFFECTS OF ATTENDING COED
VERSUS SINGLE-SEX SECONDARY SCHOOLS

Estimating the effects of attending coed versus single-sex secondary schools
is easier said than done. Ideally, we could randomly assign students to
different types of schools and then assess the outcomes of this experiment.
Because it is not possible to assign students to different types of schools,
researchers must compare existing schools as they are naturally constituted.
Interpreting results from such quasi-experiments is difficult because coed
and single-sex schools may differ on more than just gender organization.
Indeed, few American students attend single-sex schools, and those who
do comprise a select group (e.g., students enrolled in expensive private
schools or military academies).

Faced with these difficulties, researchers have relied on two other strategies: They have limited their comparisons of coed versus single-sex schools
to (a) Catholic schools or (b) non-U.S. schools. These strategies are not
without problems. It is not clear that results from Catholic schools will

generalize to public schools, and it is not clear that results from other countries will generalize to the United States. However, if similar results are found in Catholic schools and in a host of different countries, their relevance to the U.S. public school system should at least be taken seriously.

In our research, we have chosen the second strategy, and we rely on data from New Zealand. Our research is part of the Dunedin Multidisciplinary Health and Development Study. The study's history has been described by Silva (1990). Briefly, the study is a longitudinal investigation of the health, development, and behavior of a complete cohort of consecutive births between April 1, 1972 and March 31, 1973 in Dunedin, New Zealand. Perinatal data were obtained; when the children were traced for follow-up at 3 years of age, 1,139 children were deemed eligible for inclusion in the longitudinal study by residence in the province. Of these, 1,037 (91%) were assessed. The sample has been reassessed with a diverse battery of psychological, medical, and sociological measures every 2 years since the children were age 3. Data were collected for 991 subjects at age 5, 954 at age 7, 955 at age 9, 925 at age 11, 850 at age 13, and 976 at age 15.

We chose New Zealand as our setting because, relative to the United States, the New Zealand secondary school system offers a convenient natural experiment for estimating the effects of attending coed versus single-sex schools. Table 4.1 provides a guide to the New Zealand school system. New Zealand youth enter secondary schools at age 13, at which point their families choose a coed or single-sex high school. Of the girls participating in our study, 54% enrolled in coed schools and 46% enrolled in single-sex schools.

Any examination of the effects of secondary schools as developmental contexts requires that we also consider possible variations in school intake: Are there any systematic differences between students who enroll in coed versus single-sex schools that could jeopardize our ability to interpret our findings? For example, if we find that some types of school "produce" more talented students, it is necessary to ask whether those schools "take in" more talented students from the outset. This "intake" or selection effect must be understood and controlled before evaluating the effects of gender composition in schools.

To examine possible selection effects, we turned to data collected when the children in our study were ages 9 and 11—before they entered secondary schools. We examined selection effects in four areas of family and individual functioning: family values, social class, behavior problems, and intelligence.

Family Values

It is possible that parents who enroll their children in single-sex schools share a distinct value system. For example, if such parents profess religious beliefs, expect achievement, or exercise close supervision over their children, such

TABLE 4.1
A Guide to the New Zealand School System

Age	School Type
	Primary School
5	Primer 1, Primer 2
6	Primer 3, Primer 4
7	Standard 1
8	Standard 2
9	Standard 3
10	Standard 4
11*	Form I
12*	Form II
	Intermediate School
11	Form I
12	Form II
	Secondary School
13	Third Form
14	Fourth Form
15	Fifth Form (School Certificate examination)
16	Sixth Form (Sixth Form examination)
17+	Seventh Form (Bursary/Scholarship examinations)
	Tertiary Education
	University
	Polytechnics
	Colleges of education

Note. Students may leave school after 15, regardless of how far they have progressed. A relatively small percentage of students goes as far as Seventh Form—traditionally it has only been the academically bright.
*Or alternatively (and more common in cities) at age 11 and 12.

values may shape their children's behavior. Failure to control for such differences in family values could lead us to misinterpret any observed school effects.

To evaluate this possibility, we turned to the Moos Family Environment Scales (Moos & Moos, 1981; Parnicky, Williams, & Silva, 1985), which were completed by the mothers of our subjects when the sample members were 9 years old. This well-known instrument is composed of 10 subscales whose names are self-explanatory: Cohesion, Expressiveness, Conflict, Independence, Achievement Orientation, Intellectual-Cultural Orientation, Active-Recreational Orientation, Moral-Religious, Organization, and Control.

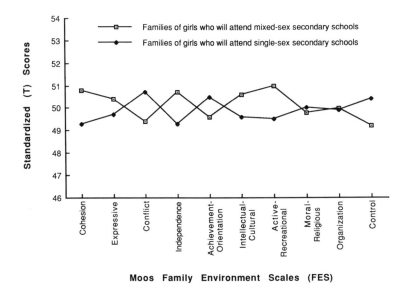

Moos Family Environment Scales (FES)

FIG. 4.1. The family environments (at age 9) of students who eventually attend either single-sex or coeducational secondary schools.

We compared the parents of students in coed and single-sex schools on all 10 family climate subscales.

Figure 4.1 presents the average profile of the family environments of children who attend single-sex schools and the average profile of the family environments of children who attend coed schools. The figure points to few meaningful differences between the groups. In fact, the biggest difference does not exceed 1.6 T-score points.

Although these parental values were not systematically linked to school choice, New Zealand parents do give careful thought to the selection of a school for their children. According to a recent survey, the main reasons New Zealand parents gave for choosing their children's school were (a) the school's "reputation" (53% mentioned), (b) locality or closest to home (53% mentioned), and (c) that previous family members had attended the same school (33% mentioned; Silva, 1987).

Social Class

The parents' occupations were rated on a 6-point scale that is used to assign social class in New Zealand (Elley & Irvin, 1972). A comparison of children attending single-sex versus coed schools revealed a statistically significant difference between them in terms of their family SES (3.1 vs. 3.4, $t = 2.1$, p

< .05). Higher SES families were more likely to enroll their children in single-sex schools. However, the magnitude of this difference is quite small.

Behavior Problems

Because of our interest in juvenile delinquency as an outcome, it is important to establish whether children with behavior problems earlier in childhood were more likely to be enrolled in coed rather than single-sex secondary schools. The Rutter Child Scales (RCS; Rutter, Tizard, & Whitmore, 1970) were filled out by parents and teachers. The RCS items regarding *antisocial, inattentive, impulsive,* and *hyperactive* behaviors were summed to provide a rating scale of *externalizing* behavior problems at age 9. We standardized and combined the parent and teacher ratings into a single score. A comparison of children attending coed and single-sex schools revealed no significant difference between them in terms of childhood behavior problems ($t < 1$).

Intelligence

The Wechsler Intelligence Scale for Children–Revised (WISC–R; Wechsler, 1974) was administered to the children by trained psychometrists within 1 month of their birthdays. A comparison of students attending single-sex versus coed secondary schools revealed a statistically significant difference between them in terms of their IQ (110 vs. 107, $t = 2.4$, $p < .05$). Students with higher IQ scores at age 11 were more likely to later attend single-sex schools, but the magnitude of this difference is quite small.

In summary, it appears that children from more advantaged social backgrounds and brighter children were slightly more likely to attend single-sex schools. Although the selection effects are quite small, these results suggest that we should control for these potentially confounding factors when evaluating school effects on delinquency and attainment, respectively.

ADOLESCENT PATHWAYS IN DIFFERENT SCHOOL CONTEXTS: THE INFLUENCE OF PUBERTAL TIMING

An examination of school effects on adolescent behavior must also acknowledge the large individual differences between students' physical development. At age 13, when New Zealand youth enter secondary schools, some students will already be "physical adults" and some will still be "physical children." The timing of puberty has profound effects on adolescents, and the extent of these effects may depend on the gender composition of the schools they attend.

Research in the United States and Europe has shown that early-maturing girls are likely to experience a more turbulent adolescence than their late-maturing peers. For example, Simmons and Blyth (1987) found several problems among early-maturing girls in their U.S. study: body image disturbances, lower academic success, and conduct problems in school. Likewise, Stattin and Magnusson (1990) reported more delinquent behavior among early-maturing girls in Sweden. We have found similar effects in New Zealand (Caspi & Moffitt, 1991).

The reported age at menarche (in months) in our New Zealand study ranged from 102 to 180, $M = 155.28$, $SD = 12.12$, median = 156, or 13.0 years of age. We assigned girls to one of three menarcheal groups: early (12:5 or younger), on time (12:6 to 13:6), and late (13:7 or older), where the early and late groups constituted the extreme 30% tails of the distribution in menarcheal age. Regardless of whether we relied on teachers' reports, parents' reports, or adolescents' self-reports, we found that the early onset of menarche was associated with the most disruptive psychosocial reactions in adolescence.

We have hypothesized that these disruptive psychosocial reactions to early puberty would be more pronounced among girls who, at age 13, make the transition to a coed secondary school than among girls who make the transition to a single-sex school (Caspi, Lynam, Moffitt, & Silva, 1993). Our reasoning is based on two lines of research.

The first reason has to do with the differential nature of social opportunities that operate in the two types of schools. Relative to single-sex schools, the gender composition of coed schools subjects girls to a greater variety of social and sexual pressures from peers. For example, previous research has shown that delinquent behavior is more normative in schools with an equal mix of boys and girls than in all-girl schools (Rutter et al., 1979). After all, boys are much more likely than girls to engage in delinquent activities (Hindelang, Hirschi, & Weiss, 1981). In such settings, then, girls are more likely to encounter delinquent role models and to be reinforced by peers for participating in delinquent activities (Giordano, 1978). In addition, girls in coed schools, especially if they are physically mature, are more likely to be exposed to the predatory attention of males. In his studies of adolescent sexuality, Udry (1988, 1990) found that androgenic hormones predicted sexual interest and noncoital sexual behaviors among females, independent of levels of physical development, but the social-stimulus value associated with advanced physical development was required for the transition to sexual intercourse among girls, independent of their hormone levels. These results indicate that males are responsive to the physical development of girls, and suggest that early-maturing girls may encounter different pressures in coed schools than in single-sex schools.

The second reason has to do with the learning climate in the two types of schools. Social–psychological studies of the high school environment suggest that coed and single-sex schools differ in more than obvious ways. Coed schools are more "pleasure oriented" than single-sex schools; they appear to place more emphasis on social affiliation and less emphasis on the control and discipline of students (Schneider & Coutts, 1982). In terms of their time management, students in single-sex schools have less free time, spend less time on extracurricular activities, and spend more time on homework (Trickett, Trickett, Castro, & Schaffner, 1982). These results suggest that early-maturing girls in single-sex schools settings are more likely to encounter institutional pressures that would curb their inclination to misbehave.

In summary, we have sought to explore the comparative influence of two different school types, and to understand how differences in the timing of pubertal development influence social behavior in these two types of schools.

EFFECTS OF SINGLE-SEX VERSUS COED SECONDARY SCHOOLS ON JUVENILE DELINQUENCY

Our analysis began with the question, Do early-maturing girls in coed schools have more contact with delinquent patterns of behavior? To answer this question, we relied on the girls' reports of peer delinquency.

When the girls were 13 years old, they were presented with a list of 58 delinquent behaviors. They were then asked the question, Do your friends, or other kids your age that you know, do these things? The 58 delinquent behaviors included 29 items tapping "norm-violating" behaviors and 29 items tapping more serious illegal behaviors. Norm-violating behaviors include items such as getting drunk, stealing money from milk bottles, and breaking windows. The more serious illegal behaviors include items such as shoplifting, breaking and entering, fighting, and using weapons. The girls sorted each of the 58 items into three piles: *I don't know anyone who has done this* (0), *Only one or two kids do it* (1), or *Lots of kids I know do it* (2). Scores were summed to create an index of familiarity with peer delinquency.

We then carried out a regression analysis, using the measure of peer delinquency as the outcome variable. The independent variables in this analysis were timing of menarche and school type. In this analysis, we first partialed out the effects associated with social class and externalizing behavior problems in late childhood.

The groups means (in z scores) from the regression analysis are shown in Fig. 4.2. There was a significant linear effect for time of menarche ($\beta = -.19$, $p < .01$); the earlier the onset of menarche, the more contact girls had with delinquent patterns of behavior. The main effect for school type was also statistically significant ($\beta = .12$, $p < .05$); girls in coed schools had more contact with delinquent patterns of behavior than their peers in single-sex schools.

To examine our hypothesis—that the effects of early puberty would be especially pronounced in coed schools—we derived a set of predictions to

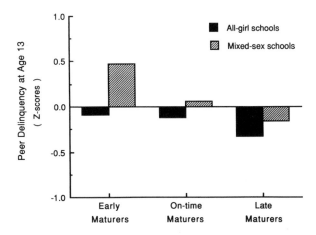

FIG. 4.2.   Peer delinquency at age 13 as a function of age at menarche and school type.

be tested in a series of planned contrasts. The results showed that (a) early-maturing girls in coed schools had more contact with delinquent patterns of behavior than their counterparts who were attending single-sex schools, $t = 2.1$, $p < .05$; (b) on-time maturing girls in coed schools had slightly more contact with delinquent patterns of behavior than their counterparts who were attending single-sex schools, $t = 1.7$, $p < .10$; and (c) late-maturing girls in coed schools did not differ from their counterparts in single-sex schools in terms of contact with delinquent patterns of behavior, $t < 1$.

Next we asked, Do early-maturing girls in coed schools also engage in more delinquent behavior? To answer this question, we relied on the girls' self-reports of their delinquency. When the girls were 13 years old, and again at 15, they completed the Self-Reported Early Delinquency instrument (SRED; described fully in Moffitt & Silva, 1988), which contains the 29 norm-violating items and the 29 illegal-behavior items mentioned earlier. Evidence about the reliability and validity of this instrument is presented in other reports (Moffitt, 1989; Moffitt & Silva, 1988).

We then carried out two regression analyses. In the first analysis, we examined self-reported delinquency at age 13; in the second analysis, we examined self-reported delinquency at age 15. The independent variables in both analyses were timing of menarche and school type. As before, we partialed out the effects associated with social class and externalizing behavior problems when interpreting the effects associated with attending different types of secondary schools.

Figure 4.3 shows the group means (in z scores) from the regression analysis performed on self-reported delinquency at age 13. The results show there was a significant linear effect for time of menarche ($\beta = -.20$, $p < .01$); the earlier

CASPI

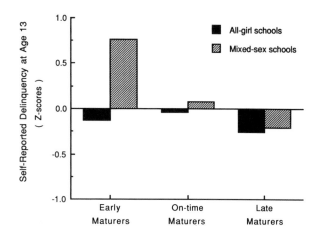

FIG. 4.3. Self-reported delinquency at age 13 as a function of age at menarche and school type.

the onset of menarche, the more girls engaged in delinquent behaviors. The main effect for school type was not statistically significant (β = .07).

To examine our hypothesis—that the effects of early puberty would be especially pronounced in coed schools—we turned again to the set of planned contrasts. The results showed that (a) early-maturing girls in coed schools engaged in more delinquent behavior than their counterparts who were attending single-sex schools, t = 3.0, p < .01; (b) on-time maturing girls in coed schools did not engage in more delinquent behavior than their counterparts who were attending single-sex schools, t < 1; and (c) late-maturing girls in coed schools did not engage in more delinquent behavior than their counterparts in single-sex schools, t < 1.

What about at age 15, 2 years later? Figure 4.4 shows the group means (in z scores) from the regression analysis performed on self-reported delinquency at age 15. In contrast to the analysis of age 13 data, the analysis of age 15 data did not reveal a clear-cut linear effect for time of menarche (β = −.11, p < .05). As can be gleaned from Fig. 4.3, early and on-time maturers did not differ from each other in terms of self-reported delinquency at age 15, but both groups differed significantly from late-maturing girls. In addition, the main effect for school type was not significant (β = .03).

As before, we used a set of planned contrasts to compare our specific predictions to the obtained data. The results showed that (a) early-maturing girls in coed schools engaged in more delinquent behavior than their counterparts who were attending single-sex schools, t = 2.0, p < .05; (b) on-time maturing girls in coed schools engaged in slightly more delinquent activities than their single-sex school counterparts, t = 1.8, p < .10; and (c) late-maturing

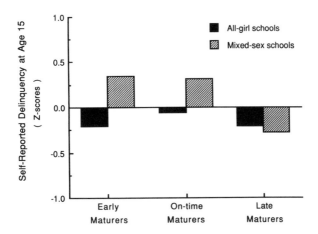

FIG. 4.4. Self-reported delinquency at age 15 as a function of age at menarche and school type.

girls in coed schools did not engage in more delinquent behavior than their counterparts in single-sex schools, $t < 1$.

Taken as a whole, the results in Figs. 4.2–4.4 suggest that girls in coed schools were more likely to become involved in delinquent behavior than girls in single-sex schools, but this school effect depended on the timing of pubertal development. Moreover, the temporal sequence of our findings suggests that, in coed schools, pubertal development first brings girls into contact with delinquent activities, after which they may begin to sample from some of these activities. We believe these results suggest that the cultural and social organization of coed schools may complicate girls' responses to the onset of puberty, especially if it is early.

Why do coed schools appear to have this effect? Rowe, Rodgers, and Meseck-Bushey (1990) recently demonstrated that adolescent problem behaviors may be "transmitted by an 'epidemic' process analogous to the epidemic transmission of infectious disease" (p. 127). The analogy to epidemic infections is merely a useful analytic device to describe a social process, according to which the likelihood that youth will engage in problem behaviors depends on the proportion of problem-behavior youth in the environment. The more problem-behavior youth, the more likely that problem behavior will "spread" to other youth. Thus, problem behaviors in adolescence are spread by contact, wherein "initiates" are "infected" by "carriers." Boys are infectious carriers. Indeed, their presence in coed school settings may serve to dilute school norms for tolerable conduct. Thus, girls in coed schools are more likely to observe delinquent behavior, to be given opportunities for participating in it, and to be reinforced for partaking in it.

68

Support for this interpretation is found in two other studies of the pubertal experience. Simmons and Blyth (1987) examined the transition to early adolescence among youth in two different educational contexts: K–6 and K–8 elementary schools. They found that early-maturing girls who began to date early suffered more self-image problems if their transition to seventh grade involved a shift from a K–6 elementary school into a junior high school than if they remained in a K–8 system. Simmons and Blyth suggested that the early-maturing girls' vulnerability in seventh grade may stem from the social and sexual pressures exerted by older males in their new peer culture.

Stattin and Magnusson (1990) also showed that the association between early maturation and delinquent behavior is influenced by the social composition of girls' social networks. Although their study did not focus on schools per se, their findings illustrate a social process that is more likely endemic to coed school settings than to single-sex settings. Specifically, Stattin and Magnusson found that early-maturing girls are likely to gravitate toward chronologically older peers. Older peers, in turn, appear to function as norm transmitters—sanctioning and even encouraging a variety of norm-breaking behaviors among early-maturing girls.

As shown in Fig. 4.5, the relationship between early maturation and norm-breaking behaviors was conditioned by peers; the relationship was strong and positive if the girls had older friends, but practically absent if the girls affiliated exclusively with same-age peers (Magnusson, 1988). In further analyses, Stattin and Magnusson showed that this effect was attributable to the role that friends played as norm transmitters. Specifically, early-maturing girls with older friends expected weaker negative reactions after engaging in

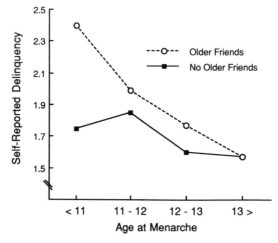

FIG. 4.5. Self-reported delinquency as a function of age at menarche and affiliation with older friends. The data are from the Individual Development and Adjustment study in Sweden (Magnusson, 1988).

delinquent activities than did girls without older friends. Thus, the social network may serve as a convoy throughout development, providing support for misbehavior.

Thus far, I have reported on age 13 and age 15 data as if they were distinct cross sections. Left unaddressed is the connection between girls' behavior across the adolescent years. First, are those girls who sample from delinquency in early adolescence likely to continue to engage in delinquency in middle adolescence? Second, does the persistence of delinquent behavior vary by school context? Our results show that there was a good deal of stability from age 13 to age 15: Those girls who engaged in delinquency at age 13 continued to engage in delinquency at age 15, $r = .5$, $p < .001$. But our results also show that this persistence was significantly more marked among girls in coed schools than among girls in single-sex schools. In coed schools, the correlation between age 13 to age 15 delinquency was .6; in single-sex schools, the correlation was half that size—.3.

These results suggest that coed schools offer favorable conditions for the persistence of delinquent behaviors because delinquent girls are more likely to find reinforcements and opportunities for their activities when in the company of boys. In contrast, the normative controls in single-sex schools appear to suppress the persistence of delinquent behaviors, possibly because delinquent girls are more likely to be viewed as deviant in these settings. Deviant individuals are often disliked, and thus are more likely to be coerced into more modal patterns—what Cattell (1982) called "coercion to the biosocial mean" (p. 353).

In summary, it appears that school contexts play an important role in regulating continuities in social development (Cairns & Hood, 1983). Delinquent activities need the support of the social group for their initiation, as well as their maintenance. As Scott reminded his audience during the 1977 presidential address to the Behavior Genetics Association, "Almost all behavior that is exhibited by members of highly social species . . . is expressed within social relationships. What little solitary behavior remains is expressed within social contexts derived from these relationships . . . the concept of the independent individual is a myth" (pp. 327–328).

EFFECTS OF SINGLE-SEX VERSUS COED SECONDARY SCHOOLS ON SCHOOL ATTAINMENT

Ideally, an evaluation of school effects on academic attainment should employ outcome measures that are not school specific. When the content of exams or the practice of grading varies across schools, it is difficult to compare students' performance. In this regard, the New Zealand school system—with its standardized national examination system—offers an important advantage for our research.

As shown in Table 4.1, the New Zealand school system provides three examinations: School Certificate, Sixth Form, and Bursary/Scholarship exams. According to the *New Zealand Official Yearbook* (1993), the School Certificate examination is taken by almost all pupils and is administered at the end of 3 years of secondary education. A candidate may enter the examination in any number of subjects, up to six, and is credited with a grade for each subject. Grades are awarded on a 1–7 scale. The Sixth Form examination is taken by the slightly smaller number of pupils who stay on in high school to satisfactorily complete a course of 1 year beyond School Certificate level. No more than six subjects can be taken. Grades are awarded on a 1–9 scale. The University Bursaries Entrance Scholarships examination is taken by a relatively small number of students during the Seventh Form, and is used in determining awards for university studies.

We have gathered both School Certificate and Sixth Form examination results for members of our study in New Zealand. With these results, we can go on to examine the comparative effectiveness of schools. We carried out a regression analysis using the School Certificate and Sixth Form examination results as the outcome measures. The independent variables in these analyses were timing of menarche and school type. In these analyses, we first partialed out the effects associated with social class and intelligence. The group means from these analyses are shown in Figs. 4.6 and 4.7, where the exam scores are presented as z scores.

With regard to the School Certificate examination, there was a trend for late-maturing girls to perform better than early-maturing girls, but this difference was not statistically significant ($\beta = .05$). The difference between school types was also not statistically significant ($\beta = -.01$). Finally, there was no significant interaction effect.

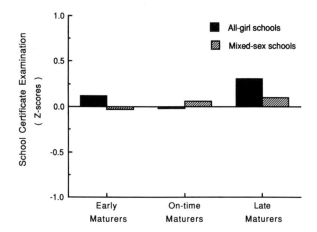

FIG. 4.6. Performance on the School Certificate examination as a function of age at menarche and school type.

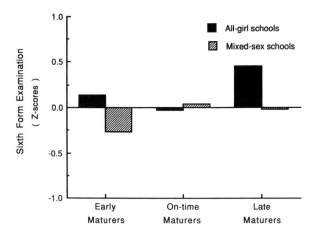

FIG. 4.7. Performance on the Sixth Form examination as a function of age at menarche and school type.

With regard to the Sixth Form examination, there was a significant linear effect for time of menarche ($\beta = .10$, $p < .05$); late-maturing girls tended to perform better than early-maturing girls. The difference between school types was statistically significant in this analysis ($\beta = -.10$, $p < .05$); girls in single-sex schools outperformed girls in coed schools even after accounting for intake differences in social class and IQ.

We used a set of planned contrasts to test the interaction between pubertal timing and school type. The results showed that (a) early-maturing girls in coed schools performed less well than their counterparts who were attending single-sex schools, $t = 2.2$, $p < .05$; (b) on-time maturing girls in coed schools did not differ in their performance from their single-sex school counterparts, $t < 1$; and (c) late-maturing girls in coed schools performed less well than their counterparts in single-sex schools, $t = 2.5$, $p < .05$.

The results from our analysis of school attainment are not as clear cut as the results from our analysis of juvenile delinquency. Still, these results provide converging evidence that early-maturing girls experience more difficulties in coed settings. Indeed, both Figs. 4.6 and 4.7 show that early-maturing girls in coed schools obtained the worst scores on their examinations—School Certificate and Sixth Form. In contrast, late-maturing girls in single-sex settings obtained the highest scores on both examinations.

CONCLUSION

Questions regarding the gender organization of schools are on the minds of many because educational reforms are sweeping the country. The chapter's opening question (Where should I send my child to school?) was not flippant. Parents wish to know about the comparative effectiveness of different types of schools, and social scientists have an obligation to try to furnish the best possible answer.

We have sought to answer this question by conducting research in New Zealand. U.S. readers may question the relevance of a study of school contexts in New Zealand for youths in the United States. Indeed, the two nations' school systems differ in important ways. Still, because the selection effects in New Zealand schools are considerably less pronounced than those in the United States, the New Zealand project offered a unique opportunity to capitalize on a "natural" experiment. Of course, our efforts to reduce "intake" differences between different types of schools—whether through conducting research in New Zealand or through the introduction of statistical controls— are not enough. It is possible that we have failed to render the two different types of schools equivalent, even with adjustments for the most relevant intake differences, and our conclusions must be interpreted accordingly.

The conclusions that we can draw are sobering, however, because they suggest no clear-cut solution to questions about the comparative effects of schools. Debates about the comparative effectiveness of schools are often reduced to dichotomous alternatives. With regard to the gender organization of schools, the question is asked: Which are better, coed or single-sex schools? Our research suggests that these debates obscure both the complexities of adolescent development, as well as the challenges that confront students, parents, and teachers.

It appears that the effects of different school environments on adolescent development depend on individual differences in pubertal timing. The gender organization of schools may influence pathways through adolescence, but this influence varies according to the timing of physical maturation. Males in the classroom are more disruptive for young women than for little girls (never mind that the "young women" and the "little girls" were born in the same year).

These findings serve to remind that the impact of biological events on behavioral development is controlled by the social context of development. These findings also suggest that uniform interventions in the gender organization of schools are useless because they will have different effects on different persons at different times. Social policies and educational reforms cannot be mandated on the basis of such conditional effects. However, conditional effects can be used to alert parents to the potential consequences that their school choice will have for their children.

ACKNOWLEDGMENTS

This work was supported by U.S. Public Health Service Grants from the Personality and Social Processes Research branch (MH-49414 to A. Caspi), the Antisocial and Violent Behavior Branch (MH-45070 to T. E. Moffitt) of the National Institute of Mental Health, and the William T. Grant Foundation. The Dunedin Multidisciplinary Health and Development Research Unit is directed by Phil A. Silva and supported by the Health Research Council of New Zealand. My thanks go to Donald Lynam, Terrie Moffitt, Ros Sidney, Phil Silva, and Sheila Williams, who have collaborated with me on the work reported in this chapter.

REFERENCES

Cairns, R. B., & Hood, K. E. (1983). Continuity in social development: A comparative perspective on individual difference prediction. In P. B. Baltes & O. G. Brim (Eds.), *Life-span development and behavior* (Vol. 5, pp. 301–358). New York: Academic Press.

Caspi, A., Lynam, D., Moffitt, T. E., & Silva, P. A. (1993). Unraveling girls' delinquency: Biological, dispositional, and contextual contributions to adolescent misbehavior. *Developmental Psychology, 29*, 19–30.

Caspi, A., & Moffitt, T. E. (1991). Individual differences are accentuated during periods of social change: The sample case of girls at puberty. *Journal of Personality and Social Psychology, 61*, 157–168.

Cattell, R. B. (1982). *The inheritance of personality and ability.* San Diego, CA: Academic Press.

Coleman, J. S. (1961). *The adolescent society.* Glencoe, IL: The Free Press.

Dale, R. R. (1974). *Mixed or single-sex school? Vol. 3. Attainment, attitudes and overview.* London: Routledge & Kegan Paul.

Elley, W. B., & Irving, J. C. (1972). A socio-economic index for New Zealand based on levels of education and income from the 1966 census. *New Zealand Journal of Educational Studies, 7*, 153–167.

Feather, N. T. (1974). Coeducation, values, and satisfaction with school. *Journal of Educational Psychology, 66*, 9–15.

Giordano, P. C. (1978). Girls, guys, and gangs: The changing social context of female delinquency. *Journal of Criminal Law and Criminology, 69*, 126–132.

Hindelang, M. J., Hirschi, T., & Weiss, J. G. (1981). *Measuring delinquency.* Beverly Hills, CA: Sage.

Lee, V. E., & Bryk, A. S. (1986). Effects of single-sex secondary schools on student achievement and attitudes. *Journal of Educational Psychology, 78*, 381–395.

Lee, V. E., & Marks, H. M. (1992). Who goes where? Choice of single-sex and coeducational independent secondary schools. *Sociology of Education, 65*, 226–253.

Magnusson, D. (1988). *Individual development from an interactional perspective.* Hillsdale, NJ: Lawrence Erlbaum Associates.

Marsh, H. W. (1989). Effects of attending single-sex and coeducational high schools on achievement, attitudes, behaviors, and sex differences. *Journal of Educational Psychology, 81*, 70–85.

Marsh, H. W., Owens, L., Myers, M. R., & Smith, I. D. (1989). The transition from single-sex to co-educational high schools: Teacher perceptions, academic achievement, and self-concept. *British Journal of Educational Psychology, 59*, 155–173.

Moffitt, T. E. (1989). Accommodating self-report methods to a low-delinquency culture: A longitudinal study from New Zealand. In M. W. Klein (Ed.), *Cross-national research in self-reported crime and delinquency* (pp. 43–66). Dordrecht, The Netherlands: Kluwer Academic Publishers.

Moffitt, T. E., & Silva, P. A. (1988). Self-reported delinquency: Results from an instrument for New Zealand. *Australian and New Zealand Journal of Criminology, 21*, 227–240.

Moos, R., & Moos, B. (1981). *Family environment scale manual.* Palo Alto: Consulting Psychologists Press.

New Zealand Official Yearbook. (1993). Wellington, New Zealand: Department of Statistics.

Parnicky, J. J., Williams, S., & Silva, P. A. (1985). Family environment scale: A Dunedin (New Zealand) pilot study. *Australian Psychologist, 20,* 195–204.

Rowe, D. C., Rodgers, J. L., & Meseck-Bushey, S. (1990). An "epidemic" model of sexual intercourse prevalences for black and white adolescents. *Social Biology, 36,* 127–145.

Rutter, M., Maughan, B., Mortimore, P., & Ouston, J. (1979). *Fifteen thousand hours: Secondary schools and their effects on children.* Cambridge, MA: Harvard University Press.

Rutter, M., Tizard, J., & Whitmore, K. (1970). *Education, health and behavior.* London: Longman.

Schneider, F. W., & Coutts, L. M. (1982). The high school environment: A comparison of coeducational and single-sex schools. *Journal of Educational Psychology, 74,* 898–906.

Scott, J. P. (1977). Social genetics. *Behavior Genetics, 7,* 327–346.

Silva, P. A. (1987). *4,000 Otago teenagers: A preliminary report from the Pathways to Employment Project.* Dunedin, New Zealand: Multidisciplinary Health and Development Research Unit, University of Otago Medical School.

Silva, P. A. (1990). The Dunedin Multidisciplinary Health and Development Study: A 15-year longitudinal study. *Pediatric and Perinatal Epidemiology, 4,* 96–127.

Simmons, R. G., & Blyth, D. (1987). *Moving into adolescence: The impact of pubertal change and school context.* New York: Aldine De Gruyter.

Stattin, H., & Magnusson, D. (1990). *Pubertal maturation in female development.* Hillsdale, NJ: Lawrence Erlbaum Associates.

Trickett, E. J., Trickett, P. K., Castro, J. J., & Schaffner, P. (1982). The independent school experience: Aspects of the normative environments of single-sex and coed secondary schools. *Journal of Educational Psychology, 74,* 374–381.

Udry, J. R. (1988). Biological predispositions and social control in adolescent sexual behavior. *American Sociological Review, 53,* 709–722.

Udry, J. R. (1990). Hormonal and social determinants of adolescent sexual initiation. In J. Bancroft (Ed.), *Adolescence and puberty: The 3rd Kinsey symposium* (pp. 70–87). New York: Oxford University Press.

Wechsler, D. (1974). *Manual of the Wechsler Intelligence Scale for Children–Revised.* New York: The Psychological Corporation.

CHAPTER FIVE

Developmental Paths in Adolescence: Commentary

Lisa J. Crockett
The Pennsylvania State University

The chapters by Huizinga (chap. 2), Cairns, Leung, and Cairns (chap. 3), and Caspi (chap. 4) raise several issues integral to an understanding of developmental pathways in adolescence. These issues include the choice of metaphors for describing developmental paths, the impact of turning points on pathways, mechanisms contributing to continuity (or discontinuity) in behavior, and the role of the social context in shaping pathways. Each of these issues is discussed in turn.

MODELS AND METAPHORS

The first issue involves the conceptualization of an individual's journey through adolescence and the selection of metaphors for describing it. Two common metaphors in the developmental literature are *pathway* and *trajectory*. Although similar in some respects, these terms reflect different assumptions about development. Pathway typically refers to a course that is already laid out, which the individual simply follows. Thus, this metaphor emphasizes the role of forces outside the person in setting that person's developmental course. Trajectory refers to the curve of a projectile in flight, which implies momentum and movement in a specified direction. Thus, this metaphor connotes a more active role for the organism; it also implies that development follows a fairly predictable course.

75

The choice of metaphors depends on one's philosophical stance (mechanistic or organismic) and, to some extent, one's disciplinary perspective. For example, sociologists Hogan and Astone (1986) argued that the term *trajectory* is innappropriate for describing the transition to adulthood because it "implies a greater amount of individual initiative than actually occurs" (p. 110). According to these authors, institutional arrangements set the expected developmental course concerning the sequence of adult role transitions, although individuals may differ in the timing and eventual success of these transitions. Hogan and Astone prefer the term *pathway*, which they defined as "a course laid out for people, strongly encouraging them to take a particular route to get from one place to another" (p. 110). Of course, other authors might reject the term *pathway* so defined because it leaves too little room for individual initiative.

It is also possible that different metaphors are appropriate for describing distinct developmental phenomena. Let us take three cases: a specific behavior, the quality of adaptation exhibited by an individual, and the individual's life course. A specific behavior, such as temper tantrums, may show a normative developmental pattern—being prevalent at certain phases of life and rare at others. Such a pattern may conform to a curve, as implied by the term *trajectory*. The term *trajectory* may also be appropriate for describing the quality of an individual's adaptation over time, especially if one presumes some degree of continuity in adaptation. That is, individuals on a positive trajectory should show a stable or increasing level of adaptation over a period of time, whereas those on a negative trajectory would be expected to show a pattern of diminishing adjustment (at least relative to peers).

Trajectory may be troublesome, however, when it is applied to the individual life course. If we think of the life course as encompassing twists and turns at critical decision points, many of which are unforeseeable (e.g., Bandura, 1982; Crockett & Crouter, chap. 1, this volume; Kagan, Kearsley, & Zelazo, 1978), trajectory seems inadequate for describing this potentially erratic pattern. If so, we must resort to the term *path* or *pathway* to describe the individual's developmental course through adolescence and beyond. The most appropriate understanding of *path*, however, is not the typical one discussed previously, but the less common usage: "a route along which something moves" (Random House, 1973, p. 973). This definition allows for an active organism with some influence over its direction and progress.

Once developmental paths are conceptualized, decisions regarding methodological approach remain. To some extent, methodological solutions depend on the resolution of the conceptual issues just discussed. For example, the use of variable-level versus person-centered data-analytic techniques depends, in part, on whether the focus is a particular type of behavior or a constellation of attitudinal and behavioral variables believed to characterize personality. Magnusson (1990) suggested that person-centered approaches are preferable for examining the development of individuals because "it is individuals who are stable [or unstable] over time, not variables" (p. 210).

Huizinga (chap. 2, this volume) provides one example of a person-centered approach to charting developmental pathways. Focusing on delinquent behavior, he defines a *pathway* as "a particular sequence of behaviors traversed by some group of individuals that is different from the sequences of behaviors followed by others." He assigns adolescents to distinct delinquency "types" based on their initial level of delinquency, and then traces transitions from each "type" to other types over the following 2-year period. Interestingly, he finds little regularity in adolescents' transitions from one delinquent status to another, although some progressions are more common than others. The factors influencing the likelihood of particular transitions are a bit clearer: Both an individual's initial delinquency status and contextual variables (e.g., contact with deviant peers) appear to affect transitions to and maintenance of aggressive types of delinquency. By expanding the longitudinal time frame to include additional data points, this method could be used to trace delinquency progressions over the entire adolescent period.

The lack of consistent patterns, however, presents an interesting problem. Although a more extended study period could yield more clear-cut patterns, this appears unlikely given the present level of inconsistency. It may be that initial delinquency status and age are insufficient for identifying groups with distinct developmental pathways. Other person or contextual variables may be needed to identify developmentally meaningful categories, or types. For example, Magnusson (1988) found that boys who were both hyperactive and aggressive in early adolescence had increased rates of criminality and alcohol abuse in young adulthood. Similarly, Caspi, Bem, and Elder (1989) found that the adult life course was influenced by personality characteristics such as shyness, ill-temperedness, and dependency. Thus, particular configurations of salient behavioral and personality characteristics may result in distinctive developmental patterns. If so, typologies based on such potent individual and contextual characteristics may prove more fruitful for identifying distinctive delinquency sequences than those focusing primarily on prior delinquent status.

THE ROLE OF TURNING POINTS

The second issue concerns the importance of turning points in the construction of developmental paths. Kagan's metaphor of a *tree* (Kagan et al., 1978) suggests that development encompasses numerous decision points where the person can select from among several alternative courses of action, each leading in a different direction. To the extent that these decision points can be predicted, they provide us with a focus of study—a window on development where we can begin to examine the mechanisms that operate to maintain or redirect individuals' paths. A focus on turning points leads to three questions: What conditions precipitate a turning point? What leads to the selection of one possible alternative over another? What are the implications of choosing one alternative over another?

The first question concerns circumstances that may set the stage for a turning point. Ecological transitions involving entry into new settings (e.g., entering a new school) or major changes in existing settings (e.g., family changes after a divorce) represent one type of potential turning point. Entry into a new setting means exposure to a new set of opportunities and pressures that may either reinforce or redirect initial behavioral dispositions. In addition, developmental changes, such as puberty or the advent of abstract reasoning, entail changes in self-perceptions and social treatment, creating an opportunity for novel person–environment interactions. Finally, entry into new social roles or statuses can initiate a turning point because these transitions involve new settings and new behavioral expectations.

Importantly, many of these potentially significant changes in young people's lives are predictable. We know, for example, that all normal children go through puberty, and we know that visual evidence of this transformation is likely to appear early in the second decade of life. Normative institutional transitions such as the move into secondary school are especially predictable. Even normative role transitions such as marriage can be anticipated for a majority of the population, although timing for an individual would be more difficult to predict. Where such changes are predictable, they provide an opportunity for the prospective study of turning points and their sequelae. Key changes in early adolescence might include puberty, school transitions, and non-normative events such as family structure changes, death or illness, and geographic relocation. Key changes in late adolescence would include moving out of the family of origin, entering college or the work force, marriage, and non-normative life events such as serious illness or unemployment. Longitudinal research could address the significance of these turning points not only for short-term behavioral change, but for the construction of life paths. Of course, not all non-normative events would be captured prospectively, and chance encounters might be missed. But periodic assessment throughout the adolescent period could catch many decision points, whose meaning and significance might only later be determined.

The second question is what leads an adolescent to adopt one possible direction over another at a particular turning point. One model of this process comes from Bandura's (1982) discussion of chance encounters. According to Bandura, such encounters are not always entirely random. Often some individual characteristic leads a person to be at a particular place at the moment when the "chance" meeting occurs. Thus, although the encounter was not anticipated, characteristics of the person led to the selection of a particular setting, making the encounter possible. By extension, individual characteristics are likely to play a role in selecting one alternative course over another at a particular turning point. For example, academically gifted adolescents are more likely to find school rewarding and are more likely to receive encouragement. Consequently, such students should be more likely to choose postsecondary education when the time for educational decisions arrives. Bronfenbrenner (1989) has referred to such individual characteristics as "developmentally instigative." Other social agents may also play a role, such as when parents choose schools for their children or when peers encourage particular forms of behavior. Finally, the broader social context plays a role because it constrains the alternatives available to the person at a given juncture in development.

The third issue concerns the consequences of choosing one possible alternative over another. When a choice of different settings is available, selecting one over another implies exposure to some opportunities and social influences to the exclusion of others. Caspi (chap. 4, this volume) provides one example of this. His analysis indicates that parents' choice of a coed or single-sex secondary school affects girls' exposure to delinquent behavior. Because boys are more involved in norm-breaking behaviors than are girls, girls in coed schools are exposed to a wider range of behaviors and to more lax norms than are those in single-sex schools. Thus, the choice of school setting has important implications for subsequent socialization.

Predicting the impact of entry into one of several alternative settings, however, involves more than understanding the general features of that setting. Caspi finds that, although girls in coed schools presumably all had the opportunity for contact with delinquent patterns of behavior, reported exposure to these patterns depended on girls' pubertal timing: Greater exposure to delinquency was concentrated among early-maturing girls. Similarly, only early-maturing girls in coed schools engaged in more delinquent behavior than their counterparts in single-sex schools. Thus, greater involvement in delinquency required both a facilitating environment and personal characteristics that increased exposure (or vulnerability) to delinquent elements. Similarly, Bandura (1982) argued that both personal and environmental characteristics affect the impact of a chance encounter (and, by extension, entry into any new setting) on an individual's subsequent life course.

Even knowing the features of both person and environment, however, may not be enough to elucidate the processes shaping an individual's response to a particular setting. For example, in Caspi's study, it would be useful to know whether early-maturing girls in coed schools were responding to greater exposure to boys in general, or to delinquent boys in particular. That is, we need to identify the *effective* social environment for these girls, not just features of the general social context. Moreover, if the key turns out to be greater contact with delinquent boys, we need to ask why this occurred:

Do delinquent boys preferentially seek the company of early-maturing girls, or are early maturers more likely than other girls to respond favorably to delinquent boys' overtures? Perhaps early-maturing girls actively seek contact with delinquent boys. Each of these possibilities points to selection processes that could lead early-maturing girls into greater contact with delinquent boys. In addition, early-maturing girls may be more influenced by delinquent models than are later maturers, even with equal exposure. Or, delinquent boys may differentially encourage early-maturing and late-maturing girls to participate in misconduct. Finally, it is possible that Caspi's early-maturing girls already had greater tendencies toward misconduct; being in a coed school simply gave them greater license to express these tendencies. In summary, to understand the impact of a new setting on adolescent behavior, we need to determine the effective social environment for a particular group of individuals, and we need to pinpoint the specific social processes influencing behavior within that social niche.

Determining the consequences of entering one setting rather than another is complicated by the selection processes discussed earlier. In many cases, the individual characteristics and social forces present at a decision point push adolescents in directions that are in some way related to their past behavior. For example, adolescents choose peer groups compatible with their own behavioral tendencies (e.g., Cairns et al., chap. 3, this volume), or parents may choose schools to enhance their child's preexisting talents or perhaps to deter former patterns of misbehavior (e.g., by sending a child to military school). In such cases, the choice occurs in response to characteristics of the adolescent, or, alternatively, to characteristics of the parents, which are, in turn, correlated with characteristics of the adolescent (Scarr & McCartney, 1983). Such selection processes may create "matches" between the person and the new context, making it difficult to separate setting effects from person effects.

MECHANISMS OF CONTINUITY

Turning points presumably offer an opportunity for changes in direction. This leads to a distinct question: What processes help maintain behavioral patterns over time, despite the interposition of turning points? One answer involves the selection processes that operate at decision points. As suggested earlier, adolescents are likely to select settings compatible with their initial dispositions, with the result that personal characteristics and socialization processes in the setting conspire to support behavioral continuity. Cairns et al. provide further clues to these processes.

Cairns et al. discuss the maintenance of antisocial behavior in the school setting. They note that this type of behavior shows an enduring presence within classrooms, despite considerable fluidity in peer-group membership. The reason for this continuity appears to be that peer groups are formed and re-formed around certain behavioral themes, including aggressiveness and deviance. Aggressive children cluster together through the process of selection: They may be excluded from prosocial groups (passive selection) and attracted to aggressive groups (active selection). Membership in the aggressive group presumably reinforces initial aggressive dispositions. Importantly, Cairns et al. note that, although membership in most groups changes considerably from year to year, as children change schools or classes, deviant adolescents tend to reshuffle themselves into new groups of deviant peers. By extension, an aggressive adolescent who moves to another school experiences a change in school environment, but the impact of that change may be trivial if he or she gravitates toward an aggressive peer group in the new location.

In summary, the tendency to end up in settings that support one's initial proclivities is likely to foster continuity in aggressive behavior. In addition, a reliance on aggressive social exchanges within and outside the group may limit opportunities for learning prosocial skills and may reinforce expectations of hostile treatment, which should, in turn, increase the probability of recurrent aggressive behavior. Caspi et al. (1989) labeled these processes *cumulative* and *interactional* continuity, respectively.

ROLE OF SOCIAL CONTEXTS

The preceding discussion suggests several points about the influence of social contexts on developmental pathways. Settings influence ongoing behavior in several ways. Apart from exposing adolescents to novel forms of behavior, which may then be imitated and adopted, settings provide an arena for the expression of preexisting behavioral dispositions. A given setting may be favorable to certain kinds of behavior and less favorable to others. Depending on the match between person and setting, a setting may either facilitate or limit the adolescent's initial behavioral tendencies (see Eccles et al., 1993). A facilitating environment does not necessarily mean that the initial behavioral tendency is rewarded; tolerance (i.e., lack of punishment) may be sufficient. Thus, as Caspi (chap. 4, this volume) suggests, coed schools may be associated with greater continuity in girls' misconduct because coed settings are less restrictive than female only settings, and thus allow delinquent tendencies to be maintained.

In all important social settings, it is important to identify the effective social context for the adolescents under study and the processes operating within it. For example, secondary schools have a number of possible peer-group niches that may reflect distinct norms and pressures (Brown & Huang, chap. 9, this volume; Clasen & Brown, 1985). Thus, the effective social context may differ for adolescents who associate with different peer groups, despite the fact that they are all embedded in the larger school setting. Moreover, school authorities may respond differentially to distinct peer groups, reinforcing and magnifying their differences (Eckert, 1989, chap. 10, this volume). An analogous process occurs in families when siblings exploit distinct niches and experience differential socialization (Dunn & Plomin, 1990).

The adolescent's capacity for selecting environments (e.g., choosing one setting over another, or choosing a particular social niche within a larger setting) suggests that the effective social environment often reflects characteristics of the adolescent (Scarr & McCartney, 1983). At the same time, individuals with distinct characteristics may have differential opportunity for active "niche picking"—gender, race, or social class may limit the social niches available within a setting, or may restrict the adolescent's freedom of movement among them. The opportunity for active niche picking may also be greater in some settings than in others. Niche picking is likely to be especially apparent in peer networks because peer associations involve a large element of choice. It may be less prominent in other contexts where the range of "niches" is more restricted and exit into alternative settings is barred. For example, some schools and neighborhoods may offer a fairly limited array of social niches from which to choose.

Differential opportunity for selecting compatible settings has implications for developmental continuity. Normally, we would expect active "niche picking" to result in positive correlations between person and environment, which would tend to foster behavioral continuity. However, niche picking may lead to changes in behavior (rather than continuity) if the available niches reflect norms at odds with the adolescent's initial dispositions. Thus, to understand the developmental consequences of "niche picking," it is important to examine the range of alternatives available within a given setting, as well as the "match" between those alternatives and characteristics of the adolescent.

CONCLUSIONS

Much remains to be done to illuminate the processes shaping adolescents' developmental paths. Influences affecting adolescents' day-to-day behavior, as well as their decisions at specific turning points, need to be elucidated. The reciprocal influences operating between adolescent and environment, and the fact that selection processes (both passive and active) are likely to increase the correlation between individual and environmental characteristics, further complicate the task of disentangling causal processes.

Furthermore, understanding adolescents' developmental pathways requires more than identifying the dynamic processes in operation at key turning points and in the settings the person enters subsequently. It requires examining the chain of events, or "series of contingencies" (Rutter, 1989), that build on each other in the developmental process, producing distinctive life paths. For example, attending poor schools appears to affect later job success indirectly—by leading to poor school attendance, which, in turn, increases the probability of early school leaving and a failure to acquire key academic credentials. The lack of academic credentials then increases the probability of erratic employment and of working in unskilled jobs (Gray, Smith, & Rutter, 1980). Such findings suggest that, in order to understand developmental pathways, the sequence of "key decisions" needs to be identified for groups of individuals, and the contingencies operating between them need to be elucidated. Although it may be useful to focus initially on small segments of time, examining the processes operating at particular turning points, ultimately the task is to place these smaller segments into the broader context of the adolescents' emerging life course.

REFERENCES

Bandura, A. (1982). The psychology of chance encounters and life paths. *American Psychologist, 37*, 747–755.

Bronfenbrenner, U. (1989, April). *The developing ecology of human development: Paradigm lost or paradigm regained?* Paper presented at the biennial meeting of the Society for Research on Child Development, Kansas City, MO.

Caspi, A., Bem, D. J., & Elder, G. H., Jr. (1989). Continuities and consequences of interactional styles across the life course. *Journal of Personality, 57*, 375–406.

Clasen, D. R., & Brown, B. B. (1985). The multidimensionality of peer pressure in adolescence. *Journal of Youth and Adolescence, 14*, 451–468.

Dunn, J., & Plomin, R. (1990). *Separate lives: Why siblings are so different.* New York: Basic Books.

Eccles, J. S., Midgley, C., Wigfield, A., Buchanan, C. M., Reuman, D., Flanagan, C., & MacIver, D. (1993). The impact of stage-environment fit on young adolescents' experiences in schools and families. *American Psychologist, 48*, 90–101.

Eckert, P. (1989). *Jocks and burnouts: Social categories and identity in the high school.* New York: Teachers College Press.

Gray, G., Smith, A., & Rutter, M. (1980). School attendance and the first year of employment. In L. Hersov & I. Berg (Eds.), *Out of school: Modern perspectives in truancy and school refusal* (pp. 343–370). Chichester, England: Wiley.

Hogan, D. P., & Astone, N. M. (1986). The transition to adulthood. *Annual Review of Sociology, 12*, 109–130.

Kagan, J., Kearsley, R. B., & Zelazo, P. R. (1978). *Infancy: Its place in human development.* Cambridge, MA: Harvard University Press.

Magnusson, D. (1988). *Individual development from an interactional perspective: A longitudinal study.* Hillsdale, NJ: Lawrence Erlbaum Associates.

Magnusson, D. (1990). Personality development from an interactional perspective. In L. A. Pervin (Ed.), *Handbook of personality theory and research* (pp. 193–222). New York: Guilford.

Random House (1973). *College dictionary.* L. Urdang (Ed. in Chief). New York: Random House.

Rutter, M. (1989). Pathways from childhood to adult life. *Journal of Child Psychology and Psychiatry, 30,* 23–51.
Scarr, S., & McCartney, K. (1983). How people make their own environments: A theory of genotype-environment effects. *Child Development, 54,* 424–435.

PART TWO

RISKS FROM WITHIN
AND WITHOUT:
RESILIENCE IN CONTEXT

CHAPTER SIX

The Knowledge Base on Resilience in African-American Adolescents

Linda F. Winfield
University of Southern California

The purpose of this chapter is to describe what is known about resilience and success among African-American adolescents, with a goal of trying to understand the protective mechanisms and sources contributing to resilience. The introduction provides a brief overview of current conceptualizations of risk and resilience. Next, a discussion is presented of four protective processes and mechanisms that foster resilience. The next section identifies sources within schools at two critical periods: the transition from grade school to middle school, and the transition from high school to college. A major objective is to delineate processes and sources of resilience within schools. The final section examines protective mechanisms within the community, focusing on the role of peers and the church. The concluding section presents methodological and conceptual considerations for further research and implications for designing effective interventions.

After the publication of *A Nation at Risk* (National Commission on Excellence in Education, 1983), educators, policymakers, and researchers overzealously applied the term *at risk* to refer to youth who are most likely to experience school failure, teen pregnancy, or some other negative developmental outcome. Although the term is relatively new when applied to youth (Richardson & Colfer, 1990), the notion of risk has long been used in medical and psychiatric research to specify conditions that make individuals susceptible to disease or mental disorders (Garmezy, 1983, 1987, 1991; Masten, Best, & Garmezy, 1990; Rutter, 1979, 1987, 1990). Some individuals are resilient and cope successfully, whereas others react negatively. The construct of *resilience* delineates individual variation in the ways that people respond to risk, stress, and adversity (Rutter, 1987). It is not a fixed attribute, but rather a combination of vulnerability or protective mechanisms that modify the individual's response to the risk situation and operate at critical points during one's life (Rutter, 1987).

Numerous studies and reviews of risk factors describe maladaptive functioning in adolescent populations (see, e.g., Natriello, McDill, & Pallas, 1990, for review of definitions and terms). Few of these studies consider competence, adaptation, or resilience. Even fewer identify African Americans as the sample, which confirmed Graham's (1992) documented scarcity of empirical research on African Americans in mainstream psychology.

Studies focusing on risk and deficiencies tend to describe educational practices and policies, such as remediation, designed to make racial/ethnic groups "equal" to their White middle-class counterparts. Consequently, there is little understanding of the diversity of skills and talents possessed by these students (see Slaughter, 1988, for a discussion of deficit models and their implications for educational interventions for African-American children). Another outcome of the remediation focus is the tendency to "blame the victim," and to suggest that the causes for being at risk for failure come from the lives, families, communities, or cultures of the student, rather than from the social, political, and economic conditions of the nation.

Sociological studies examining the achievement and attainment of African-American young adults generally criticize the traditional models, which emphasize individual, social–psychological factors as those that influence outcomes (Epps & Jackson, 1985; Wilson & Allen, 1987). Factors such as influential others and aspirations, tend to mediate the effects of earlier social circumstances (e.g., one's schooling or family history). Over the course of the life span, events and transitions modify individual trajectories (Elder, 1985).

Structural factors such as differential access to society's resources, inequities in opportunities, and inadequate schooling restrict opportunities for upward mobility (Allen & Farley, 1987; Epps & Jackson, 1985; Wilson & Allen, 1987). For African-American young adults, tracking (Braddock, 1990; Lee & Bryk, 1988), gender (Edwards, 1979; Jackson, 1973; Lee, Winfield, & Wilson, 1991), employment opportunities (Braddock & McPartland, 1987; Wilson, 1987), and economic climate (Wilson, 1987) have also been linked to levels of attainment. Although this literature mostly focuses on high school and early adult years, it illustrates how structural factors leave youth vulnerable and form the basis for determining the most productive ways to alter the paths of African-American adolescents.

Gordon (1982) provided an important perspective on students from racial/ethnic groups:

> In earlier work, great attention was given to the characteristics of these populations and the ways in which they differed from the so-called majority popu-

lation. As that work progressed, we have come to realize that it was in error . . . by implying they represented a relatively homogeneous group. They do not. . . . They have poverty and low status and certain kinds of neglect and maltreatment as common characteristics, but in terms of their other characteristics they vary as much within this group as they do between the lower- and higher-status groups. . . . Ethnic and class status is important for political purposes but relatively unimportant for pedagogical purposes. (p. 1975)

Similarly, Berry (1989) noted: "The old labels of the past have inferred cognitive, motivational, self-esteem, and learning deficits of Black children, youth, and college-age young adults should be looked at with a jaundiced eye" (p. 288). This is particularly true, and is illustrated by the following example. I had been in a particular urban school conducting observations for several months. One day after school, one of the first-grade special education students was missing when his mother came to pick him up at school. The teacher and principal called school security and the police, searched the building, and questioned other children in the class. They could not locate the boy anywhere. The next day when I went to school, I asked the principal what had finally transpired. Apparently, after school, this first grader's mother was late in coming to pick him up, and he knew he had an appointment at the clinic downtown. The school routinely provided bus and transportation tokens for large numbers of students. So this particular student caught the mass transit system to get to the bus stop, took the bus downtown, and walked the three or four blocks to make sure he was on time for his clinic appointment. The point is that this student—a first grader classified as special education—was able to negotiate a complicated transportation system. Think of all the higher order cognitive skills that were required for him to accomplish this task. Once his mother did not get to school on time, he had to make an inference that she was not coming, devise a plan, use memory, and execute his plan to get to his scheduled appointment (Winfield, 1982).

More recent research identifies the positive coping and resilience of poor African-American children and their families. Some researchers have identified and studied characteristics of higher and lower achieving, low-income African-American children and young adults, as well as the family groups and classroom settings in which they participated (Clark, 1983; Nelson-Le Gall & Glor-Scheib, 1985; Nelson-Le Gall & Jones, 1990; Scott-Jones, 1987; Spencer, Brookins, & Allen, 1985; Winfield, 1988, 1991a). An emerging knowledge base, of which these studies are a part, shows the diversity of competencies and attitudes among poor African-American children, families, and communities.

Learning and development can best be understood within an ecological perspective (Bronfenbrenner, 1979) and over the life span of an individual. For African-American students, this means considering how the triple cultural bind—of belonging to the mainstream, the African-rooted culture, and a status-oppressed racial/ethnic group (Boykin, 1986; Nettles & Pleck, 1994)—affects their lives. This perspective also suggests the need for critical interdisciplinary research that goes beyond the individual to focus on institutions such as schools and the community, within which learning and development occur.

To develop models that present a positive trajectory of adolescence, the focus must necessarily shift from the notion of at risk to that of resilience. From this perspective, the critical issues in education now become the need to determine the protective processes and mechanisms that will reduce risk and foster resilience, rather than the need to dwell on who is at risk or what factors put one at risk. More importantly, how can schools, administrators, teachers, community groups, and policymakers enhance and foster the development of these protective processes? Garmezy (1983) suggested that protective factors fall into three categories: aspects of the child's disposition, family cohesion, and supportive persons in the environment. Competent African-American children from urban ghettos who were exposed to poverty and prejudice exhibited protective factors that included a wider array of social skills, positive peer and adult interactions, and a higher degree of social responsiveness and sensitivity (Garmezy, 1983).

Teachers rated these students lower in defensiveness and aggressiveness, and higher in cooperation, participation, and emotional stability. The students tended to have a positive sense of self, a sense of personal power rather than powerlessness, and an internal locus of control, and they believed they were capable of exercising a degree of control over their environment. Their parents were concerned and participated in education, provided direction in everyday tasks, and were aware of their children's interests and goals. Although an intact family was not a requirement, it was important that the children had at least one significant adult involved in their lives. An alternative conceptualization by Rutter (1987) notes: "Protection does not reside in the psychological chemistry of the moment but in the ways in which people deal with life changes and in what they do about their stressful or disadvantageous circumstances. Particular attention needs to be paid to the mechanisms operating at key turning points in people's lives when a risk trajectory may be redirected onto a more adaptive path" (p. 329).

The appealing aspect of this concept is the way it incorporates the interaction of personal and individual factors and environmental circumstances. During adolescence, general goals, talents, and attitudes are shaped by both personal characteristics and a person's experiences within a particular sociocultural milieu. These factors continuously interact with and modify opportunities or obstacles encountered by the individual. Furthermore, the choices an adolescent makes will affect the social roles occupied later in life, the stability of role performance, and the individual's attainment over the life course (Clausen, 1991). Clausen's notion of "planful competence" implies a level of self-confidence and self-awareness in adolescence, such that students can make rational decisions concerning their future. In order to do this, students need to know something about their abilities, skills, and interests, in addition to some social skills. They also need to know something about their available options, and be able to reflect on how to maximize them. A similar concept was found among those better adjusted young women who had been institutionalized as youngsters. As adolescents, these women actively planned and often changed their adult lives more positively. They accomplished this by controlling their own fertility and selecting a more appropriate marital partner (Quinton & Rutter, 1988). The authors suggest that positive experiences at school during adolescence did not simply reflect better functioning at that time, but were associated with much planning and forethought concerning employment and marriage prospects.

PROTECTIVE PROCESSES FOSTERING RESILIENCE

Rutter (1987) identified four main processes, which are used here to discuss the knowledge base on schools and communities and the development of resilience among African-American youth. These include: (a) reducing negative outcomes by altering either the risk or the child's exposure to the risk, (b) reducing the negative chain reaction following risk exposure, (c) establishing and maintaining self-esteem and self-efficacy, and (d) opening up new opportunities.

Reducing Negative Outcomes

Rutter proposed two ways to reduce the impact of risk. A rather dramatic example of altering the risk or child's exposure to risk are those programs in which the child is totally removed from his or her environment and sent away to private schools (Domhoff & Zweigenhaft, 1991). This scenario provides an extreme case of reducing the exposure to risk, however it remains as one alternative. For many inner-city children impacted by alcohol or drug use among parents or family members, physically leaving the environment is not an option. These children experience inconsistent parenting, abuse, and neglect in a variety of ways, and typically they must "fend" for themselves. In one school site, the principal discovered that chronic lateness and absenteeism among kindergarten and first-grade children was largely because they had to get themselves up, dressed, and out of the house. The children indicated they had no one to wake them up. The principal had the Home School Association purchase alarm clocks to be distributed to these children. In addition, she formed a "walking pool," whereby older students in the neighborhood were assigned to walk past younger students' houses and walk with them to school.

Many students from severely chaotic or abusive homes come to schools with hostility and anger, which contribute to classroom behavioral problems. Often looks or comments between students ignite physical altercations, causing disruption in classrooms. One teacher started each morning by allowing the third-grade students 15 minutes to cry and scream and get everything out "from the night before" before settling down to classwork. For many of these students, violence and abuse was an everyday occurrence. In another school, the teachers and principal formed a "SWAT Team," which came into classrooms on call when students became too disruptive or emotional, or were in crisis. This group was trained in positive disciplining techniques and defusing charged emotional situations. What these examples indicate is that, in the classroom and school, solutions were attempted to reduce the child's exposure to risk. Unfortunately, merely working with children on an individual basis is not entirely successful because a more effective intervention occurs within the family unit. However, school personnel attempted to do something within their sphere of control. These interventions served, in some slight way, to alter the child's exposure to the risk. Another group of protective mechanisms reduces the negative chain reactions that follow risk exposure.

Reducing the Negative Chain Reaction

What typically happens following gang involvement, dropping out of school, or teen pregnancy is a downward negative spiral that proves too difficult to overcome. Without an intervention, students cannot go on to recover from that particular event in their lives. Some of the recovery programs for students who drop out of school have been found to be very effective, particularly where students are given part-time jobs and are allowed to come to school at different hours than traditional schools. The flexibility, additional counseling support, smaller classes, and experiential learning are designed to prevent the negative chain reaction that occurs due to lack of education.

With appropriate intervention, a similar positive outcome occurs for adolescent mothers. Scott-Jones and Turner (1990) found that education mediated the impact of teenage pregnancy on income. The negative outcomes of adolescent pregnancy are diminished for teenage mothers who receive prenatal care, home support, adequate child care, and additional education (Scott-Jones, 1991). The same event, if accompanied by different adaptations, can lead to a different path. In studies of adolescent childbearing, Furstenburg (1976) found that African-American adolescent girls encountered a number of decisions after the birth: putting the child up for adoption, abandoning the child, getting a job, completing school, or obtaining additional information. If they did get a job, because of low skill levels and inadequate education, it did not cover child-care and household expenses. If other adults were present in the household and provided a source of economic and emotional support to the young mother, she could go on to complete school. However, if the young mother's response was additional births, this path led to persistent economic dependence and poverty.

At an earlier age, severe disruptive behavior, chronic absenteeism, or lack of academic progress often signal a risk exposure. In one urban school, a Pupil Support Team was formed to discuss, on an ongoing basis, individual children's academic and social problems and unusual home circumstances (Winfield, Hawkins, & Stringfield, 1992). This team consisted of a counselor, teachers, the principal, a school community coordinator, the school psychologist, and so on. The purpose was not to refer students to special education, but to brainstorm about what options, resources, and strategies could be used to provide support to distressed students. Typically, a teacher would request a meeting about an individual student who was having some type of problem. The solutions included having a teacher spend extra time before or after school or at lunch time with a troubled student, obtaining a decent pair of shoes for a child who failed to attend school because of the holes in his or her shoes, or arranging for an eye exam. Other solutions included obtaining resources from the church or community for counseling, food, shelter, and referrals for social work or mental health. In many cases, this latter option was rarely used because, within many of these impoverished communities, there were no mental health or social welfare clinics, and parents and students were required to travel distances outside of the community for services. Typically, schools serve as clearinghouses. Educators are proficient at identifying problems, but because of insufficient resources or commitment, interventions occur sporadically if at all. In order to develop resilience, this scenario must change.

Establishing and Maintaining Self-Esteem and Self-Efficacy

The third mechanism—self-efficacy—concerns how individuals feel about themselves, their environment, and their competence in handling life's obstacles, as well as their perceptions of control in determining outcomes. For individuals in high-risk situations, these self-concepts develop as a result of interpersonal relationships with significant others and by successfully completing tasks. Self-esteem and self-efficacy are developmental processes that are learned primarily in two ways: in positive interactions with peers or adults, and in successful accomplishment of a task (be it academic, music, art, or athletics). Self-esteem is not something that is learned in a decontextualized manner. It is not learned by completing a series of lessons in commercially available programs. Similarly, self-efficacy develops when students learn they have some control over certain things in their environment and that they are not helpless. African-American youth with a high sense of personal efficacy performed better academically than their counterparts who lacked this component of self (Gurin & Epps, 1974). Rutter (1979) indicated that: "Both home and school will have an impact through a variety of mechanisms which include helping the child to achieve competence, recognizing and appreciating achievement in a wide range of activities, and ensuring that the focus is on that which is done well rather than on the areas of failure" (p. 63). The following example, taken from case studies in an urban elementary school, highlights this point:

> I spent every afternoon observing a reading group conducted by the reading teacher, Mrs. S. Every lunch time, afternoon, and after school, the same little girl, Adrienne, would come into Mrs. S.'s room. I later learned that, at times, Adrienne even left her classroom to come to the room. Mrs. S. gave her small tasks to perform, such as putting labels on books, stacking books, and delivering books to other classrooms, and she also encouraged Adrienne to read the titles and sound out unfamiliar words, along with other positive encouragement to boost her reading skills. When I asked Mrs. S. about the young girl, she indicated that Adrienne had been in a pull-out reading program in third and fourth grades with her, but that the program did not serve fifth graders. Mrs. S. indicated that Adrienne would always want to hang around after reading group so much so that Mrs. S. had to force her to go back to class. She later found out from the school counselor that Adrienne was physically and sexually abused at home. Mrs. S. indicated: "Adrienne really enjoys helping me out and when it is not interfering with her classroom time, I usually allow her to do that. Sometimes I have to chase her home after school."

This youngster was gaining a lesson in self-efficacy and self-esteem by accomplishing tasks and having positive interactions with an adult. Those accomplished tasks, part-time jobs, involvement with youth-serving agencies, and church experiences provide valuable positive lessons in self-efficacy for many inner-city students (Winfield, 1982).

Opening Up of Opportunities

The fourth mechanism—opening up of opportunities—reflects the scope of options available at critical points in an individual's life. For example, it is important to finish school and attain skills and credentials. Those who drop out or do not receive a high school diploma forego later opportunities for protective experiences (Rutter, 1987). When specific programs offer opportunities for students to acquire skills and invest in prosocial activities, they foster persistence. Nettles (1991) found that students who participated in activities sponsored by community-based programs expressed more certainty of graduating from high school, an increased sense of personal control, a heightened academic self-concept, and increased efforts to achieve future goals.

Another critical point during adolescence where opportunities are lost is when young teenage girls become pregnant. The difficulties of finishing school, caring for an infant, and obtaining financial support are typically overwhelming and perpetuate poverty conditions. Protective factors that facilitated teenage mothers remaining in school included family support for achievement, a sense of personal motivation, and support for schooling from caring adults in the community (Danzinger & Farber, 1990). Stevenson and Rhodes (1991) indicated that there were no differences in areas of personality, environment, and family and social relationships between African-American girls who avoid pregnancy and those who do not. However, Scott-Jones and White (1990) found that beginning sexual activity was significantly related to educational expectations, age, presence of a girlfriend or boyfriend, and the mother's educational level.

In assessing the impact of adolescent childbearing, Scott-Jones (1991) indicated that the ability to alter the negative chain reaction following pregnancy depends on whether adolescent mothers receive additional training and education. She found that education is a more powerful influence on adult economic status than is the experience of adolescent pregnancy. Resilient adolescent mothers are more likely to have strong social networks within the family and community, adequate child care, and opportunities to continue their education.

For African-American males, participation in athletics can be considered both a risk and a protective mechanism. In high schools, athletics has provided scholarships and opportunities to go on into higher education—an opportunity that many of these youngsters would not have had. The risk is that many of these students attend college, but do not graduate. Policies implemented can result in more or less opportunity for some students. The National Collegiate Athletic Association (NCAA) proposition 48 (1983), which attempted to strengthen minimum academic standards for participation in Division I institutions by implementing a minimum score on the SAT and a minimum grade point average (GPA), had a disproportionate impact on African-American male eligibility (Taylor, 1986). Athletic participation as a source of protection does not occur in isolation. Just as there are multiple risks, some of which interact or potentiate the others (Rutter, 1979), protective processes also work together. In reality, they are mixed, as seen in a comment made to me by a high school sophomore from a single-parent family who was captain of his school basketball team. I asked why he was getting all Fs in his courses, when last semester he made all Bs and Cs. He replied, "The courses are boring besides last semester—it was basketball season, I was bookin (studying)." I said, "Oh?" He replied, "Yea, you have to keep a C average in order to play. Now I hang out with my boys through the week . . . but 'dey won't let me drink or drug 'cause they know I'm the one who wins the games. Dey my boys, dey look out for me." This student has academic promise, but is only motivated to perform academically during basketball season. Thus, he does not reap all the protective benefits of athletic participation (Braddock, Royster, Winfield, & Hawkins, 1991). However, he enjoys a higher status among his peers who seemingly protect him from the drug culture that is so pervasive and could close off any opportunity he might have for postsecondary education or full-time employment. In reality, the processes, risks, and individual characteristics are not easily discovered or separable.

Figure 6.1 illustrates the framework for a knowledge base on the resilience of African-American youth, and is suggested as a beginning to identify the protective mechanisms and sources of resiliency factors. However, a critical gap exists in understanding how and why some adolescents succeed in overcoming adverse circumstances. An example of resilience is a student's decision to remain in school when few job opportunities or rewards are visible (Ogbu, 1987), or when students experience negative peer pressure. Yet little is known about the source of resilience, the protective mechanisms, or the process used by the individual that makes such a decision possible.

SOURCES OF RESILIENCE
AND PROTECTIVE MECHANISMS

The following sections examine sources of protection within middle and high schools that enable students to cope with the multiple pressures of adolescence and put them on positive pathways toward successful adult functioning. The sources are not mutually exclusive; in reality, they co-occur in a reciprocal manner. Although studies of resilience have occurred over the last decade, only a few have included African-American adolescents.

Protective Mechanisms	SCHOOLS		COMMUNITY		
	Schools	Classrooms	Family	Peers	Policymakers
1. Reduction of risk impact					
2. Reduction of negative chain reaction					
3. Self-esteem, self-efficacy					
4. Opening of new opportunities					

FIG. 6.1. Resilience, schooling, and development among African-American youth (from Winfield, 1991b).

Thus, the knowledge base is limited, and some of the discussion of how these processes interact is speculative.

Schools

For African-American students and their families, education and schooling has been traditionally viewed as a mechanism for upward social mobility (Clark, 1983). Research on schooling in low-income and disadvantaged schools in the late 1960s and early 1970s sought to identify characteristics of school environments that facilitate achievement among these youth (Purkey & Smith, 1983; Rutter, Mortimer, Ouston, & Smith, 1979; Venezky & Winfield, 1979; Winfield, 1991b). Only Rutter's study documented how school characteristics contributed to positive coping and behavioral outcomes other than academic achievement. Rutter et al. found that factors such as academic emphasis, teacher actions during lessons, availability of incentives and rewards, and extent to which children were able to take responsibility were all related to students' disruptive behavior and absenteeism.

The study further suggested that, apart from altering students' perceptions and reactions to stressful events, schools should operate in two other ways. First, positive relationships with peers or other adults outside the family may mitigate the effect of stress. Second, students who experience personal success in school or within the peer group will develop a high self-esteem and a positive sense of work (Rutter, 1987). Also critical to long-term persistence in education are the opportunities afforded to students who are successful at each grade level in school.

Transition to Middle School. The middle school years may be difficult for many students as they cope with the rigors of preadolescence. For African-American youth who may be from extremely impoverished families, the transition to middle school will be even more stressful as they cope with negative peer pressure, biological changes, and other potential stressors. Krasner (1992) found several protective factors related to school achievement that were common to high-achieving White, African-American, and Mexican-American eighth graders in the National Education Longitudinal Survey (NELS 88). These factors included parents' expectations and being enrolled in gifted programs. However, protective factors unique to the African-American population included fathers' occupation levels and after-school supervision. Teacher variables that were important were teaching experience and instructional strategies, such as the amount of time spent teaching the whole class. The schools attended by high-achieving African-American students were safer and had higher teacher expectations in terms of amount of homework and textbook coverage. There was less time spent disciplining and less time teaching small groups.

In a similar study of high-achieving eighth graders (i.e., those who scored at or above the population mean on measures of reading proficiency on the National Assessment of Educational Progress, 1985), Lee et al. (1991) found that families of high-achieving African-American students were also in a considerably higher economic group than their lower achieving counterparts. However, both groups were more likely to reside in urban areas. High-achieving African-American students reported a higher proportion of working mothers (75%), compared with the 70% reported by below-average achievers.

There were similarities and differences among the schools that both high-achieving and low-achieving African-American students attend. The percentage of African-American students and faculty are relatively high. The enrollment and student-to-faculty ratio show little difference between groups. The schools that high-achieving African-American students attend generally have a higher average socioeconomic status (SES), greater student commitment, an enriched curriculum, and fewer students in remedial reading programs than do the schools their low-achieving counterparts attend. Both groups of students watched an average of 4 hours of television daily. However, the high achievers reported having better grades, that they read more pages during school and for homework, and that they did more homework than the low achievers.

These studies suggest some expected, as well as unanticipated, protective sources. First, having a working parent, either father or mother, suggests better economic conditions for African-American students. Co-occurring with this source of protection are instrumental behaviors on the part of parents, such as after-school supervision and getting students enrolled in gifted programs, which result in higher student commitment and better academic behaviors (e.g., more homework and reading). At the school level, although these are all urban schools, the curriculum, culture, and level of teacher expectation in terms of what students are expected to cover differs substantially for high-achieving African Americans. The enrollment in gifted programs is unexpected in that the percentage of minority students enrolled is typically very low. In other studies, this variable was one of several that differentiated between high- and low-achieving schools at the eighth-grade level (Winfield, 1991a). I speculate that this source not only indicates parental monitoring, but also influences teacher expectations and serves as a mechanism for providing support against negative peer pressure for academically successful African Americans.

The Role of Athletics in Middle School. Rutter (1987) indicated that self-esteem and self-efficacy are based largely on an individual's ability to successfully complete those tasks that are most important to the individual. Several aspects of athletic participation may facilitate the processes of academic resilience and attainment for African-American male students. In order to participate in interscholastic and intramural sports, the students must usually meet the school's minimum achievement requirements. For African-American male students, this adds an academic incentive to other intrinsic incentives already associated with sports activities.

Perhaps even more important are those behaviors shared by sports and academics. Athletic training requires considerable practice and conditioning, obeying the rules of fair competition, cooperating with other students to achieve goals, persisting in the face of losses, analyzing constructively, and compensating for competitive weaknesses. Athletic participation, then, may be seen as a mechanism that forces and facilitates academic responsiveness and provides the rationale and tools for academic effort—even in the face of disasters (Braddock et al., 1991).

Braddock et al. examined the relationship between interscholastic and intramural athletic participation and academic resilience for eighth-grade males in the NELS 88 data. This study found that links exist between athletic participation and several indicators of pro-academic investment behaviors and attitudes. Athletes involved in interscholastic sports were less likely to misbehave in school, more likely to enjoy core curriculum classes, and more likely to be judged by their teachers as fully participating in class work. These positive relationships appeared to be unaffected by other background characteristics (e.g., age, SES, standardized test scores, and family composition) or school characteristics. The analyses indicated that sports participation is positively associated with the aspirations of African-American eighth-grade males to enroll in academic or college preparatory programs in high school and with plans to complete high school and attend college. Participation is also related to self-esteem and positive peer relations. We speculate that the effects co-exist and are mutually reinforcing. That is, adolescents involved in sports may receive direct benefits in the form of discipline and training, and have had more incentives to perform academically. However, they enjoy a certain status within schools, and they select a set of peers with similar values of discipline and motivation compared with adolescents not involved in sports. The concept of "niche building" suggests that individuals seek out environments that include peers who are compatible and stimulating (Scarr & McCartney, 1983). Thus, once set in motion, a protective factor may serve as a catalyst for a constellation of sources that project some adolescents on more positive pathways toward adulthood.

Transition to High School. In studies examining the postsecondary plans and aspirations of African-American students, social origin and individual psychological factors have not had the explanatory power that earlier models predicted. One study of the post-high school plans and aspirations of

African-American and White high school seniors found that, although the chances of college entry declined substantially among African Americans between 1977 and the mid-1980s, this drop could not be attributed to a change in values or motivation (Hauser, 1987). However, education and career aspirations are powerful predictors of later success among African Americans. One study found that career aspirations were closely associated with enrollment in a postsecondary institution and educational attainment 7 years beyond high school (Alexander & Garibaldi, 1983). Other studies have noted that the educational aspirations of African-American students from supportive family backgrounds were relatively high regardless of parents' level of education and occupation (Clark, 1983; Ginsburg & Hanson, 1986; Martin, 1986). In fact, factors such as parents' general level of encouragement and concern, students' belief in the work ethic and religious convictions, and peers' educational values served as important protective mechanisms. This constellation of variables was twice as important in predicting African-American student performance than variables measuring family background (Ginsburg & Hanson, 1986; Hanson & Ginsburg, 1986). African-American adolescents who were academically successful in high school were found to have a good attitude, strong belief in themselves, good coping skills, motivation, and determination. These students expended a great deal of effort in academic pursuits (Geary, 1988). Other protective mechanisms included participation in class and extracurricular activities, particularly athletics. Although teachers' expectations were important, teachers typically evaluated students' potential for success primarily by attitude and effort expended, and felt that success or failure was the sole responsibility of the students, rather than the teachers' beliefs, knowledge, or techniques (Geary, 1988).

Wilson-Sadberry, Winfield, and Royster (1991) examined the influences on the postsecondary attainment of African-American adolescents in a nationally representative sample of high school and beyond (HS&B). We explored the effects of peers, counselors, families, educational preparation, and aspirations on attainment. Two obstacles that typically hinder the attainment of African-American males—unemployment and becoming a father—were included as mediating variables. The study compared African-American males who completed high school and received postsecondary training with a comparable group who completed high school only. A majority (66%) continued on in postsecondary schooling. About 17% were in the highest SES quartiles, compared with most who were in the lowest quartile.

No differences existed between the two groups with respect to their fathers' influence on their plans after high school. Approximately two thirds of each group indicated that fathers had from "somewhat to a great deal of influence." In contrast, 58.5% of the African-American males with postsecondary training attributed a great deal of influence to their mothers, compared with 50% of those who did not go on.

Differences in Influences Outside the Family. The influence of counselors on postsecondary plans was mixed. For those males who continued their schooling, one third felt that the counselor had no influence on their plans, as did a slightly higher percentage of those who did not continue. However, 22% who continued their education felt that the counselor had a great deal of influence, compared with 13% of those who did not go on. The differences can be attributed to differences in access to postsecondary education, as well as differences in the quality of in-school counseling available to young African-American males. Approximately 75% of those who continued felt that their teacher had "somewhat to a great deal of influence," compared with 64% who did not go on. One fourth who continued attributed no influence to teachers.

In contrast to the moderate influence of teachers and counselors, peers appear to have considerable influence. A sizable number of the young males who continued their education described their best senior friend as the following: has a strong academic profile, gets good grades, is interested in school, attends classes regularly, and plans to go to college.

Differences in Academic Preparation and Aspirations. Significant differences in curriculum track exist between the two groups. Students who continued their education were twice as likely to be in the academic track, whereas 83% who did not continue were in vocational and general tracks. Similarly, a sizable proportion of males who continued had grades of C or better (61% vs. 50%). There were significant differences in aspirations between the two groups of males. Over two thirds of those who continued their education aspired to a 4-year or advanced degree. Only 7% of those who continued had no plans, compared with over a third of those who did not continue.

In summary, sources of protection for African-American males who had completed high school and continued their postsecondary schooling included slightly better economic status with strong maternal influence on plans, academically inclined peers, better academic preparation, and higher aspirations. For a small proportion, the school guidance counselor's influence was important.

Those African-American males who completed high school but did not continue tended to be from lower SES families, with few significant others influencing their decision. They were more likely to have been enrolled in the vocational and general curriculum, and were more likely to have earned the lowest grades. Thus, their tendency was to not continue with postsecondary educational plans.

Differences in Mediating Factors. The young men who completed only high school tended to be older than the average high school graduate, which suggests the likelihood of grade-level retention as a possible factor in their lower attainment and reduced educational goals. Roughly one third of these young men had children; consequently, their need to work might have interfered with further schooling. Interestingly, the presence or absence of the young men's fathers was not related to differences between the groups. In both cases, slightly under 50% of the young men reported that their fathers lived elsewhere.

Differences in Unemployment Rates. Young African-American men who attended high schools in counties where the unemployment rate was between 7% and 9% were more likely to have graduated from high school and attended postsecondary schooling. Thus, it appears that the unemployment rate does affect the degree to which further education is pursued by students. Furthermore, young men who had only completed high school were more likely to enlist in the armed forces. Almost a quarter of the group pursued this vocational option, compared with 14% in the higher attainment group. However, the military may serve as a source of protection for these students, and they may use this as a vehicle for continuing their education. Elder (1986) found that early entrants into the military—those that enlisted before finishing high school—eventually all earned high school diplomas and continued into college either while in the service or after. Many of these entrants had previous academic difficulties in traditional school, and would not have been able to afford higher education without educational benefits from the GI bill. Moreover, during the service, these entrants—who during adolescence had been ranked the most inept on social competence, ambition, self-adequacy, and assertiveness—demonstrated dramatic gains in psychological health and competence. Thus, the military may serve as a source of protection for many African-American males who do not pursue postsecondary education.

Summary

Several protective factors were significant in continuing the education of African-American males. Family SES is important because of the financial and human resources that become available to support and encourage academic success and planning, which needs to occur during adolescence. Additionally, these students may select similar-type peers, be in the academic track, and thus be more motivated to achieve higher grades. Higher grades lead to more options in terms of course selection and college admissions and planning. Fine (1991) found that differences between minority dropouts and graduates is the belief in a linear relationship between education and opportunity—dropouts do not have these beliefs. Together these studies suggest the co-occurrence of protective sources; that is, regardless of SES, students from supportive home environments that value education and academic success have higher aspirations. These students set goals and are more likely to be in academic programs and receive higher grades, which is an indicator of higher motivation. They also derive benefits from participation in extracurricular activities, including athletics. They are more likely to select positive peers and receive more favorable reactions from teachers. All of these sources increase self-efficacy and open up new opportunities.

However, the link between aspirations and actual entrance into postsecondary institutions may be problematic because of family financial resources. For those students who apply to college and do not attend, socioeconomic factors are important (Arbeiter, 1987; Lee, 1985). In addition to valuing and encouraging academic success, an important protective factor is money, particularly with cuts in financial aid. Slightly more than half of the students who never attended college (based on first follow-up of HS&B) were in the lowest SES quartile. A significant proportion of 1980 African-American seniors (31%) applied to college, but were not attending 2 years later (Lee, 1985). In a study of 189 African-American high school seniors in a large, northern urban school, 55% of the sample had applied to college within 1 month of graduating, whereas only 33% of those who had applied anticipated that their families would pay all or most of their college expenses. More than 33% of the youngsters who did not apply to college cited "lack of money" as the most important reason for not applying. Females at each income level were more likely than males to apply for college admission (Medley & Johnsen, 1976). This suggests that structural factors may serve as risks and are important in determining the college attendance rates of African-American students. These factors include the degree to which financial aid in the form of work study, grants, and scholarships are available, and the degree to which colleges and universities recruit youngsters from minority groups (Blackwell, 1990; Thomas, 1981).

COMMUNITY

Community associations have offered opportunities for and served as a source of protection and developing leadership in the African-American community (Woodard, 1986). The community plays an important role in students' intellectual and psychosocial development (Nettles, 1991). Nettles (1992) defined the *community involvement process* as the means whereby protective mechanisms are provided or set in motion. Students who participated in activities sponsored by community-based programs were more certain that they would graduate from high school, had an increased sense of personal control, had a heightened academic self-concept, and increased their efforts to achieve future goals. Community-based programs offer opportunities and provide a sense of task accomplishment for African-American students.

Nettles' analysis, based on evaluations and studies of various community-based programs, indicates that school-based clinics are only partially effective in reducing the risk-taking behaviors of African-American adolescents. However, programs that promote resilience by extending opportunities typically denied to African-American students often provide social support, adult helpers, options for students to experience success, and outlets for students to invest and discover their interests and talents.

Other protective sources within the community, based on Ogbu's (1987) cultural-ecological model of urban youth, suggest that specific competencies are acquired. Mutual exchange is based on the notion of reciprocity, which exists in poor, urban neighborhoods (e.g., I'll watch your front door, if you watch mine for me). Other competencies suggested by Ogbu include conventional employment, clientship, hustling, pimping, entertainment, and collective struggle. These competencies are generally referred to as "street smarts," which typically are not compatible with school success, but are necessary for survival in the street. In order to protect themselves from the risk associated with street culture, young adolescents may acquire some or all of these competencies. However, the degree and level to which these skills are learned or applied is a function not only of individual characteristics, but also mediators in the environment (e.g., amount of exposure to "street culture," amount of parental supervision, other out-of-school learning opportunities, athletics, and church involvement). Adolescents who survive the streets and avoid involvement with the drug culture—if given the appropriate mentoring, opportunity, and education to translate these competencies into legal and traditional avenues (e.g., in corporate America)—might be highly successful. Former gang members in South Central Los Angeles started and maintained a very successful bodyguard and protection service.

PEERS

External support from peers and other adults differentiated resilient children from peers of the same sex who had problems coping in adolescence (Garmezy, 1983; Werner & Smith, 1982). I speculate that those adolescents who become academically successful have selected peer groups in accordance with their own value system. When youths form social bonds to family and school, they are less likely to develop attachments to negative peer groups because the behaviors rewarded in family and school are incompatible with those likely to be rewarded by negative peers (Hawkins & Lam, 1987). However, during the middle school years, peer-group relationships become increasingly important, and the positive influence of supportive parenting is undermined by the absence of peer support for achievement (Steinberg, Dornbusch, & Brown, 1992). For African-American adolescents, and especially males, the peer group also acts as a stressor, exerting a negative influence on academic learning (Fordham, 1988; Fordham & Ogbu, 1986; Trotter, 1981). Fordham (1988) described the struggle that African-American adolescents face in having to choose between their community and the school, which reflects the dominant views of society. Some adolescents adopt an "oppositional social identity" as their response to the conflict between school and community-based standards of achievement. The oppositional identity has grown out of the need for group affiliation among African Americans as a means of coping with mistreatment and negative stereotypes.

Another option that these adolescents may choose, according to Fordham, is to become part of the school culture by minimizing their ties to the African-American community. As they limit their association, African-American adolescents free themselves to adopt the standards of the school and dominant society, and to seek individualistic achievements. Adolescents who isolate themselves from the African-American community tend to do well in school (Fordham, 1988).

Clark (1991) noted that rejection of an African-American social identity is not without some cost to the adolescent. First, there is the stigma associated with being successful in school. Academically successful adolescents are likely to be rejected and belittled by their peers for their accomplishments. Second, evidence suggests that the failure to adopt one's ethnic identity may be associated with low self-esteem. Trotter (1981) found significant differences in self-esteem and attitudes toward school and the perception of peers' attitudes between high- and low-achieving African-American males. There were also significant differences on academically related issues, such as the importance of good grades, studying, doing homework, and cooperating with teachers.

Clark indicated that "African American adolescents who are academically resilient have developed support systems that help them be successful in and out of school" (p. 46). She reported that social support provides two major functions: "To contribute to adjustment and development, and to provide a buffer against stress that can result in physical and psychological illness" (p. 45). The sources of support systems for African-American adolescents are in developing friendships and obtaining support from peers and school personnel.

Friends affect adolescents' attitudes and feelings toward school and themselves. Adolescents who performed successfully had friends who shared similar values and put forth more effort (Patchen, 1982; cited in Clark, 1991). Clark found that factors such as positive peer interactions in multicultural settings and the development of social support systems in and out of schools can promote academic resilience among African-American adolescents. Recommended solutions include mentorship programs, developing extracurricular activities, recognizing and rewarding academic achievement, and community service (Clark, 1991; Garibaldi, 1992).

It is clear from this discussion and the previously cited studies that peers serve as either a source of protection or a stressor in determining the trajectory of African-American adolescents, particularly males. Although there is no clear answer to this dilemma, this source operates reciprocally with a number of other protective sources, such as family cohesion and values, individual characteristics, school academic culture, and options and opportunities. To illustrate, an article in the Los Angeles Times (Mitchell, 1993) described the situation of a 16-year-old African-American male, Rashawn, who was expelled from school for carrying a gun. Rashawn was being raised by his grandmother, because his father was never around and his mother was addicted to drugs. He was described as having a "criminal record and an unfocused future." Rashawn was involved with the Crips and purchased a gun with money his grandmother had given him to buy school clothes. The gun was purchased for protection after he was shot at while riding in a car with his friends. His grandmother had high expectations for Rashawn, feared for his life, and anonymously alerted school officials. He was immediately expelled with no guarantee of return, because the school district policy called for automatic expulsion for a student caught carrying a gun. Rashawn was sent to juvenile camp for 6 months because he was on probation from a previous drug-selling conviction. While at camp, he tried to figure out what he could do to turn things around, particularly since his 16-year-old girlfriend had given birth to their son. He indicated that he did not want to be like his father and wanted to be a better role model for his own son. However, when he was released, he returned to the same environment with more time, no support, and no plans. His probation officer indicated that he was struggling, doing alright, and not violating. However, Rashawn was similar to a number of the others of his 50-client caseload in that he indicated: "These are kids who haven't been exposed to a lot of things. They really want to do something but they don't know what to do." While Rashawn expressed aspirations for employment, he did not follow through on a prospective job application or a home-study program, but attended a rap concert where another teenager was shot and killed. He was eligible to reapply for school in September and should have entered the eleventh grade but barely had enough credits to qualify as a freshman. He did not know where things had gone wrong, nor what he needed to get his life back on track. There are few options for youngsters like Rashawn, who have to redirect themselves and who have few protective sources but multiple risks and stressors. From the story, it appears that his grandmother intervened in the situation; however, options following the intervention were unavailable. It remains to be seen what will happen with this young male.

ROLE OF THE FAMILY

The family can be a source of support. Clark (1983) identified family socialization patterns that differentiated high- and low-achieving African-American high school seniors from low-income families. He found that parents of the high achievers were more likely to exhibit positive attitudes toward academic pursuits, as well as behaviors that reinforced these attitudes (i.e., establishing norms, monitoring children's performance, and teaching problem-solving and social skills). Families that are successful in motivating African-American adolescents have strong educational values and expectations, encourage academically related activities, are optimistic, and have a strong sense of control (S. Johnson, 1992).

Studies of the African-American family document the importance of the extended family's support as a protective mechanism for children against a hostile, racist, societal environment (McAdoo, 1981; Nobles, 1981; Sudarkasa, 1981). Fine and Schwebel (1991) reviewed the literature on resiliency in African-American children from single-parent families. They reported that academic achievement is unrelated to family structure, and that the effects of maternal employment on the achievement of elementary school children from single-parent families were positive. One study of naturally occurring assertive behaviors among preschool children found that these children were more assertive.

Fine and Schwebel indicated "that Black single-parent families are cohesive, flexibly led, as school-achievement oriented as two-parent families, and may tap into external support to help them achieve their goals" (p. 30). During in-depth interviews with 25 African-American single mothers—in the areas of parenting, sense of family, and finances—they found that the mothers developed innovative ways to meet financial obligations, coped fairly well, and reported a strong sense of organization and cohesiveness within the family. Numerous authors have noted the importance of an extensive kinship network, and some evidence suggests that this support replaces the income of their ex-husbands (Takai, 1981; cited in Fine & Schwebel, 1991).

External support systems are critical. Several studies have discussed the importance of African-American male role models, and that some children in single-parent households lack the opportunity to develop supportive relationships with their fathers. However, as emphasized by Fine and Schwebel, the data do not directly indicate the presence of other males in the children's lives (e.g., uncles, grandfathers, mothers' boyfriends, or older brothers who may all provide support and serve as role models).

Scott-Jones and Nelson-Le Gall (1986) emphasized the supportive environment and highly developed networks of kin and friends, and the positive value given to children in African-American families. Although factors within single-parent African-American families promote resilience, no evidence suggests that African-American children in single-parent families cope more effectively than they would if they came from two-parent families (Fine & Schwebel, 1991). Family composition has little relationship to school achievement except that it serves as a proxy for income level (S. Johnson, 1992).

ROLE OF THE CHURCH

Although there has been a considerable amount of media attention devoted to the role of youth service organizations in solving adolescent youth problems (National Collaboration for Youth, 1990), few empirical investigations have studied the effect these organizations have as a source of developing resilience. Many religious organizations provide youth services. Several studies have found that religion is associated with educational attainment and competence (Brown & Gary, 1991; Masten, Best, & Garmezy, 1990). One protective mechanism within the African-American community has traditionally been the church, which has helped alleviate the psychological stress of institutional racism and inequalities that youth encounter daily.

The church acts in both an instrumental and a spiritual role to provide youth with alternative coping mechanisms (Woodard, 1992). The instrumental aspect involves child care, tutoring, general education diploma (GED) and job training programs, and advocacy groups. Although not well documented, the spiritual aspect may provide adolescents with a "sense of coherence" (Antonovsky, 1979). This construct, as a characteristic of resilient youth and children in Kauai (Werner, 1987; Werner & Smith, 1982), is the confidence that one's internal and external environments are predictable, that problems will be resolved reasonably well, and that one can cope with life's inevitable stresses. Antonovsky (1979) suggested that individuals develop a generalized way of viewing the world as more or less coherent by approximately age 30. The more an individual's life experiences are characterized by consistency and the ability to shape outcomes, the more one is likely to view the world as coherent and predictable. This construct may be reinforced by religion and church attendance.

Some evidence suggests that high-achieving African-American adolescents are more likely to have particular religious values (Ginsburg & Hanson, 1986). Inner-city African-American youth who attended church more frequently had significantly higher school attendance and employment than other inner-city African-American youth (Freeman, 1986). Moreover, values of students, parents, and peers were twice as predictive of academic achievement as family background (Ginsburg & Hanson, 1986). Others have also noted the relationship between religious values and success (Clark, 1983; Ginsburg & Hanson, 1986; Hanson & Ginsburg, 1986). As levels of religious socialization increase, educational attainment among African-Americans also increases, irrespective of particular denomination or family structure (Brown & Gary, 1991). These findings suggest that one important source of protection for African-American adolescents may be the value system inherent in religious organizations or spiritual communities.

A "sense of coherence" also appears to be related to a sense of personal efficacy—one of the protective mechanisms discussed. The reciprocity and co-occurrence of these mechanisms are once more suggested from empirical evidence. Strong positive relationships exist among achievement, competence, and the attitudes of students' self-concept with regard to learning and success in school, and students' feeling of control over their environment (e.g., believing that hard work pays off; Coleman et al., 1966). The variable of control over environment was more strongly related to achievement than was family background and school variables. Similarly, 45% of the variance in student achievement after controlling for race, SES, and community was attributed to students' sense of futility within the school social system (Brookover & Schneider, 1975). This relationship suggests that students' understanding of their role in school determines, to some extent, how well they perform.

One study reported that low-income African-American students who experienced failure blamed their failure on stable factors, such as ability (Broderick & Sewell, 1985). These students largely perceived outcomes as out of their control and resistant to change. However, the research on the attribution pattern of African-American children from low-income homes has not yielded consistent results (Broderick & Sewell, 1985). Because of the high proportion of minority students who fail academically in schools, Graham (1989) noted that motivation theorists will have to incorporate the dynamics of failure into theories.

METHODOLOGICAL, CONCEPTUAL, AND POLICY CONSIDERATIONS

As with most human behavior, the processes and mechanisms involved in the development of resilience among African-American adolescents are complex. It would make researchers' jobs much easier if there were a rational, linear progression of mechanisms, processes, and events over the life course that might explain and predict which adolescents would make the transition to become well-functioning, productive adults. For example, Elder (1985) noted that events and transitions modify life trajectories, and that four sets of variables must be taken into account: (a) the nature of the event or transition, and its severity, duration, and so on; (b) the resources, beliefs, and experiences people bring to the situation; (c) how the situation/event is defined; and (d) resulting lines of adaptation as chosen from available alternatives.

Another intricate model examines risk and protective factors with multiple domains (e.g., biology/genetics, social environment, perceived environment, personality, and behavior), which then have reciprocal effects on adolescent risk behaviors that lead to life outcomes. There is a growing awareness that the social context influences adolescent risk behaviors (Jessor, 1993). Social context is not only composed of the unique sociocultural frames of reference or results of empirical research on African Americans. It is also necessary to view the larger societal context for understanding resilience among African-American youth. In this country, race matters. The high levels of poverty and unemployment, the disproportionate amount of negative media portrayal of African Americans, the "Rodney King" incident, the repetition of homicide in the news media, murder and incarceration rates of African-American youth, overt discrimination, and racism in the 1990s all have direct and negative effects on the psyche of African Americans, particularly the young (Stroman, 1991; K. A. Johnson, 1991; Berry, 1980). In one study, African-American males who had high goals, such as aspiring to college, were much more likely to achieve them than those who did not (Wilson-Sadberry, Winfield, & Royster, 1991). The mere fact that aspirations were significant, given the larger social context, suggests that buffers/protective processes had to be of much greater impact to reduce the negative distractions, such as peers. Processes such as support and encouragement from significant adults on an ongoing basis, personal efficacy, and academic achievement are all critical to long-term success. As Ogbu (1987) identified some years ago, the larger societal context has to be considered. However, the context has changed substantially since his study, so that it is more than the job ceiling and prospects for employment. I suspect that the current negative influences in the larger society depress motivation for performance and persistence.

The development of resilience occurs over the life span. Unfortunately, unlike the Berkeley studies, which followed Caucasian males for 20–30 years, there are no longitudinal databases that followed African Americans over a long period of time. These studies began in the late 1920s and identified samples during childhood, documenting growth patterns, personality traits, and home environment. Samples were contacted at intervals throughout adolescence and adulthood (see Eichorn, 1981, for a description of the studies). Thus, we are left with cross-sectional studies to piece together the process. Many of the studies cited in this chapter are secondary data analyses of large-scale, national datasets. These studies allow us to test some general notions concerning relationships between variables. However, they (a) are correlational and do not allow us to get at cause and effect, and (b) are typically very poor for understanding social process or what was occurring in the individual's life at that particular point in time. To address the first issue, research that follows students over a critical transition period would be useful, however it is costly and takes time to collect longitudinal data. Large urban school districts, which have the capability of maintaining a longitudinal dataset, typically retain achievement, attendance, behaviors, and grades on students, but typically do not have the staff or resources to analyze these data. In these datasets, individual students could be followed from kindergarten through twelfth grade. Another avenue for collecting longitudinal data is through programs such as "I have a dream" and similar ventures, which promise students a college scholarship if they complete high school. These programs provide a naturally occurring laboratory in which to study the development of resilience. Typically, students are selected at the completion of sixth grade, at which time they are given tutoring, mentoring, and other resources typically not available to low-income students in their neighborhoods. Carefully designed qualitative evaluations of these programs would test some of the hypotheses on the interactions of risk and protective mechanisms.

To address the second issue of understanding social interaction and process, additional case studies of individuals within these longitudinal samples would get in-depth information on decision making and interactive influences. Qualitative studies at critical points (e.g., following the death of a parent, teenage pregnancy) are needed to provide the thick description of social process untapped by questionnaire items. Thus, an appropriate paradigm would be situational and capture the person/environment interaction. From this discussion, it is clear that what is *not* needed are short-term studies (unless they are interventions), in which scales are constructed and administered to children at age 3, labeling them *resilient* and *nonresilient* for life.

There *is* a need to identify schools, classrooms, and institutions that provide protective mechanisms to African-American youth. Much of the research on effective schools conducted in the late 1960s and 1970s focused on the school- and teacher-level variables related to student achievement during a 1- or 2-year period, and thus did not provide a longitudinal view of student persistence in school. Moreover, with the exception of the Rutter (1979) study, the focus of effective schools was standardized achievement tests, and these studies did not include behavioral outcome measures. Moreover, this research omits individual, social–psychological variables, such as attributions and effort, which may be as important to developing resilience and long-term success as developing cognitive skills.

What do institutions do to protect African-American students? Traditionally, the success rates of historically African-American institutions have been documented (Garibaldi, 1991). These institutions grant bachelor degrees to more African-American students than do predominantly White institutions. Remarkably, these institutions admit youngsters with less academic preparation and less resources (both human and financial), and yet a large number of these students go on to graduate schools to pursue advanced degrees.

Some studies have indicated that the more nurturing environment, smaller classes, and so on make the difference. These institutions provide models of how protective processes function at an institutional level.

At the level of individual characteristics, the issues of sex role, race, SES, and academic preparation are critical to consider for future research as well as interventions. There needs to be more research focused on sex differences because males and females respond differently to stress (Rutter, 1979). In a study on sex differences in National Assessment of Education Progress (NAEP) reading proficiency, African-American females had higher scores after controlling for family background and academic behaviors at fourth grade, but not at eighth and eleventh grades (Winfield & Lee, 1986). Consistent with other studies of within-race sex differences (Hare, 1985, 1988), we speculated that differences at the earlier grades were due, in part, to the differential response and expectations given by teachers in elementary school settings to African-American males. However, by middle school, males and females were more similar in their performance. This might be influenced by differential dropout rates. We know very little about differential responses to stress and protective mechanisms. Interventions might look very different depending on sex.

Graham (1989) discussed the confounding of racial and social class variables in studying motivations of the African-American population. Middle-SES African-Americans in her study had an adaptive attributional pattern that was different from that of Whites and lower status African-Americans (Graham, 1984). These differences had been previously undetected. Studies of resilience typically focus on lower SES students, however, they also need to examine middle-class African Americans as a source of information about motivation and persistence in minority populations. There is a need to incorporate studies on the values, attitudes, and attributions that have proved to promote persistence and long-term success.

The lack of academic preparation of high school youth is a risk factor for many African-American youth. Findings from the National Assessment of Educational Progress (1985) indicate that fewer African-American than White eleventh graders read at the level expected of college freshmen. Nineteen percent of African-American eleventh graders read at the "adept" proficiency level, compared with 47% of Whites. Others have documented the cumulative effects of tracking on the academic performance and postsecondary attainment of African Americans (Braddock, 1989, 1990). African-American students do not initially start out behind their White counterparts; rather, the gap begins around third grade. The interventions in schools, classrooms, and communities must begin prior to middle and high school.

Social policies such as funding of Headstart have affected urban youngsters' opportunities and access in schools and classrooms (Hawkins, 1991; Swanson & Spencer, 1991). From the findings in this chapter, in addition to early intervention, there is a need for supportive significant adults who interact in a positive manner with students, and additional opportunities to explore various talents in community-based or school-related programs. Unfortunately, in most major urban school districts—faced with budget cuts— art, music, gym, and shops are the first programs to go. Having these options available are critical for some students' motivation and long-term persistence.

Finally, it is necessary to shift people's thinking from risk to resilience, particularly teachers, principals, and other adults working with youth. This requires a change in the beliefs, structures, and policies that are currently in practice. Expectations are a part, but not all, that must change. If I ask teachers about IQ, a majority will say it is fixed and immutable, and that there is not much that can be done to change it. They feel intelligence is largely genetic, and that there are racial/ethnic group differences. Most teachers might also agree that environment plays a part. However, because of the extremely impoverished homes from which many students come, teachers feel that students are incapable of performing academically. Thus, when these belief systems are ingrained and fixed in teachers' minds, it makes no sense to talk about changing expectations, planning for long-term success, using protective mechanisms, or developing resilience in inner-city and disadvantaged children. Unfortunately, individuals' perceptions, beliefs, and attitudes are not easily changed. Within the control of school administrators and teachers is the ability to change the structures, language, and policies that impact individual belief systems. Schools and classrooms must incorporate diversity training, multiethnic views, curricula, and so on, but also be critically examined for congruence with the four protective processes discussed earlier. Currently, policies such as tracking, readiness testing, Chapter I, special education, and ability grouping may serve the needs of some students, but for the most part they do not act as protective mechanisms. There needs to be a critical rethinking of what we do with and to African American and other racial/ethnic minority students to provide necessary protective mechanisms to foster resilience and success.

REFERENCES

Alexander, L., & Garibaldi, A. (1983, April). *The relationship of educational and career aspirations of Black students to college matriculation and completion.* Paper presented at the annual meeting of the American Educational Research Association, Montreal, Quebec, Canada.

Allen, W., & Farley, R. (1987). *The color line and the quality of life in America.* New York: Russell Sage Foundation.

Antonovsky, A. (1979). *Health, stress and coping.* San Francisco: Jossey-Bass.

Arbeiter, S. (1987). Black enrollments: The case of the missing students. *Change, 19*(3), 14–19.

Blackwell, J. (1990). Blacks and Hispanics in the educational pipeline. In G. E. Thomas (Ed.), *U.S. race relations in the 1980s and 1990s challenges and alternatives.* Washington, DC: Hemisphere.

114 WINFIELD

Berry, G. L. (1980). Children, television, and social class roles: The medium as unplanned educational curriculum. In E. L. Palmer & A. Dorr (Eds.), *Children and the faces of television* (pp. 71–81). New York: Academic.

Berry, G. L. (1989). Afro Americans and academic achievement: Pathways to excellence. In G. L. Berry & J. K. Asamen (Eds.), *Black students* (pp. 286–294). Newbury Park, CA: Sage.

Boykin, W. (1986). The triple quandary and the schooling of Afro-American children. In U. Neisser (Ed.), *The school achievement of minority children* (pp. 57–92). Hillsdale, NJ: Lawrence Erlbaum Associates.

Braddock, J. H. (1989). *Tracking: Implications for African American students.* Baltimore, MD: The Johns Hopkins University, Center for Research on Disadvantaged Students.

Braddock, J. H. (1990). *Tracking: Implications for student race/ethnic subgroups.* Baltimore, MD: The Johns Hopkins University, Center for Research on Effective Schooling for Disadvantaged Students.

Braddock, J. H., & McPartland, J. (1987). Social science evidence and affirmative action policies: A reply to the commentators. *Journal of Social Issues, 43*(1), 133–143.

Braddock, J. H., Royster, D. A., Winfield, L. F., & Hawkins, R. (1991). Bouncing back: Sports and academic resilience among African-American males. *Education and Urban Society, 24*(1), 113–131.

Broderick, P., & Sewell, T. (1985). Attributions for success and failure in children of different social class. *The Journal of Social Psychology, 125*(5), 591–599.

Bronfenbrenner, U. (1979). *The ecology of human development.* Cambridge, MA: Harvard University Press.

Brookover, W. B., & Schneider, J. M. (1975). Academic environments and elementary school achievement. *Journal of Research and Development in Education, 9*(1), 82–91.

Brown, D. R., & Gary, L. E. (1991). Religious socialization and educational attainment among African Americans: An empirical assessment. *Journal of Negro Education, 60*(3), 411–426.

Clark, M. L. (1991). Social identity, peer relations, and academic competence of African American adolescents. *Education and Urban Society, 24*(1), 41–52.

Clark, R. (1983). *Family life and school achievement. Why poor Black children succeed and fail.* Chicago: University of Chicago Press.

Clausen, J. S. (1991). Adolescent competence and the shaping of the life course. *American Journal of Sociology, 96*(4), 805–842.

Coleman, J. S., Campbell, E. Q., Hobson, C. J., McPartland, J., Mood, A., Weinfeld, F. D., & York, R. L. (1966). *Equality of educational opportunity.* Washington, DC: U.S. Government Printing Office.

Danzinger, S. K., & Farber, N. B. (1990). Keeping inner-city youths in school: Critical experience of young Black women. *Social Work Research and Abstracts, 26,* 32–39.

Domhoff, G. W., & Zweigenhaft, R. L. (1991). *Blacks in the White establishment: A study of race and class in America.* New Haven, CT: Yale University Press.

Edwards, O. (1979). Cohort and sex changes in Black educational attainment. *Sociology and Social Issues, 59,* 110–120.

Eichorn, D. H. (1981). Samples and procedures. In D. H. Eichorn, J. A. Clausen, N. Haan, M. P. Honzik, & P. H. Mussen (Eds.), *Present and past in middle life* (pp. 33–51). New York: Academic.

Elder, G. H. (1985). Perspectives on the life course. In G. H. Elder (Ed.), *Life course dynamics: Trajectories and transitions, 1968–1980* (pp. 23–49). Ithaca, NY: Cornell University Press.

Elder, G. H. (1986). Military times and turning points in men's lives. *Developmental Psychology, 22*(2), 233–245.

Epps, E. G., & Jackson, K. W. (1985). *Educational and occupational aspirations and early attainment of Black males and females.* Atlanta, GA: Southern Education Foundation.

Fine, M. (1991). *Framing dropouts: Notes on the politics of an urban public high school.* Albany, NY: State University of New York Press.

Fine, M. A., & Schwebel, A. I. (1991). Resiliency in Black children from single-parent families. In W. A. Rhodes & W. K. Brown (Eds.), *Why some children succeed despite the odds* (pp. 23–40). New York: Praeger.

Fordham, S. (1988). Racelessness as a factor in Black students' school success: Pragmatic strategy or Pyrrhic victory? *Harvard Educational Review, 58*(1), 54–84.

Fordham, S., & Ogbu, J. (1986). Black students' school success: Coping with the burden of "acting White." *The Urban Review, 18*, 176–206.

Freeman, R. B. (1986). Who escapes? The relation of churchgoing and other background factors to the socioeconomic performance of Black male youth from inner city tracts. In R. B. Freeman & H. J. Holzer (Eds.), *The Black youth employment crisis* (pp. 353–356). Chicago: University of Chicago Press.

Furstenberg, F. F. (1976). *Unplanned parenthood: Social consequences of teenage childbearing.* New York: The Free Press.

Garibaldi, A. M. (1991). The role of historically Black colleges in facilitating resilience among African American students. *Education and Urban Society, 24*(1), 103–112.

Garibaldi, A. M. (1992). Educating and motivating African American males to succeed. *Journal of Negro Education, 61*(1), 4–11.

Garmezy, N. (1983). Stressors of childhood. In N. Garmezy & M. Rutter (Eds.), *Stress, coping, and development in children* (pp. 43–84). New York: McGraw-Hill.

Garmezy, N. (1987). Stress, competence, and development: Continuities in the study of schizophrenic adults, children vulnerable to psychopathology, and the search for stress-resistant children. *American Journal of Orthopsychiatry, 57*(2), 159–174.

Garmezy, N. (1991). Resiliency and vulnerability to adverse developmental outcomes associated with poverty. *American Behavioral Scientist, 34*(4), 416–430.

Geary, P. A. (1988, April). *Defying the odds?: Academic success among at-risk minority teenagers in an urban high school.* Paper presented at the annual meeting of the American Educational Research Association, New Orleans, LA.

Ginsburg, A. L., & Hanson, S. L. (1986). *Values and educational success among disadvantaged students* (Contract No. 300-83-0211). Washington, DC: U.S. Department of Education.

Gordon, E. (1982). Urban education. In H. E. Mitzel (Ed.), *Encyclopedia of educational research* (Vol. 4, 5th ed., pp. 1973–1980). New York: Macmillan.

Graham, S. (1984). Communicating sympathy and anger to Black and White children: The cognitive (attributional) antecedents of affective cues. *Journal of Personality and Social Psychology, 47*, 40–54.

Graham, S. (1989). Motivation in Afro Americans. In G. L. Berry & J. K. Asamen (Eds.), *Black students* (pp. 40–68). Newbury Park, CA: Sage.

Graham, S. (1992). Most of the subjects were White and middle class. Trends in published research on African Americans in selected APA journals, 1970–1989. *American Psychologist, 47*(5), 629–639.

Gurin, P., & Epps, E. (1974). *Black consciousness, identity, and achievement.* New York: Wiley.

Hanson, S. L., & Ginsburg, A. L. (1986). *Gaining ground: Values and high school success* (Contract No. 300-83-0211). Washington, DC: U.S. Department of Education.

Hare, B. (1985). Reexamining the achievement central tendency: Sex differences within race and race differences within sex. In H. P. McAdoo & J. L. McAdoo (Eds.), *Black children, social, educational and parental environments* (pp. 139–155). Beverly Hills, CA: Sage.

Hare, B. (1988). African-American youth at risk. *Urban League Review, 12*, 25–38.

Hauser, R. M. (1987). *Post-high school plans of Black high school graduates: What has changed since the mid-1970s?* CDE Working Paper 87-26, University of Wisconsin, Center for Demography and Ecology.

Hawkins, A. F. (1991). Becoming preeminent in education: America's greatest challenge. *Harvard Journal of Law and Public Policy, 14*(2), 367–395.

Hawkins, J. D., & Lam, T. (1987). Teacher practices, social development, and delinquency. In J. Burchard & S. N. Burchard (Eds.), *Prevention of delinquent behavior* (pp. 241–274). Beverly Hills, CA: Sage.

Jackson, J. J. (1973). Black women in a racist society. *Planning for Higher Education, 17*(3), 43–57.

Jessor, R. (1993). Successful adolescent development among youth in high risk settings. *American Psychologist, 48*(2), 117–126.

Johnson, K. A. (1991). Objective news and other myths: The poisoning of young Black minds. *Journal of Negro Education, 60*(3), 328–341.

Johnson, S. (1992). Extra-school factors in achievement, attainment and aspiration among junior and senior high school-age African American youth. *Journal of Negro Education, 61*(1), 99–119.

Krasner, D. V. (1992). *Risk and protective factors and achievement of children at risk.* Unpublished doctoral dissertation, University of California, Los Angeles.

Lee, V. (1985). *Access to higher education: The experience of Blacks, Hispanics, and low socioeconomic status Whites.* Washington, DC: American Council on Education, Division of Policy Analysis and Research.

Lee, V. E., & Bryk, A. S. (1988). Curriculum tracking as mediating the social distribution of high school achievement. *Sociology of Education, 61*(2), 78–94.

Lee, V. E., Winfield, L. F., & Wilson, T. (1991). Academic behaviors among high-achieving African American students. *Education and Urban Society, 24*(1), 65–86.

Martin, O. L. (1986, April). *An analysis of Black high school students' postsecondary plans: Educational excellence or economic survival?* Paper presented at the annual meeting of the American Educational Research Association, San Francisco, CA.

Masten, A. S., Best, K. M., & Garmezy, N. (1990). Resilience and development: Contributions from the study of children who overcame adversity. *Development and Psychopathology, 2,* 425–444.

McAdoo, H. P. (1981). *Black families.* Beverly Hills, CA: Sage.

Medley, M. L., & Johnsen, K. P. (1976). The economics of college plans among Black high school seniors. *Journal of Negro Education, 45*(2), 134–140.

Mitchell, J. L. (1993, July 12). Expelled for having guns, youths must reclaim selves. *Los Angeles Times,* pp. A1, A20.

National Assessment of Educational Progress. (1985). *The Reading Report Card: Progress toward excellence in our schools. Trends in reading over four assessments, 1971–1984* (Report No. 15-R-01). Princeton, NJ: Educational Testing Service.

National Collaboration for Youth. (1990). *Report on the nationwide project Making the Grade.* Washington, DC: Author.

National Commission on Excellence in Education. (1983). *A nation at risk.* Washington, DC: U.S. Department of Education.

Natriello, G., McDill, E. L., & Pallas, A. M. (1990). *Schooling disadvantaged children: Racing against catastrophe.* New York: Teachers College Press.

Nelson-Le Gall, S., & Glor-Scheib, S. (1985). Help-seeking in elementary classrooms: An observational study. *Contemporary Educational Psychology, 10,* 58–71.

Nelson-Le Gall, S., & Jones, E. (1990). Cognitive-motivational influences on children's help seeking. *Child Development, 61,* 581–589.

Nettles, S. M. (1991). Community involvement and disadvantaged students: A review. *Review of Educational Research, 61*(3), 379–406.

Nettles, S. M. (1992). Community contributions to school outcomes of African American students. *Education and Urban Society, 24*(1), 132–147.

Nettles, S. M., & Plenck, J. (1994). The multiple ecologies of risk and resilience in African American adolescents. In R. J. Hagerty, N. Garmezy, M. Rutter, & L. R. Sherrod (Eds.), *Stress, coping, and development: Risk and resilience in children*. New York: Cambridge University Press.

Nobles, W. W. (1981). African-American family life: An instrument of culture. In H. P. McAdoo (Ed.), *Black families* (pp. 77–86). Beverly Hills, CA: Sage.

Ogbu, J. (1987). Variability in minority school performance: A problem in search of an explanation. *Anthropology and Education Quarterly, 18,* 312–333.

Purkey, W., & Smith, M. (1983). Effective schools: A review. *Elementary School Journal, 84*(4), 427–452.

Quinton, D., & Rutter, M. (1988). *Parenting breakdown: The making and breaking of intergenerational links.* Brookfield, VT: Avebury.

Richardson, V., & Colfer, P. (1990). Being at-risk in school. In J. I. Goodlad & P. Keating (Eds.), *Access to knowledge: An agenda for our nation's schools* (pp. 107–124). New York: College Entrance Examination Board.

Rutter, M. (1979). Protective factors in children's responses to stress and disadvantage. In M. W. Kent & J. E. Rolf (Eds.), *Primary prevention of psychopathology: Vol. 3. Social competence in children* (pp. 49–74). Hanover, NH: University Press of New England.

Rutter, M. (1987). Psychosocial resilience and protective mechanisms. *American Journal of Orthopsychiatry, 37*(3), 317–331.

Rutter, M. (1990). Psychosocial resilience and protective mechanism. In J. Rolf, A. Masten, D. Cichetti, K. Nuechterlein, & S. Weintraub (Eds.), *Risk and protective factors in the development of psychopathology* (pp. 181–214). New York: Cambridge University Press.

Rutter, M. B., Mortimer, P., Ouston, J., & Smith, A. (1979). *Fifteen thousand hours: Secondary schools and their effects on children.* Cambridge, MA: Harvard University Press.

Scarr, S., & McCartney, K. (1983). How people make their own environments: A theory of genotype–environment effects. *Child Development, 54,* 424–435.

Scott-Jones, D. (1987). Mother-as-teacher in the families of high- and low-achieving low-income Black first-graders. *Journal of Negro Education, 56,* 21–34.

Scott-Jones, D. (1991). Adolescent childbearing: Risks and resilience. *Education and Urban Society, 24*(1), 53–64.

Scott-Jones, D., & Nelson-Le Gall, S. (1986). Defining black families: Past and present. In E. Seidman & J. Rappaport (Eds.), *Redefining social problems* (pp. 83–100). New York: Plenum.

Scott-Jones, D., & White, A. B. (1990). Correlates of sexual activity in early adolescence. *Journal of Early Adolescence, 10,* 221–238.

Scott-Jones, D., & Turner, S. L. (1990). The impact of adolescent childbearing on educational attainment and income of Black females. *Youth and Society, 22,* 35–53.

Slaughter, D. (1988). *Black children and poverty: A developmental perspective.* San Francisco: Jossey-Bass.

Spencer, M., Brookins, G., & Allen, W. (Eds.). (1985). *Beginnings: The social and affective development of Black children.* Hillsdale, NJ: Lawrence Erlbaum Associates.

Steinberg, L., Dornbusch, S. M., & Brown, B. B. (1992). Ethnic differences in adolescent achievement: An ecological perspective. *American Psychologist, 47*(6), 723–729.

Stevenson, H., & Rhodes, W. A. (1991). Risk and resilience in teenagers who avoid pregnancy. In W. A. Rhodes & W. K. Brown (Eds.), *Why some children succeed despite the odds* (pp. 79–91). New York: Praeger.

Stroman, C. A. (1991). Television's role in the socialization of African American children and adolescents. *Journal of Negro Education, 60*(3), 314–327.

Sudarkasa, N. (1981). Interpreting the African heritage in Afro American family organization. In H. P. McAdoo (Ed.), *Black families* (pp. 37–53). Beverly Hills, CA: Sage.

Swanson, D. P., & Spencer, M. B. (1991). Youth policy, poverty, and African-Americans: Implications for resilience. *Education and Urban Society, 24*(1), 148–161.

118   WINFIELD

Taylor, J. T. (1986, April). *Using political solutions to address educational problems: The impact of increased academic standards on Black student athletes.* Paper presented at the annual meeting of American Educational Research Association, San Francisco, CA.

Thomas, G. E. (1981). *Black students in higher education: The conditions of blacks in the 1970s.* Westport, CT: Greenwood.

Trotter, J. R. (1981). Academic attitudes of high achieving and low achieving academically able Black male adolescents. *Journal of Negro Education, 50*(1), 54–62.

Venezky, R. L., & Winfield, L. F. (1979). *Schools that succeed beyond expectations in reading* (Studies on Education, Technical Report No. 1). Newark: University of Delaware. (ERIC Document Reproduction Service No. ED 177 484).

Werner, E. E. (1987). Vulnerability and resiliency in children at risk for delinquency: A longitudinal study from birth to young adulthood. In J. D. Burchard & S. N. Burchard (Eds.), *Prevention of delinquent behavior* (pp. 16–43). Beverly Hills, CA: Sage.

Werner, E. E., & Smith, R. S. (1982). *Vulnerable but invincible: A study of resilient children.* New York: McGraw-Hill.

Wilson, J. W. (1987). *The truly disadvantaged: The inner city, the underclass and public policy.* Chicago, IL: University of Chicago Press.

Wilson, K. R., & Allen, W. R. (1987). Explaining the educational attainment of young Black adults: Critical familial and extra-familial influences. *Journal of Negro Education, 56*(1), 64–76.

Wilson-Sadberry, K., Winfield, L. F., & Royster, D. A. (1991). Resilience and persistence of African-American males in postsecondary enrollment. *Education and Urban Society, 24*(1), 87–102.

Winfield, L. F. (1982). *Case studies of inner urban schools and reading achievement.* Unpublished doctoral dissertation, University of Delaware, Newark, DE.

Winfield, L. F. (1988). *An investigation of high vs. low literacy proficient Black young adults. Final report to the Rockefeller Foundation.* Philadelphia, PA: Temple University, Center for Research on Human Development and Education.

Winfield, L. F. (1991a). Characteristics of middle grades schools implementing minimum competency testing programs. *Research in Middle Level Education, 15*(1), 31–44.

Winfield, L. F. (1991b). Resilience, schooling and development in African American youth: A conceptual framework. *Education and Urban Society, 24*(1), 5–14.

Winfield, L. F., Hawkins, R., & Stringfield, S. (1992). *A description of Chapter I schoolwide projects and effects on student achievement in six case study schools* (CDS Report #37). Baltimore, MD: Johns Hopkins University, Center for Research on Effective Schooling for Disadvantaged Students.

Winfield, L. F., & Lee, V. (1986, August). *Gender differences in reading proficiency: Are they constant across racial/ethnic groups?* Paper presented at the annual meeting of the American Psychological Association, Washington, DC.

Woodard, M. D. (1986). Voluntary association membership among black Americans: The post-civil rights era. *The Sociological Quarterly, 28*(2), 285–301.

Woodard, M. D. (1992, September). *Youth in the African American church: Alternative coping mechanisms for the 21st century.* Paper presented at the fourth annual international conference for Society and Resource Management, University of Wisconsin, Madison, WI.

CHAPTER SEVEN

Social Context and Adolescence: Perspectives on Development Among Inner-City African-American Teens

Linda M. Burton
Kevin W. Allison
Dawn Obeidallah
The Pennsylvania State University

The study of development among adolescents has been a topic of interest to social scientists for over half a century (Adelson, 1986; Coleman, 1961; Feldman & Elliott, 1990; Hoffman, 1980; Modell, 1989; Petersen, 1988). Although this interest has generated a rich theoretical and empirical knowledge base on the biological, social, psychological, and moral development of White middle-class adolescents, issues concerning the influence of social context on the developmental experiences of ethnic/racial minority or economically disadvantaged teens are rarely addressed (Holliday, 1989; Jarrett, 1990; Seidman, 1991; Spencer & Dornbusch, 1990). For example, a systematic exploration of what constitutes normal development among inner-city, economically disadvantaged, ethnic/racial minority teens has yet to appear in the adolescent development literature (Bell-Scott & Taylor, 1989; Feldman & Elliott, 1990; Gibbs, 1985; McLoyd, 1990; Spencer, 1990). The lack of systematic conceptual and empirical explorations of social context and development among ethnic/racial minority and economically disadvantaged teens raises serious questions concerning the applicability of mainstream developmental models to the study of their life course (Murray, Smith, & West, 1989). Is adolescence a clearly delineated developmental stage among ethnic/racial minority and economically disadvantaged teens? What are the parameters of development among these adolescents? How does social context influence the developmental experiences of poor African-American, Hispanic, Native-American, Asian-American, or White adolescents?

Ecological and life-course perspectives on development underscore the importance of examining the relationship between social context and the developmental paths of economically disadvantaged and ethnic/racial minority subgroup teens (Brofenbrenner, 1979; Elder, Modell, & Parke, 1993; Jarrett, in press; Ogbu, 1981; Silbereisen, Eyferth, & Rudinger, 1986). These perspectives suggest that the social contexts of economically disadvantaged communities and families may have differential effects on the developmental life course of ethnic/racial minority teenagers (Allison & Takei, 1994; Conger, Conger, Elder, & Lorenz, 1993; Dornbusch, Ritter, & Steinberg, 1991; Elder, 1974; Garbarino, Kostelny, & Dubrow, 1991; Seidman, 1991; Williams & Kornblum, 1985). Within these contexts, there may be distinct ideologies, role expectations, behavioral practices, and means of marking the entry to and exit from adolescence that reflect individual and familial responses to surviving in economically deprived and high-risk environments (Burton, 1990; Garbarino et al., 1991; Merry, 1981). Thus, identifying the contextual meaning of adolescent development among specific racial/ethnic and economic subgroups is an important and necessary enterprise in developing theories that are sensitive to the experiences of non-White and poor teens (Allison & Takei, 1993; Jones, 1989).

This chapter explores the relationship between context and development among economically disadvantaged, inner-city African-American adolescents. We argue that traditional mainstream perspectives of adolescent development may have limited applicability to some inner-city African-American teens. In certain community and family contexts, adolescence may be an ambiguous life stage, with role expectations and definitions of developmental success that differ from those experienced by middle-class teenagers (Holliday, 1989; McGee, 1982). Using insights from existing ethnographic accounts of African-American families and qualitative data from an ongoing ethnographic study of urban African-American families, this chapter addresses three issues. We outline dimensions of social context that may influence the distinctiveness of adolescence as a developmental stage among inner-city African-American teens. We use case-history data from our ongoing ethnographic study of urban, low-income African-American families to further illuminate the impact of these dimensions on teens' perceptions of adolescence and the life course. We discuss the implications of these issues for future research on social context and the developmental pathways of urban African-American teens.

ADOLESCENT DEVELOPMENT, SOCIAL CONTEXT, AND AFRICAN-AMERICAN TEENS

Adolescence is typically defined, in contemporary American society, as a transition period marking the change from childhood to adulthood. Occurring between the ages of 11–20, normative adolescent development is characterized by qualitative biological, social, and cognitive changes for the individual (Elliot & Feldman, 1990). The onset of puberty is the biological marker that signals the beginning of adolescence as a life-course phase (Brooks-Gunn & Reiter, 1990). At the cognitive level, it is believed that adolescents, through the development of abstract reasoning, begin to acquire a more complex and integrated notion of self, the ability to be self-reflective, and the capacity to make social comparisons and entertain thoughts about future expectations (Graber & Petersen, 1991; Keating, 1990). At the social level, adolescence is characterized as a life period when individuals develop stronger ties with peers and develop increasingly autonomous relationships with their parents and family (Steinberg, 1990; Youniss & Smollar, 1985).

In mainstream contexts, social institutions and families provide specific guidelines concerning the role expectations and behaviors of adolescents. For example, schools plan developmentally appropriate curriculum and activities for teens. Parents offer directives to adolescents concerning their place in families and society. Under these directives, adolescents are often reminded that they are no longer children, but are not yet adults. Although the activities adolescents engage in are designed to prepare them for adulthood, in most cases, adolescents are not allowed to fully assume adult responsibilities (i.e., parenthood) or engage in the behaviors of adult life until their post-teenage years.

In other contexts, however, the directives concerning appropriate adolescent roles and behavior may be quite ambiguous. Particularly for economically disadvantaged teens, adolescence may not be defined as a distinctive stage that occurs between childhood and adulthood (Bush & Simmons, 1987; Hamburg, 1974). For example, ethnographic accounts of the lives of economically disadvantaged African-American teens living in inner-city "ghettos" suggest that, in adapting certain skills to survive in their environments and in assuming adult responsibilities such as primary caregivers of siblings, many teens move from childhood to adulthood without experiencing the intermediate stage of adolescence (Hippler, 1971; Jarrett, 1990; Jeffers, 1967; Kotlowitz, 1991; Ladner, 1971; MacLeod, 1987; Silverstein & Krate, 1975; Stack, 1974; Sullivan, 1989; Williams, 1978; Williams & Kornblum, 1985). In his ethnographic description of the life course of an African-American male, Coles (1964) underscored this point with this question: "Is a sixteen-year-old [African American] boy who has lived in stark, unremitting poverty, worked since eight, earned a living since fourteen, married at 15, and soon to be a father, a child?" (p. 319).

In a review of existing historical and ethnographic accounts of the lives of African-American families, Burton, Obeidallah, and Allison (1993) suggested that there are five dimensions of social context that contribute to the ambiguity of adolescence as a developmental stage in the lives of some inner-city African-American teens. The literature indicates that these dimensions emerge in the contexts of communities and families where there are limited economic, social, political, spiritual, and emotional resources for children to experience the "luxury" of adolescence before fully assuming adult responsibilities. The five dimensions include: (a) the inconsistencies teens experience across different social institutions with respect to "expected adolescent behavior," (b) the lack of clarity in developmental boundaries in age-condensed families, (c) the overlapping social worlds of teens and their parents, (d) perceptions of an accelerated life course, and (e) alternative contextual definitions of successful developmental outcomes.

Structural Inconsistencies in the Definition of Adolescent Roles

Burton et al. indicated that one of the most pervasive patterns that emerged in their review of ethnographic literature on inner-city African-American families concerns inconsistent expectations between parents and social institutions regarding teenagers' social roles. Although some researchers believe that inconsistencies in adolescents' experiences across different social settings are common, because of contextual influences, such as economic deprivation, these inconsistencies are often exacerbated among inner-city teens (Davis & Dollard, 1964; Lerner, 1986).

A common inconsistency in the developmental expectations of teens involves the divergent role expectations between school life and home life (Clark, 1983). School systems generally expect adolescents to adhere to mainstream educational aspirations, adult-monitored activities, and academic protocols. In this context, adolescents are often treated like "older children." At home, however, some inner-city adolescents are treated like "grown folks"—often saddled with adult responsibilities that are in direct conflict with the "older child" treatment and adult monitoring they receive in school (Burton & Jarrett, 1992). For example, an adolescent Mexican male from a migrant or illegally immigrated family may work a full-time job to support his extended family while being expected to adhere to a subordinate "teenager" role in school (Allison & Takei, 1994). MacLeod (1987) recounted the school–family conflict experienced by an inner-city African-American male teen:

> I got seven brothers. . . . My brother Joe had to quit school when he was sixteen years old, just because my father was an alcoholic. He had to go out and get a job. . . . But Joe was out gettin' a job at sixteen to support all the kids. . . . He's our father. That's what he really is. He's our father. . . . Every penny that my brother got he threw right into the house. Cuz my mother can't work. She almost died three times. (p. 51)

Williams and Kornblum (1985) further illustrated the point in the comments of a young African-American adolescent living in Harlem, New York:

I went to work in a restaurant in the back of a bar. I was 11 years old at the time. My schedule was one that most grown people would never had survived. I woke each morning, went to school, and when school was out I went directly to work. I got off work at 1:00 A.M. each night, no earlier, but sometimes later. I went home, did whatever I had to do, went to sleep and to school in the morning. (p. 19)

These examples suggest that the "adult" expectations of families and the "older child" behavior expectations of schools send adolescents mixed messages concerning their life stage. These mixed messages render adolescence an abridged or ambiguous developmental stage among teens who are struggling to survive in challenging environments. The implications of mixed messages and the ambiguity of adolescence as a developmental stage are far reaching in terms of how teens may interpret their own behaviors. "Older child" behavior is rewarded in one context, whereas it may be a liability in another. Thus, teens may be forced to choose one behavioral style over the other. For many inner-city teens, that choice results in a premature transition to adulthood.

Age-Condensed Families, Developmental Stages, and Blurred Intergenerational Boundaries

A second source of ambiguity in defining adolescence as a distinct life stage concerns the context of age-condensed families (Bengtson, Rosenthal, & Burton, 1990). Age-condensed families are characterized by a relatively narrow age distance between generations, typically 13–17 years. The age-condensed structure is prevalent in families where teenage childbearing has occurred consistently across generations (Burton, 1990; Burton & Dilworth-Anderson, 1991).

Previous research has highlighted the importance of examining the impact of age-condensed family structures on family members (Burton & Dilworth-Anderson, 1991). In age-condensed families, the developmental boundaries and roles of family members are often blurred. For example, consider the description of a four-generation age-condensed family identified in Burton's (1995) ethnographic study of multigeneration, teenage childbearing families. In this family, the child generation includes both a young mother (age 15) and her child (age 1), the young-adult generation is composed of a 29-year-old grandmother, and the middle-aged generation includes a 43-year-old great grandmother. As a result of the closeness in generational ages, chronological and developmental challenges often become inconsistent with generational positions. This is evident by the fact that the adolescent mother, as a function of giving birth, is launched into the young-adult role status; however, she remains legally and developmentally a member of the child generation. Similarly, the young-adult female has moved to the status of grandmother. Grandmother status is typically associated with middle-aged women. Further, the middle-aged woman has been propelled to the status of great grandmother—a role usually referring to women in their later years (Burton, in press; Burton & Bengtson, 1985).

Associated with the age-condensed family structure is the weakening of parental authority over developing children. For instance, the nature of the generational proximity between parents and their teenage offspring encourage these family members to behave in ways consistent with sibling roles, rather than roles characterized by parental hierarchy. The result is that parents often confront difficulties in disciplining their children.

The lack of clarity in family roles and developmental boundaries can contribute to the ambiguity of families identifying adolescence as a distinct life-course stage. The ambiguity is further enhanced by the concomitant overlapping of social worlds that parents and children in age-condensed families often experience.

The Overlapping Worlds of Teen and Their Parents

A third theme concerning the ambiguity of adolescence as a life-course stage involves the overlapping world of teens and their parents. Bronfenbrenner (1986) suggested that parents are involved in certain life contexts that have limited access for their children. These contexts include the work world and parents' peer networks. In some ways, the child's limited access to these worlds may help to differentiate the developmental status of parents and their offspring.

However, within some inner-city African-American communities and families, the distinction between the worlds of adults and children is often blurred. The blurring of this distinction may create difficulties in families identifying mutually exclusive developmental stages among its members. This point is echoed throughout ethnologies of African-American youth. Overlaps in social roles and relationships occur across multiple levels for teens and their parents (Stack, 1974).

The overlapping worlds of teens and their parents are particularly evident in the relationships between mothers and daughters in age-condensed families (Hembry, 1988). In a description of the behaviors of a young mother and her fifth-grade daughter, Kim, Ladner (1971) described the overlap:

> Kim's behavior was similar to that of her mother's and her 16-year-old sister. She cursed and occasionally imitated sex with her 12-year-old boyfriend. Frequently, she also had to baby-sit with the two year olds while their parents were away, help her mother prepare meals, clean house and face the bill collectors when her mother was in hiding because she didn't have the money. (p. 56)

A similar example of overlap is found in Kotlowitz's (1991) *There Are No Children Here*. In his treatise of the survival of a young family in a Chicago ghetto, Kotlowitz described a situation where a young mother, La Joe, just learned that her federal aid had been cut off. She immediately turned to her 12-year-old son, Lafeyette, for emotional support: "He was the only person she felt she could talk to about it. It was as if he were as much a husband as he was a son." She recognized this overlap and stated, "The things I should have been talking to (her husband) about I was talking to Lafie. But I didn't have anyone to talk to. Lafie became a twelve-year-old man that day" (Kotlowitz, 1991, p. 97).

The Accelerated Life Course

A fourth theme that is related to development and adolescence among inner-city African Americans concerns notions of the accelerated life course. The accelerated life course is based on an individual's view that he or she has a foreshortened life expectancy (Burton, 1991; Coles, 1967).

A truncated view of the length of one's life course reflects the realities of life expectancy and mortality rates in African-American populations. The life expectancies at birth are 63.7 years for African-American males and 72.3 for African-American females, compared with 70.7 years and 78.1 years for White males and females, respectively (Farley & Allen, 1987). In addition, the mortality rate of African-American men ages 25–44 is notably higher than the rate of their White counterparts. In 1984, the mortality rate of African-American men in this age range was 2–2.5 times higher than that of White men (Farley & Allen, 1987). Although precise estimates by socioeconomic status (SES) are not available, it has been suggested that the mortality rate is even higher at younger ages for poor African Americans (Jackson, 1988). High death rates are related to the consequences of poverty, including limited access to quality medical care, deficient diets, and substandard living environments (Burton, 1990; Gibbs, 1989).

Given the realities of lower life expectancies, it is plausible that some African-American teens may envision survival to a "ripe old age" as an unlikely prospect. The truncated vision of the life course is even more enhanced by the high rates of incarceration experienced by young African-American males (Staples, 1985). MacLeod (1987) reported three youths' responses to the question, What will you be doing in twenty years? Their comments include the following:

Stoney: Hard to say. I could be dead tomorrow. Around here, you gotta take life day by day.

Boo-Boo: I dunno. I don't want to think about it. I'll think about it when it comes.

Frankie: I don't know. Twenty years. I may be dead. I live a day at a time. I'll probably be in the pen. (p. 61)

The impact of an accelerated life course surfaces in the trajectories of friendships, as well. Liebow (1967) discussed this aspect of friendships in *Tally's Corner*:

> As if in anticipation of the frailty of personal relationships, to get as much as he can from them while they last and perhaps hopefully to prolong them, the man hurries each relationship toward a maximum intensity, quickly upgrading casual acquaintances to friends, and friends to best friends and lovers. This rush to upgrade personal relationships, to hurry them on to increasingly intense levels of association, may itself contribute to a foreshortening of their life span, prematurely loading the incumbents with expectations and obligations which their hastily constructed relationships simply cannot support. (p. 217)

Perceptions of a foreshortened life course has important implications for the adolescent development experience. If young children perceive that they have a limited life expectancy, such as those portrayed in Kotlowitz's (1991) *There Are No Children Here*, they may attempt to move from childhood to adulthood without taking the time to be "adolescents." This trajectory may be most pervasive in what Garbarino et al. (1991) described as "war zones and inner city neighborhoods plagued by violence and crime" (p. 376). In these environments, children witness the loss of life among the very young on a fairly regular basis. Under these circumstances, it is quite tenable to believe that children, as well as adults, accelerate their developmental transitions.

Developmental Outcomes

In assessing developmental outcomes for inner-city African-American teens, researchers have tended to use traditional outcomes measured in studies of White teens. These measures include the completion of high school, the presence or absence of a premarital teen pregnancy, and the attainment of stable legitimate employment (Allison & Takei, 1994). Although these are clearly important developmental outcome markers, they do not exhaust the potential range of successful developmental outcomes that inner-city African-American teens experience in their contexts. In their ethnographic studies of African-American families, Stack and Burton (1993) noted that a teen's commitment to care for a frail elderly relative is considered a successful outcome in a number of contexts. This outcome runs counter to mainstream perspectives on adolescent development, which suggest that adolescence involves a process of individuation and separation from family (Powers, Hauser, & Kilner, 1989).

Divergent contextual perspectives on developmental outcomes, in addition to the other dimensions outlined here, suggest that adolescence as a distinct developmental stage among inner-city African-American teens may be ambiguous at best. We argue that the ambiguity is related to inconsistencies in life-stage expectations that teens experience in the context of families, communities, and social institutions. This ambiguity may result in a corollary to Kotlowitz's (1991) *There Are No Children Here*. Building on his premise, might we as social scientists say of some inner-city teens, there are no adolescents here?

ADOLESCENT DEVELOPMENT: INSIGHTS
FROM AN ETHNOGRAPHIC STUDY

Description of the Study

Case-history data from an ongoing ethnographic study of inner-city African-American families are now presented to further illustrate the dimensions that create ambiguity in the delineation of adolescence as a developmental stage. The study, which began in June 1989, is being conducted in a northeastern city where 51% of the population is African American. Data collection involves the systematic use of multiple qualitative strategies to identify prevailing community and family norms concerning life-course development for urban African-American children, teens, and adults. Five qualitative data-collection strategies are employed: field observation (community ethnography); focus groups; life-history interviews with teens and their families; participant–observation in family activities; and in-depth interviews with ministers, school officials, health-care providers, school counselors, grassroots political activists, and informal community leaders.

The field observations have been conducted over a 5-year period, and involve observational assessments and discussions with residents in 18 neighborhoods. These assessments focus on residents' perceptions of neighborhood context and community-based norms concerning developmental life-course stages among African Americans. For each of the 18 neighborhoods, a preliminary profile reflecting the physical characteristics of the community (e.g., exposure to neighborhood dangers), as well as prevailing community norms (e.g., norms concerning life-course transitions), were developed (see Burton, Price-Spratlen, & Spencer, in press, for a detailed description of the neighborhood profiles).

The focus-group strategy involved generating nine groups of four to six African-American community residents to discuss specific issues concerning the culture of neighborhoods and developmental outcomes for children, teens, and adults. Each of the focus-group sessions were videotaped. Two of the groups included mid-life and elderly females, three were composed of adolescent and young-adult females, two were composed of adolescent and young-adult males, and two involved mid-life and elderly males. The groups represented a range of generational and socioeconomic strata, and included members from each of the 18 neighborhoods studied.

In-depth life-history interviews were conducted with members of 48 multigenerational African-American families residing in the community. These interviews explored the meaning of neighborhood context in the lives of family members, and also identified family beliefs and perceptions of life-course stages. The 48 families were distributed equally across four socioeconomic strata: persistently poor, working poor, transient poor, and working class. At least one family lived in each of the 18 neighborhoods studied, and all families had children between the ages of 10–18. In addition to the in-depth interviews, participant–observation in family events such as weddings, baby showers, and holiday celebrations provided baseline data on family practices concerning markers of life-course transitions.

The interviews with formal and informal community leaders (e.g., ministers, neighborhood gatekeepers) provided additional perspectives on neighborhood context and community norms. Informal and formal community leaders also provided feedback on how accurately community perceptions of life-course development were reflected in the data.

Seven African-American field researchers collected qualitative data using these five strategies. The data generated using the multiple strategies were transcribed and then analyzed using the grounded-theory approach (Glaser & Strauss, 1967). The grounded-theory approach is a style of analyzing qualitative data using a specific coding scheme to generated a profile of conceptual themes and relationships among variables that emerge in the data (Strauss, 1987). Several themes emerged in the qualitative data concerning the meaning of adolescence as a developmental stage among African Americans and the relevance of traditional indicators of developmental outcomes in the lives of these teens. These themes were consistent with those identified in the review of the existing literature on the life course of African-American teens.

Findings

Structural Inconsistencies in the Definition of Adolescent Roles. Most of the teens involved in the study were members of families that were barely surviving economically. As such, the teens often had to take on adult roles in their families. These roles involved assuming primary care of the household, as well as assuming surrogate-parent responsibilities for younger siblings. Many of the teens had engaged in these roles since the age of 8.

Although most of the teens involved in the study were expected to behave as adults in their families, they were often treated, as one respondent stated, "as stupid, irresponsible, incompetent White teenagers" in school. Steven, a 15-year-old who participated in this study, stated:

> Sometimes I just don't believe how this school operates and thinks about us. Here I am a grown man. I take care of my mother and have raised my sisters. Then I come here and this know nothing teacher treat me like I'm some dumb kid with no responsibilities. I am so frustrated. They are trying to make me something that I am not. Don't they understand I'm a man and I been a man longer than they been a woman.

The experiences of Candyce, a 13-year-old mother, further illustrate the point. Candyce, a seventh grader, had a 6-week-old baby at the time of her interview. She, like many of her friends, is also responsible for taking care of the household and providing primary parenting for her three younger siblings.

Shortly after the birth of her child, Candyce, one of the girls in our sample, went through what appeared to be an episode of depression. Out of concern for her, we approached the school counselor about the possibility that Candyce may have been experiencing postpartum depression. The school counselor indicated the following: "There is no way a teenager can have postpartum depression. She's just a kid who is lazy and doesn't want to do work. You know how teenagers are." In a later conversation with Candyce, we discussed her perception of where she was in life and how various people in her school and her church treated her. She stated: "I am a grown woman. Why these people keeping keep treating me like a kid. I don't even know what being a kid is like."

The profiles of these two respondents are similar to the structural inconsistencies described by inner-city African-American teens in the ethnographic literature. These inconsistencies often resulted in our respondents feeling confused about their roles as teenagers. Tony, a 15-year-old male involved in our study, summarized these sentiments best: "Do this, do that. School says one thing. Momma says another. Am I a young man, grown man, or a child. You tell me!"

Age-Condensed Families and Developmental Stages.   The most common age structure found in the families studied was the age condensed. In several of the families, the age distance between generations was only 14 years. The minimal age distance between generations in these families often resulted in the blurring of developmental role boundaries and expectations, particularly between parents and their children. For example, daughters and mothers in several of the families behaved like siblings toward each other, rather than like parents and adolescent children. The narrowness in age distance between generations created some dissonance with respect to how the parents and teens thought about themselves developmentally. Yvonne, a 16-year-old ninth grader from the sample, remarked: "My mom and me seem to be going through the same things at the same time. Like dealing with that relationship stuff. So what does that make me a woman or a kid?"

Comparable statements were made by the young men in the study with respect to their fathers. Darrell, a 15-year-old, had this to say about his relationship with his 33-year-old father: "I don't really know what my place is. I don't seem like a teenager because I hang with my old man [father]. We is buds! We're no different from each other. I guess we both just men."

The Overlapping Worlds of Teens and Their Parents. Among the families studied, the differentiation between the worlds of parents and children was not often clear, and thus fostered an environment where the adolescents became confused regarding their roles. For example, because of the high unemployment rate among African-American males in the neighborhoods studied, teenage sons and their adult fathers often competed for the same jobs in fast-food restaurants. For example, James, a 16-year-old, commented: "It's hard for a man to get a job here. Sometimes me and my friends go to apply for a job, and our fathers and grandfathers are trying for the same jobs, too! It's not fair." Moreover, given the limited number of marriageable African-American males in these communities, mothers and their teen daughters often competed for the same male partners. Under such circumstances, it is difficult to differentiate developmental stages between parents and adolescents. As one 18-year-old young lady stated: "It's hard to have ever thought about myself as a teenager when I've had boyfriends as old as my mom's boyfriends since I was 14."

The Accelerated Life Course. The mortality and incarceration rates for African-American males whose families were involved in the study was notably high. In each of the 48 families interviewed, at least one male relative under age 21 was incarcerated or killed during the course of the study. As such, a significant number of the teen males interviewed did not expect to either live past the age of 21 or stay out of prison. Consequently, when asked to reflect on the developmental stage of adolescence as part of their life course, most of the young men replied as did Sam, a 17-year-old high school senior: "Me, a teenager! Be for real lady. Who's got time for that. I'm a man. I'd better be one before I lose my life out on these streets."

This view of the accelerated life course was also shared by females in the study. The mothers, sisters, and girlfriends of the young men expressed sentiments comparable to those voiced by 16-year-old Tara: "I don't expect James [her boyfriend] to be around too long. He lives fast. He has to. Most of his friends are dead or in jail. I expect the same will happen to him."

Developmental Outcomes

Contextual data gathered in the study indicated that the teens living within the various neighborhoods studied had limited educational exposure, opportunities, resources, and related employment options. Given these limited opportunity paths, many of the teens did not achieve traditional adolescent developmental outcomes, such as high school completion. However, the data suggest that the teens, as well as some of their parents and community residents, had alternative perspectives about what merited a successful developmental outcome in their environment. The outcomes reported by those who participated in the study are categorized into three groups: outcomes that reflect cultural and situational success, outcomes that represent the realities of survival in the community, and outcomes that suggest new possibilities for success.

Cultural and Situational Outcomes. Three types of alternative outcomes emerged in this category: the "Revised American Dream," the achievement of adult status, and the development of cultural and sex role identities. Each outcome implicitly emphasizes present well-being as opposed to long-term success. The adolescents' focus on immediate and readily apparent symbols of success underlies the fact that legitimate avenues to success are severely restricted in their environment: The restriction relates to systematic racism and classim found in the contexts in which they live.

The "Revised American Dream" concerns the adolescent's ability to own clothing and jewelry as indicators of success. This external manifestation of success is relevant for the individual, as well as his or her family. Many of the adolescents and their families took pride in being able to dress well. Roger, a 16-year-old tenth grader, remarked: "We don't have much money but at least I always look good in my clothes. That's important to me. It makes me feel good, like I'm doing something I can be proud of when I dress fine."

The second outcome, the achievement of adult status, can be considered a ubiquitous indicator of a positive outcome. Adult status, self-sufficiency, and autonomy were manifest among the teens in their ability to be economically independent—whether it be financed through traditional employment, aid to families with dependent children, or illegal means. It was also reflected in their ability to father or give birth to a child. Regardless of the source of achieving "adult status," a number of the respondents suggested that becoming an adult as soon as possible in the teen years was a positive life-course outcome.

The final category of cultural and situational outcomes concerns the teen's ability to be comfortable with his or her cultural and sex role identities. One mother offered this representative statement: "As long as my son Alan knows that he is a man and he can be proud of being a Black man that's alright with me. That's how I know he is a success right now. And no one can tell me any different."

Community Realities. The harsh community realities that many African-American teens face daily are clearly intertwined with the indicators of successful developmental outcomes in this category. Among many urban male youth in high-risk environments, participation in sports has served as a chosen pathway or trajectory to financial success. However, the odds against achieving success through these routes are high. Subsequently, participation in the drug industry has provided risky, although highly profitable, employment opportunities for a number of youth with good odds for financial success. However, the high-risk nature of this option, and the associated community violence, has made the simple physical survival of an African-American male in many urban communities the only relevant indicator of a successful adolescent outcome. As Stephon, a 14-year-old eighth grader, stated: "I know I'm successful because I know how to survive on the streets. I bet them rich White kids couldn't do what I do."

In addition to sports and street survival, the ability to make it out of the community, even if it only meant transferring and surviving in a school outside the school district, was considered a success. Cherise, a 17-year-old eleventh grader, commented: "All my homies think I'm something because I go to school across the river now. Me and my momma worked a thing to get me in school over there. And I'm making it too."

New Possibilities. The last category of outcomes that emerged in the qualitative data represents developmental successes for which adolescents, particularly African Americans, are rarely given credit. The first outcome reflects success in terms of spiritual development and involvement in religious activities. Although traditionally conceptualized in the research literature as a coping strategy, many people in the African-American community consider spiritual integrity and harmony to be the most important indicator of positive adjustment.

The second outcome concerns fostering the development of one's creative talents. The expression of creativity in such contextually relevant modes, such as rapping, voguing, dancing, and "doing hair and nails well," was acknowledged by most of the respondents involved in the ethnographic component of the study as a viable successful outcome.

The third outcome involves the range of roles provided for teens within specific family and community contexts. Within families and communities, teens may serve important roles as facilitators of familial cohesion, as interpreters and negotiators of social institutions for elderly family and community members, and as peacemakers and contributors to cohesion in communities.

A community leader's description of Anthony, a 19-year-old high school dropout, illustrates the point: "Anthony may not have finished high school, and he may not have a job, but he is the treasure of our community. He helps the young mothers around the neighborhood with their kids. He does the grocery shopping for some of the old folks around here who can't get out. And he keeps the peace between rival street gangs in the community."

DISCUSSION AND CONCLUSION

The purpose of this chapter was to examine dimensions of social context that may influence the distinctiveness of adolescence as a developmental stage among inner-city African-American teens. Five dimensions related to community and family contexts and adolescent development were examined: (a) the inconsistencies that teens experience across different social institutions with respect to "expected adolescent behavior," (b) the lack of clarity in developmental boundaries in age-condensed families, (c) the overlapping social worlds of teens and their parents, (d) perceptions of an accelerated life course, and (e) inconsistencies in mainstream and contextual definitions of successful developmental outcomes. Using insights provided in existing ethnographic accounts of African-American families, and an ongoing qualitative study of urban African-American teens and their families, this discussion suggests that adolescence may be a relatively ambiguous developmental life stage among some inner-city African-American teens. That ambiguity has implications for how we study and implement interventions for adolescents who develop in high-risk and economically disadvantaged contexts.

Our primary objective here was to provide alternative ways to think about adolescence as a developmental experience among teens who grow up in contexts that are not White, middle class, nor identified as *mainstream*. The teenagers described in this chapter are those who live in community and family contexts where, for the most part, teens operate at the level of survival on a daily basis. These are teenagers who have difficulty garnering resources to meet their basic needs, and thus experience greater challenges in thriving and coping in their environments. This statement is not to imply that all inner-city African-American teenagers have the same experience. Clearly, there is tremendous heterogeneity in the experiences of African-American adolescents (Jones, 1989). Nonetheless, it is important to incorporate the experiences of these inner-city teens who continuously operate at the level of survival in conceptual models of adolescent development.

The issues presented here are arguably preliminary, but they nonetheless have implications for future research and interventions for inner-city and economically disadvantaged minority teens. First, these issues raise questions concerning the "conceptual starting points" of studies on development among African-American adolescents. In particular, the discussion of the ambiguity of adolescence as a developmental life stage among some inner-city teens suggests that, before social scientists superimpose existing adolescent developmental frameworks on the study of teens in diverse environments, they must first determine if adolescence is a distinctively defined stage of the life course in that environment (Dilworth-Anderson, Burton, & Turner, 1993). As cross-cultural studies indicate, adolescence may not be a universal life-course experience (Adelson, 1986). Consequently, if mainstream perspectives on adolescent development are applied in contexts where they do not fit, researchers may be generating inaccurate and uninterpretable profiles of the development of teens in that context.

Second, this discussion raises questions concerning the prevalence of adolescence as an ambiguously defined life stage among economically disadvantaged and ethnic/minority teens. The ideas presented here draw on a sparse ethnographic literature and an exploratory qualitative study; as such, they are not necessarily representative of patterns in larger populations. Currently, however, there are no existing large-scale studies that examine the nature of development among economically and ethnically diverse subgroups of teens. Do teens in diverse contexts experience inconsistencies in how their families and schools define their roles? Is the prevalence of assuming adult responsibilities early in the life course more prevalent for poor African-American, Hispanic, Native-American, Asian-American, and White adolescents? Clearly, large-scale studies that examine both within-group and across-group variability in these experiences are needed to address these questions.

Finally, the ideas presented in this chapter challenge those who develop adolescent interventions to identify what constitutes normal development in certain contexts and how that definition of *normalcy* is reflected in contextual perspectives of successful adolescent outcomes. Current interventions are often designed using a mainstream template, and thus promote that teens achieve outcomes that are "traditionally" defined as successful (e.g., completion of high school). Within these intervention programs, teens may not be acknowledged for the contextually defined successful outcomes (e.g., taking care of an elderly relative) they achieve. What impact does that lack of recognition have for the teen achieving nontraditional outcomes? What implications does a commitment by the teen to certain types of contextually defined successes mean for their long-term developmental trajectories?

Clearly, the ideas outlined here raise more questions than answers. However, these "ways of thinking" about development among inner-city African-American teens prods us to reexamine the paradigms that guide current research and interventions directed toward economically disadvantaged and ethnic/racial minority adolescents. How will alternative ways of thinking about development affect the use of traditional conceptual frameworks in the study of social context and development among economically disadvantaged and ethnic/racial minority teens? Will research that incorporates nontraditional conceptual models of development yield more accurate assessments of the relationship between social context and the developmental pathways of economically and racially disadvantaged teen populations?

ACKNOWLEDGMENTS

The research reported in this chapter was supported by grants to Linda Burton from the William T. Grant Foundation and a FIRST Award from the National Institute of Mental Health (No. R29 MH46057-01), and by a supplemental grant from the William T. Grant Foundation to Kevin Allison.

REFERENCES

Adelson, J. (1986). *Inventing adolescence*. New Brunswick, NJ: Transaction.

Allison, K., & Takei, Y. (1993). Diversity: The cultural contexts of adolescents and their families. In R. M. Lerner (Ed.), *Early adolescence: Perspectives on research, policy, and intervention* (pp. 51–69). Hillsdale, NJ: Lawrence Erlbaum Associates.

Bell-Scott, P., & Taylor, R. (1989). The multiple ecologies of black adolescent development. *Journal of Adolescent Research, 4*(2), 119–124.

Bengston, V. L., Rosenthal, C., & Burton, L. M. (1990). Families and aging. In R. Binstock & L. George (Eds.), *Handbook of aging and the social sciences* (pp. 263–287). New York: Academic Press.

Bronfenbrenner, U. (1979). *The ecology of human development*. Cambridge, MA: Harvard University Press.

Bronfenbrenner, U. (1986). Ecology of the family as a context for human development: Research perspectives. *Developmental Psychology, 22*(6), 723–742.

Brooks-Gunn, J., & Reiter, E. O. (1990). The role of pubertal processes in the early adolescent transition. In S. S. Feldman & G. R. Elliott (Eds.), *At the threshold: The developing adolescent* (pp. 16–53). Cambridge, MA: Harvard University Press.

Burton, L. M. (1990). Teenage childbearing as an alternative life-course strategy in multigeneration black families. *Human Nature, 1*(2), 123–143.

Burton, L. M. (1991). Caring for children. *The American Enterprise, 2*(3), 34–37.

Burton, L. M. (1995). Intergenerational family structure and the provision of care in African-American families. In K. W. Schaie, V. L. Bengston, & L. M. Burton (Eds.), *Intergenerational issues in aging*. New York: Springer.

Burton, L. M., & Bengston, V. L. (1985). Black grandmothers: Issues of timing and meaning in roles. In V. L. Bengston & J. F. Robertson (Eds.), *Grandparenthood: Research and policy perspectives* (pp. 61–77). Beverly Hills, CA: Sage.

Burton, L. M., & Dilworth-Anderson, P. (1991). The intergenerational family roles of aged Black Americans. *Marriage and Family Review, 16*(3/4), 311–330.

Burton, L. M., & Jarrett, R. L. (1992). *Studying African-American family structure and process in underclass neighborhoods*. Paper presented at the annual meeting of the American Sociological Association, Cincinnati, OH.

Burton, L. M., Obeidallah, D., & Allison, K. (1993). *The dynamic link between context and adolescent development.* Unpublished manuscript, The Pennsylvania State University.

Burton, L. M., Price-Spratlen, T., & Spencer, M. B. (in press). On ways of thinking about and measuring neighborhoods: Implications for studying context and developmental outcomes for children. In G. Duncan, J. Brooks-Gunn, & L. Aber (Eds.), *Neighborhood poverty: Context and consequences for development.* New York: Russell Sage.

Bush, D. M., & Simmons, R. G. (1987). Gender and coping with the entry into early adolescence. In R. C. Barnett, L. Brener, & G. K. Baruch (Eds.), *Gender and stress* (pp. 129–150). New York: The Free Press.

Clark, R. M. (1983). *Family life and school achievement: Why poor black children succeed or fail.* Chicago, IL: University of Chicago Press.

Coleman, J. S. (1961). *The adolescent society.* New York: Glencoe.

Coles, R. B. (1967). *Children of crisis: A study of courage and fear.* Boston, MA: Little, Brown.

Conger, R. D., Conger, K. J., Elder, G. H., & Lorenz, F. D. (1993). Family economic stress and adjustment of early adolescent girls. *Developmental Psychology, 29*(2), 3206–3219.

Conger, R. D., Elder, G. H., Lorenz, F., Simons, R., & Whitbeck, L. (1992). A family process model of economic hardship and adjustment of early adolescent boys. *Child Development, 63,* 526–541.

Davis, A., & Dollard, J. (1964). *Children of bondage: The personality development of Negro youth in the urban south.* New York: Harper & Row.

Dilworth-Anderson, P., Burton, L. M., & Turner, W. (1993). The importance of values in the study of culturally diverse families. *Family Relations, 42,* 238–242.

Dornbusch, S. M., Ritter, L. P., & Steinberg, L. (1991). Community influences on the relation of family statuses to adolescent school performance: Differences between African Americans and non-Hispanic Whites. *American Journal of Education, 38*(4), 543–567.

Elder, G. H., Jr. (1974). *Children of the great depression.* Chicago, IL: University of Chicago Press.

Elder, G. H., Jr., Modell, J., & Parke, P. (Eds.). (1993). *Children in time and place: Intersecting historical and developmental insights.* New York: Cambridge University Press.

Elliott, G. R., & Feldman, S. S. (1990). Capturing the adolescent experience. In S. S. Feldman & G. R. Elliott (Eds.), *At the threshold: The developing adolescent* (pp. 1–14). Cambridge, MA: Harvard University Press.

Farley, R., & Allen, W. R. (1987). *The color line and the quality of life in America.* New York: Russell Sage Foundation.

Feldman, S. S., & Elliott, G. R. (Eds.). (1990). *At the threshold: The developing adolescent.* Cambridge, MA: Harvard University Press.

Garbarino, J., Kostelny, K., & Dubrow, N. (1991). What children can tell us about living in danger. *American Psychologist, 46*(4), 376–383.

Gibbs, J. T. (1985). Black adolescents and youth: An endangered species. *American Journal of Orthopsychiatry, 54,* 6–21.

Gibbs, J. T. (1989). Black adolescents and youth: An update on an endangered species. In R. L. Jones (Ed.), *Black adolescents* (pp. 3–27). Berkeley, CA: Cobb & Henry.

Glaser, B., & Strauss, A. (1967). *The discovery of grounded theory.* Chicago: Aldine.

Graber, J. H., & Petersen, A. C. (1991). Cognitive changes at adolescence: Biological perspectives. In K. R. Gibson & A. C. Petersen (Eds.), *Brain maturation and cognitive development: Comparative cross-cultural perspectives* (pp. 253–279). Hawthorne, NY: Aldine de Gruyter.

Hamburg, B. A. (1974). Early adolescence: A specific and stressful stage of the life cycle: In G. V. Coelho, D. A. Hamburg, & J. E. Adams (Eds.), *Coping and adaptation* (pp. 102–124). New York: Basic Books.

Hembry, K. F. (1988). *Little women: Repeat childbearing among black, never-married adolescent mothers.* Unpublished dissertation, University of California, Berkeley, CA.

Hippler, A. E. (1971). *Hunter's point: A black ghetto.* New York: Basic Books.

Hoffman, M. L. (1980). Moral development in adolescence. In J. Adelson (Ed.), *Handbook of adolescent psychology* (pp. 295–343). New York: Wiley.

Holliday, B. G. (1989). Trailblazers in black adolescent research: The American Council on Education's studies on Negro youth personality development. In R. L. Jones (Ed.), *Black adolescents* (pp. 29–48). Berkeley, CA: Cobb & Henry.

Jackson, J. J. (1988). Growing old in Black America: Research on aging in Black populations. In J. Jackson (Ed.), *The Black American* (pp. 3–16). New York: Springer.

Jarrett, R. L. (1990). *A comparative examination of socialization patterns among low-income African-Americans, Chicanos, Puerto Ricans, and Whites: A review of the ethnographic literature.* New York: Social Science Research Council.

Jarrett, R. L. (in press). Community context, intrafamilial processes, and social mobility outcomes: Ethnographic contributions to the study of African-American families and children in poverty. In M. B. Spencer & G. K. Brookings (Eds.), *Ethnicity and diversity.* Hillsdale, NJ: Lawrence Erlbaum Associates.

Jeffers, C. (1967). *Living poor: A participant observer study of choices and priorities.* Ann Arbor, MI: Ann Arbor Publishers.

Jones, R. L. (Ed.). (1989). *Black adolescents.* Berkeley, CA: Cobb & Henry.

Keating, D. (1990). Adolescent thinking. In S. S. Feldman & G. R. Elliott (Eds.), *At the threshold: The developing adolescent* (pp. 54–89). Cambridge, MA: Harvard University Press.

Kotlowitz, A. (1991). *There are no children here.* New York: Doubleday.

Ladner, J. A. (1971). *Tomorrow's tomorrow: The black woman.* New York: Anchor Books.

Lerner, R. M. (1986). *Concepts and theories of human development* (2nd ed.). New York: Random House.

Liebow, E. (1967). *Tally's corner: A study of negro street corner men.* Boston, MA: Little, Brown.

MacLeod, J. (1987). *Ain't no makin' it: Leveled aspirations in a low-income community.* Boulder, CO: Westview.

McGee, E. (1982). *Too little, too late: Services for teen-age parents.* New York: Ford Foundation.

McLoyd, V. C. (1990). The impact of economic hardship on black families and children: Psychological distress, parenting, and socioemotional development. *Child Development, 61,* 311–346.

Merry, S. (1981). *Urban danger: Life in a neighborhood of strangers.* Philadelphia, PA: Temple University Press.

Modell, J. (1989). *Into one's own: From youth to adulthood in the United States 1920–1975.* Berkeley, CA: University of California Press.

Murray, C. B., Smith, S. N., & West, E. H. (1989). Comparative personality development in adolescents: A critique. In R. L. Jones (Ed.), *Black adolescents* (pp. 49–62). Berkeley, CA: Cobb & Henry.

Ogbu, J. V. (1981). The origins of human competence: A cultural ecological perspective. *Child Development, 52,* 413–429.

Petersen, A. C. (1988). Adolescent development. In M. R. Rosenzweig (Ed.), *Annual review of psychology* (pp. 583–607). Palo Alto, CA: Annual Reviews.

Powers, S. I., Hauser, S. T., & Kilner, L. A. (1989). Adolescent mental health. *American Psychologist, 44,* 200–208.

Seidman, E. (1991). Growing up the hard way: Pathways of urban adolescents. *American Journal of Community Psychology, 19*(2), 173–205.

Silbereisen, R. K., Eyferth, K., & Rudinger, G. (Eds.). (1986). *Development as action in context: Problem behavior and normal youth development.* New York: Springer-Verlag.

Silverstein, B., & Krate, R. (1975). *Children of the dark ghetto: A developmental psychology.* New York: Praeger.

Spencer, M. B., & Dornbush, S. M. (1990). Challenges in studying minority youth. In S. S. Feldman & G. R. Elliott (Eds.), *At the threshold: The developing adolescent* (pp. 123–146). Cambridge, MA: Harvard University Press.

Stack, C. B. (1974). *All our kin: Strategies for survival in a Black community.* New York: Harper & Row.

Stack, C. B., & Burton, L. M. (1993). Kinscripts. *Journal of Comparative Family Studies, 24*(2), 157–170.

Staples, R. (1985). Changes in Black family structure: The conflict between family ideology and structural conditions. *Journal of Marriage and the Family, 47*(4), 1005–1013.

Steinberg, L. (1990). Autonomy, conflict, and harmony in the family relationship. In S. S. Feldman & G. R. Elliott (Eds.), *At the threshold: The developing adolescent* (pp. 255–276) Cambridge, MA: Harvard University Press.

Strauss, A. (1987). *Qualitative analysis for social scientists.* Cambridge: Cambridge University Press.

Sullivan, M. (1989). *Getting paid: Youth crime and work in the inner-city.* Ithaca, NY: Cornell University Press.

Williams, M. (1978). Childhood in an urban black ghetto: Two life histories. *Umoja, 2,* 169–182.

Williams, T. M., & Kornblum, W. (1985). *Growing up poor.* Lexington, MA: Lexington Books.

Youniss, J., & Smollar, J. (1985). *Adolescents' relations with mothers, fathers, and friends.* Chicago: University of Chicago Press.

CHAPTER EIGHT

Lessons About Adolescent Development From the Study of African-American Youth: Commentary

Susan M. McHale
The Pennsylvania State University

The chapters by Winfield (chap. 6) and Burton, Allison, and Obeidallah (chap. 7) provide a vivid picture of the lives of youth who are growing up in circumstances seen by most researchers only in media snapshots. These are youth who skip school at a very young age to carry out important family responsibilities; who at an early age have witnessed so much violence and death that they acquire "truncated" views of their own life spans; and who at far too young an age recognize that many opportunities for success in the mainstream culture are closed to them.

This portrait of disadvantaged African-American youth calls into question some of our ideas about what is fundamental to human nature and human development: Concepts and theories with seemingly universal application may be specific to the relatively privileged individuals of the majority (Western) culture. As such, knowledge gleaned from the study of minority youth in demanding life circumstances may push us to new levels in our understanding of human development. In the following discussion, I focus on several of the ideas presented in the two preceding chapters. I highlight the ways in which these may inform existing research and theory in two areas: the study of adolescent development, and the literature on intervention for at-risk youth.

ISSUES IN ADOLESCENT DEVELOPMENT

In describing the experiences of economically disadvantaged African-American youth, Burton et al. point out that their observations challenge contemporary ideas about adolescent development on a least two fronts. First, for

139

these youth, adolescence does not appear to be a clear developmental stage. Growing up in "age-condensed families" where the developmental boundaries between generations are obscured, shouldering heavy family responsibilities (e.g., housework, child care, and even breadwinning activities), and experiencing an "accelerated" life course mean that, by the time they reach sexual maturity, many of these youth already have assumed the roles and status of adults. Discussions of adolescence as a distinct phase of human development often point out that, within a historical context, the prolonged postponement of adult social status following sexual maturity is a relatively recent phenomenon in Western societies. This prolonged period of dependency has come to be an accepted and even institutionalized part (e.g., via schooling) of the lives of socioeconomically advantaged youth. Nonetheless, ambiguity and dysynchrony in the "mainstream" adolescent role (such as cognitive sophistication and sexual maturity in the context of emotional, social, and economic dependency) have been blamed for some of the psychological and behavioral problems of this developmental period. The vignettes in the Burton et al. chapter illustrate that role ambiguity and dysynchrony are even more profound in the experiences of inner-city minority youth. Their interview data convey the confusion and hostility that characterize these youths' subjective experiences of role ambiguity.

The Burton et al. observations also led the authors to question the kinds of "outcome" measures employed in analyses of these young people's development and well-being. Traditional measures of success, they argue, fail to capture the attitudes and expectations that influence adolescents' everyday behavior and ideas about future goals, attitudes, and expectations emanating from cultural norms, as well as from the reality of closed opportunities. To understand the trajectories of disadvantaged minority youth, researchers need to evaluate their adaptation in context.

The Burton et al. observations highlight the importance of including minority populations in research on adolescent development and behavior. As noted, the findings from research on youth outside the mainstream test the limits of contemporary concepts and theories of adolescent development. In this discussion, I elaborate on insights provided by Burton et al. and Winfield's portraits of African-American youth with respect to two areas of developmental research: work on adolescent personality development, and work on adolescent adjustment.

The Role of the "Self" in Development

With respect to personality development, Caspi and his colleagues outlined a "paradoxical theory of personality coherence" (Caspi, Lynam, Moffitt, & Silva, 1993; Caspi & Moffitt, 1993). Central to this theory is the accentuation hypothesis, which holds that dispositional differences between individuals will become most apparent in stressful and ambiguous situations. This is because organisms are "goaded into action" in response to uncertainty; those actions and behaviors are oriented at "reinstating predictability" in the environment (Caspi et al., 1993, p. 5). In Caspi's view, reactions to the unfamiliar represent the most consistent and valid indices of individual differences in personality. One implication of this perspective is that youth in risky environments show their true colors by their reactions to the stresses and ambiguities in their everyday lives; youths' reactions to such pressures represent what is central and unique to their personalities.

As noted earlier, however, when we study mainstream populations and a limited range of human experience, the ideas we develop about human behavior also may be limited. Examples of how an analysis of mainstream populations may limit our thinking are comments by Caspi et al. (1993) about why unpredictability and ambiguity forces the organism into action: "How to obtain food? How to construct shelter? How to avoid predators? *Of course, modern humans are seldom exposed to comparable levels of life-threatening uncertainty.* . . . In response to such threats all organisms seek to reinstate predictability . . . motivated by a basic drive to preserve fitness" (pp. 4–5; italics added). The stories we have been told about the lives of youth in a northeastern U.S. city in 1993 suggest that life-threatening uncertainty is an all too common part of poor, urban, minority children's everyday experiences. Statistics about hunger and disease among Third World children suggest that life-threatening uncertainty is all too pervasive in the experience of the modern child.

Burton et al. provide an alternative perspective on what human organisms do in response to life-threatening uncertainty: They shut down. In their analyses of "copers," "thrivers," and "survivors," these investigators suggest that, at an extreme level, stress can undermine the press for actions that promote survival. At an extreme level of stress, differences between individuals disappear and "numbness" and "hopelessness" set in.

Analyses of minority youth have additional and possibly more profound implications for personality theories that posit the existence of an integrated core "self." To the extent that such theories were developed in the context of the majority culture, they fail to capture the reality of minority individuals' experience of living in two cultures. Observations of the *psychic duality* (term used by Burton et al.) or *oppositional identities* (Winfield's description, coined by Fordham & Ogbu, 1986) of African-American youth describe the experiences of adolescents who live in two worlds: two worlds with orthogonal, if not competing, demands and values.

In reconciling theoretical conceptions of personality with the data provided about African-American youths' struggles with establishing an integrated identity or sense of self, one could argue that the "same" underlying personality structure may be manifested—albeit in different, culturally appropriate ways—in two different worlds. Suggesting that an "extroverted personality" is simply manifested in different ways in different cultural contexts, however, fails to capture the profound differences in minority individuals' experiences of separate realities. Alternatively, personality theorists might argue that the failure of minority individuals to establish an integrated identity, personality, or sense of self is indicative of psychopathology or deviance. The analyses in the two preceding chapters show that such theories are ethnocentric and deny the everyday realities of African-American people in a White world. To understand the range of human experience, however, researchers need to abandon concepts and theories that were developed through the study of the (relatively) powerful and privileged.

Measurement strategies also need to be modified. Techniques for assessing self-related constructs such as self-esteem, identity, or personality either implicitly or explicitly seek comparisons against an unspecified norm or reference group. On Rosenberg's (1979) frequently used Self-Esteem scale, for example, adolescents are asked to consider whether they are "a person of worth, at least on an equal plane with others." On another commonly used measure for studying adolescents' self-esteem—Harter's (1988) Self-Perception Profile—adolescents are asked to pick the teenager who is most like themselves. An example is: "Some teenagers feel that they are socially accepted, but other teenagers wish that more people their age liked them." An adolescent from a minority background would probably answer such questions very differently, depending on whether the reference group was a minority or mainstream one. Yet existing measurement strategies assume a unitary reference group or focus of social comparison.

Understanding the "Outcomes" of Development

A second area in which the study of disadvantaged minority youth may promote new insights about adolescent development pertains to the study of adolescent adjustment. The argument by Burton et al.—that common measures of "successful" adaptation fail to account for the cultural norms and opportunities of disadvantaged minority youth—was highlighted earlier. In addition to targeting the kinds of outcomes researchers measure, both Burton et al. and Winfield question the more general conceptualization of outcomes that many researchers use in describing individual development and well-being.

Much of the existing research on adolescents' health and development is based on an assumption of the "perfectibility" of the human organism. Existing frameworks suggest that, through judicious imposition of a safe and stimulating environment and supportive social experiences, "healthy" (healthier) development may be fostered. Recognizing the diversity of adolescents' interests, goals, and personal qualities, some theorists (e.g., Lerner, 1986) have also pointed out that environments and experiences must be matched to the needs of individual adolescents if development is to be optimized.

What the study of minority youth makes apparent, however, are the choices and trade-offs that are involved in adolescents' strivings for successful or adaptive "outcomes." In the case of these adolescents, decisions made at a young age may have far-reaching consequences, including: the choice between individualistic achievement (e.g., in school) versus racial/ethnic identity formation (through involvement in the peer culture), the exchange of economic well-being for the dangers involved in the drug trade, and the trade-offs involved in devoting family resources toward one child's success at the expense of the success of other family members. What emerges from these observations is a conceptualization of individual adaptation that is inconsistent with the notion of human perfectibility. This alternative model suggests that optimization in one arena of individual functioning may come at the expense of accomplishments in another.

Discussing another "minority" population—older adults—Baltes and Baltes (1990) noted that: ". . . development is never only a gain. This is so because every developmental change is an adaptive specialization. . . . Because of this specialization, any given developmental process that entails a positive change in some kind of adaptive capacity also contains the loss of other developmental capacities and future options" (pp. 16–17). Baltes and Baltes cited information pertaining to cognitive, biological, and social development in making the point that adaptation involves both gains and losses. In this work, studying aging processes provided insights about developmental processes that apply to all periods of the life span.

McHale and Crouter (in press) made a similar argument with respect to research on children's adjustment and family relationships. They noted the following:

> At the level of the individual, accomplishments in one domain are pursued at the expense of skills in another, and personal accomplishments may come at the price of interpersonal relationships. At the level of the family, promoting the needs and interests of one member may give rise to differences [in well-being and development] among individuals within the family. . . . Conceptual and analytic approaches that ignore these patterns paint a deceptively simple portrait of individual and family functioning. (p. 23)

Among advantaged youth and families, the illusion that one can "have it all" may be partly responsible for widespread belief in the "perfectibility" of human adaptation. Although the choices made by more advantaged adolescents (e.g., what sport to play, what electives to take, what college to attend) may be less obvious given their lack of immediate negative implications, they are nonetheless decisions to pursue skills and experiences in one domain at the expense of those of another. Studying youth who are more obviously faced with the necessity to make choices—often between life-threatening options or between the lesser of two evils—provides us with a more complex and possibly more accurate picture of how human systems work.

Understanding human systems, however, requires a conceptual and analytic approach, wherein the organization or integrity of the individual's experiences is maintained. As Magnusson (1988) noted, "an individual functions as a totality . . . each aspect of the structures and processes that are operating (perceptions, plans, values, goals, motives, biological factors, conduct, etc.) takes on meaning from the role it plays in the total functioning of the individual" (p. 22). Studying adolescents' personal characteristics (e.g., race, school achievement, behavior problems), experiences (e.g., parents' disciplinary style, peer norms), or contexts (e.g., neighborhood or school characteristics) as if these factors operate independently of one another provides an inaccurate picture of human development.

The premises of Magnusson's "personological" approach contrast sharply with those of the "variable-oriented" approaches that are employed to address normative questions about human behavior and development. These more commonly employed, variable-oriented approaches often ignore the natural confounds that exist among potential "independent" variables of interest (e.g., race, peer norms, neighborhood characteristics). Efforts directed at assessing the "variance accounted for" by one measure in predicting another (i.e., strategies designed to measure the connections between variables) mean that "the individual is then important only because he provides the measures for the variables" (Magnusson, 1988, p. 20).

Magnusson suggested that variable-oriented approaches are inadequate for the study of human development because they are grounded in a mechanistic tradition and because they test reductionistic, linear, and noninteractive hypotheses. Strategies consistent with a personological approach include: (a) a descriptive goal of understanding what personal and contextual qualities actually co-occur in the lives of young adolescents; (b) a longitudinal design wherein individuals with different patterns of characteristics are followed over time; and (c) a focus on the question of how objectively similar experiences may have different implications for individuals with different personal characteristics who are growing up in different contexts. The understanding gleaned from such endeavors will have important implications for the development of intervention strategies directed at promoting adolescent development, the topic to which I now turn.

IMPLICATIONS FOR INTERVENTION

Stories of the everyday experiences of disadvantaged youth initially make the challenges of intervention appear overwhelming. Both Burton et al. and Winfield's observations highlight two particularly important challenges. The first pertains to the "systemic" nature of the risks faced by the adolescents in their studies. In the two preceding chapters, the authors make it clear that tinkering with one component of the system may alleviate risks in one area of adolescents' lives; however, fixing one problem can exacerbate problems in other domains of adolescents' experiences. A second challenge has to do with the "structural" basis of these adolescents' risk status: Many of these youths' difficulties are grounded in social and economic discrimination and concomitant limitations in opportunities. These important underlying causes of these adolescents' risk status, however, are difficult to target for intervention. Thus, many interventions are directed at the skills, attitudes, and behaviors of the "victims" of inequality.

Burton et al. and Winfield highlight the difficulties involved in effecting change in these adolescents' lives, but they also provide important insights about characteristics of effective intervention efforts. First, Winfield's analysis of factors that promote "resiliency" in at-risk youth provides some ideas about where interventions might begin in addressing the needs of disadvantaged youth. Her chapter describes how both individual factors and contextual factors constitute important intervention targets. Both Burton et al. and Winfield suggest that the subjective experiences of the youth who are the targets of intervention efforts are fundamentally important. Knowing the values and attitudes of these adolescents, understanding their personal goals, and recognizing their interpretations of their life situations are essential if an effective intervention plan is to be designed and implemented. Only by appreciating the adolescents' points of view can we understand the choices they have already made and evaluate the competencies they have already developed. These choices and competencies, in turn, will have implications for their developmental trajectories.

In short, it is important to understand how these youth have adapted to a risky and challenging environment, and to see their behaviors and goals in context. It is equally important that such a "relativistic" assessment be balanced by the recognition that certain of these adolescents' choices may have disastrous consequences. Given existing options, an adolescent's decision to join a gang or become involved in the drug trade may be "adaptive" in the short run, but lead to imprisonment and early death.

As noted, although many of the problems these youth face are based in structural factors, the difficulties involved in changing social and economic institutions mean that interventions often are directed at changing the attitudes and behaviors of the adolescents who are the victims of societal inequities. For example, interventions designed to promote life skills and foster self-esteem and feelings of efficacy have become increasingly popular approaches for the prevention and amelioration of problems in adolescent adjustment and health. Given young adolescents' increasing cognitive sophistication—including self-reflection and future-oriented thinking abilities, in combination with their increasing autonomy and independence—intervention strategies aimed at "self-development" may be developmentally appropriate for young adolescents. The philosophical grounding of such interventions in the "organismic" notion of the "active" organism (Lerner, 1986) also presents an attractive alternative to mechanistic emphases on biological and environmental "determinants" of youths' developmental trajectories.

Although self-determination is an important factor in healthy development, we cannot hold adolescents' low self-esteem or disintegrated identities entirely to blame for their poor adaptation. The "down side" of a focus on building life skills and personal efficacy is that we may come to blame the victims of social and economic circumstances. A second problem is that inculcating youth with the notion that they have control over their own destinies, in contexts where social and economic opportunities are actually quite limited, is questionable on ethical grounds. This is why Winfield's emphasis on "opening up new opportunities" is so important in any intervention effort. Recognizing the role that contextual forces play in adolescents' adaptation means that, in addition to changing adolescents' behaviors and attitudes, interventions must also be directed toward changing the contexts of adolescents' development.

Insights from Caspi and Moffit's (1993) analysis of factors central to personality change provide guidelines for interventionists interested in contextual change (see also Crockett & Petersen, 1993). According to these authors, in addition to placing individuals in novel roles and situations, previous behavioral patterns must be "knifed off" and "scripts" for new social patterns provided if significant personality change is to be effected. Adolescence is a time of transition and, as such, an opportunity for effecting meaningful change in youths' developmental trajectories. What Caspi and Moffit's analysis also tells us, however, is that circumstances must be structured so that there is "a strong press to behave . . . previous responses are actively discouraged . . . [and] clear information is provided about how to behave adaptively . . ." (p. 264).

In short, the existing literature, including the work described in this volume, provides many ideas about characteristics of effective intervention programs for adolescents. The challenge that continues to face us is communicating what we know, in convincing ways, to practitioners and policymakers—whose job it is to effect change in the lives of youth.

REFERENCES

Baltes, P. B., & Baltes, M. M. (1990). Psychological perspectives on successful aging: The model of selective optimization with compensation. In P. B. Baltes & M. M. Baltes (Eds.), *Successful aging: Perspectives from the behavioral sciences* (pp. 1–34). New York: Cambridge University Press.

Caspi, A., Lynam, D., Moffitt, T. E., & Silva, P. A. (1993). Unraveling girls' delinquency: Biological, dispositional and contextual contributions to adolescent misbehavior. *Developmental Psychology, 29,* 19–30.

Caspi, A., & Moffitt, T. E. (1993). When do individual differences matter? A paradoxical theory of personality coherence. *Psychological Inquiry, 4,* 247–271.

Crockett, L., & Petersen, A. (1993). Adolescent development: Health risks and opportunities for health promotion. In S. Millstein, A. Petersen, & E. Nightingale (Eds.), *Promoting the health of adolescents* (pp. 13–37). New York: Oxford University Press.

Fordham, S., & Ogbu, J. (1986). Black students' school success: Coping with the "burden of acting White." *The Urban Review, 18,* 176–206.

Harter, S. (1988). *Manual for the Self Perception Profile for Adolescents.* Unpublished manuscript, University of Denver, Denver, CO.

Lerner, R. M. (1986). *Concepts and theories of human development* (2nd ed.). New York: Random House.

Magnusson, D. (1988). *Individual development from an interactional perspective.* Hillsdale, NJ: Lawrence Erlbaum Associates.

McHale, S. M., & Crouter, A. C. (in press). The family contexts of children's sibling relationships. In G. Brody (Ed.), *Sibling relationships: Their causes and consequences.* Norwood, NJ: Ablex.

Rosenberg, M. (1979). *Conceiving the self.* New York: Basic.

PART THREE

INTERRELATIONS AMONG SOCIAL CONTEXTS

Examining Parenting Practices in Different Peer Contexts: Implications for Adolescent Trajectories

B. Bradford Brown
Bih-Hui Huang
University of Wisconsin–Madison

As individuals make the transition from childhood into adolescence, many features of their social world are transformed. Certainly one of the most dramatic transformations occurs in the area of peer relations, with the emergence of peer "crowds"—groups by which a teenager's reputation and status among peers are demarcated (Brown, 1990). The function of these crowds, especially the direction and degree of influence on adolescent attitudes and behavior relative to the influence of parents, has been hotly debated. Some portray adolescent peer groups as the locus of antisocial or antiadult peer pressures that pull teenagers away from the prosocial influence of parents and other adults (Bronfenbrenner, 1970; Coleman, 1961). Others maintain that parents and peer groups develop separate spheres of influence, such that teenagers will follow the advice of parents on certain issues and the advice of peers on other matters (Brittain, 1963; Larson, 1972). In this chapter, we provide a different perspective on the linkage between the family and the peer group in adolescence. Rather than regarding them as independent or antagonistic influences on adolescents, we view them as interdependent, such that parenting practices can be expected to have a different impact on teenagers in different peer-crowd contexts.

PARENTAL INFLUENCES IN ADOLESCENCE

Although some theories propose that parents' power of influence is sharply reduced at adolescence (Freud, 1958), a host of empirical evidence refutes this notion. Particularly interesting is the body of research demonstrating that parents' childrearing strategies, or "parenting styles," can have a significant impact on a variety of teenage behaviors (Steinberg, 1990). These studies identify a set of "authoritative" parents; namely, those who establish high expectations for a teenager's behavior, grant the child autonomy to make decisions, yet also maintain close and affectionate relationships with the child. Such parents, especially in contrast to "neglectful" parents who display the opposite set of characteristics, tend to have teenage offspring who are successful in school, shy away from drug use and delinquent activity, and have positive self-images (Lamborn, Mounts, Steinberg, & Dornbusch, 1991; Maccoby & Martin, 1983). Other dimensions of parenting, beyond those that define such parenting styles, can also influence adolescents. For example, when parents encourage their child's educational efforts through attending school functions, monitoring homework, or modeling learning behavior, the child tends to display higher achievement and educational aspirations (Entwisle, 1990; Steinberg, Lamborn, Dornbusch, & Darling, 1992). To be sure, much of the association between parenting behaviors and an adolescent's characteristics are the cumulative effects of years of childrearing efforts. Yet it seems clear that, even in adolescence, parents can do a great deal to facilitate or inhibit adaptive behaviors in their children.

In studying parenting effects, investigators typically only examine teenagers as a whole. There have been some efforts to disaggregate samples into different ethnic or socioeconomic groups, which suggest that the effects of parenting practices are surprisingly consistent across these contexts (Steinberg, Mounts, Lamborn, & Dornbusch, 1991). Efforts to study the effects of parenting in different peer contexts, especially naturally occurring peer contexts (rather than groupings arbitrarily derived by the researcher), are rare indeed.

PEER GROUPS AS SOCIAL CONTEXTS

Perhaps researchers have ignored peer groups, in part, because they believe that the peer context is essentially the same for all teenagers, or is adequately differentiated by such individual characteristics as sex, ethnicity, or social class (Hollingshead, 1949; Peshkin, 1991). Yet contemporary studies of the adolescent social world provide compelling evidence that the teenage peer culture is actually composed of a disparate set of peer groups, or crowds. Crowds represent clusters of young people perceived to act in predictable ways and to share common beliefs, such that each crowd features a distinct "provisional identity" or prototypic lifestyle (Brown, 1990). The norms of some crowds correspond closely to conventional adult values and expectations, helping members to move easily through adult-controlled institutions such as school (Brown, Lohr, & Trujillo, 1990; Eckert, 1989). Other crowds endorse a strictly deviant lifestyle, eschewing school achievement in favor of more problematic behaviors. Still other groups display a curious mixture of prosocial and antisocial norms: Members are expected to put genuine effort into school achievement, but also participate in weekend rituals of drug use and sexual activity. In short, crowds offer a wide array of peer contexts—from primarily prosocial to essentially antisocial (as judged by adult norms).

Of course, young people's affiliation with certain crowds is by no means random or haphazard. Teenagers tend to associate with the crowd whose norms offer the best "fit" with their own values and interests, at least as they are perceived by peers. Indeed, crowd labels are meant to define who a person is or how a person acts, rather than who a person "hangs out" with (i.e., an adolescent's reputation among peers, rather than his or her cluster of friends). Being a jock does not necessarily imply interacting exclusively (or even primarily) with fellow jocks, although, understandably, there is a tendency to draw one's close friendships disproportionately from within one's own crowd (Brown, Mory, & Kinney, 1994).

The fact that teenagers are as much assigned to a crowd by peers as they are able to choose their own peer-group affiliation has important implications for the way in which crowds influence teenagers. It means that young people face pressures to live up to their crowd's norms not only from fellow crowd members but from other peers as well (who expect them to conform to their reputation). Thus, escaping a crowd's influence is not as easy as withdrawing membership. One must change one's attitudes and behaviors, alter one's image among peers, and gain acceptance by a new crowd—not always an easy matter given the exclusionary nature of certain crowds (Eckert, 1989; Eder, 1985; Kinney, 1992). This gives the peer crowd more stability of influence than one might expect from other, more voluntary social contexts. In essence, affiliation with a certain crowd sets teenagers off on a certain trajectory—or, perhaps more accurately, continues them along the trajectory in which they entered adolescence—and increases the difficulty of shifting that trajectory in a different direction.

LINKING PARENTING PRACTICES TO PEER CONTEXTS

The image of the family and peers as separate social worlds for teenagers is quickly being replaced by an understanding of the important linkages between them. For example, a number of studies have provided indications that parenting practices—probably throughout childhood as well as into adolescence—endow young people with certain characteristics that predispose them to association with a certain crowd, rather than other peer groups (Brown, Lamborn, Mounts, & Steinberg, 1993; Feldman & Wentzel, 1990; Whitbeck, Simons, Conger, & Lorenz, 1989). It also seems sensible that, as teenagers enter certain crowds, parents may adjust their childrearing behaviors in response to crowd norms. When suddenly confronted with the defiance or deviance that defines *druggie* and *punk* peer cultures, a parent may "clamp down" on curfew or car privileges in an effort to stifle the child's errant behavior. Yet the connection between parenting practices and crowd affiliation is not so strong that parents of youth in a given crowd display a uniform set of parenting strategies. In fact, it is not clear that a given parenting strategy would have an equivalent effect among members of different crowds.

This prompts us to explore another possible link between parents and peers. This link is predicated on the assumption that peer crowds will act as a filter for the effects of other socializing agents, including parents. Teenagers who belong to crowds whose norms or prototypic behaviors are neither remarkably prosocial nor antisocial should display a modal pattern of association between parenting practices and child outcomes: Adaptive behaviors will vary directly with the degree to which parenting practices promote such behaviors. In more extreme peer contexts, however, the effects of parenting should grow more complex. On the one hand, there may be an enhancing effect, in which crowd members are especially boosted toward desirable outcomes by positive parenting, but also buffered against the ill effects of negative parenting practices. On the other hand, there may be an exacerbating effect, in which the crowd context makes negative parenting particularly debilitating and dampens the benefits of positive parenting practices. What's more, we suspect that the filtering effect of crowd contexts will be stronger among younger than older adolescents because of the waning salience of crowd affiliations across the teenage years (Brown, Eicher, & Petrie, 1986), and stronger among girls than boys because of girls' heightened interpersonal sensitivity and their somewhat more dependent relationship with parents during adolescence (Berndt, 1982; Furman & Buhrmester, 1985).

ARE CROWDS REALLY DISTINCT SOCIAL CONTEXTS?

Before examining whether crowd affiliation moderates the effects of parenting practices on adolescent behavior, it seems prudent to establish that different crowds are, indeed, distinctive social contexts for adolescents. Previous studies have established that adolescents attribute a different set of characteristics to each major crowd in their school (Brown et al., 1990), and that members of various crowds differ in the types of peer pressures they perceive (Clasen & Brown, 1985). Ethnographers also have emphasized the distinctive "cultures" or lifestyles that characterize the crowds they have studied (Eckert, 1989; Kinney, 1993; Larkin, 1979). Yet it is possible that these simply represent overblown stereotypes, or that they only apply to the core members of crowds who are most often the subjects of ethnographic investigations. Does the wider membership of each crowd reflect the attributes that are supposed to make their crowd distinctive from all others?

To address this question, we conducted a preliminary study among middle and high school students (Grades 7–12) in two midwestern communities. Participating schools in one community served a predominantly rural, but socioeconomically diverse population; the other schools, located in a larger city, drew primarily from working-class households. Like the schools they attended, the vast majority of participants (90%) were Euro-American.

Through a "Social Type Rating" (STR) peer-nomination technique, described in detail elsewhere (Clasen & Brown, 1985), we identified core and peripheral members of each school's major crowds and invited them to complete a self-report questionnaire. In addition to members of particular crowds, the sample included students best classified as *floaters* (for whom there was little consensus among peer raters about the crowd to which they belonged), as well as a set of *unknowns* (who simply were not recognized by a majority of raters). About 85% (n = 810) of those invited successfully completed the questionnaire, which included measures of (a) prosocial attitudes and behavior: students' grade point average (GPA; converted to the standard 4-point scale) and the importance they attached to school-related issues such as getting along well with teachers, never cutting class, or graduating from high school; and (b) antisocial behavior: frequency of illicit drug use and minor delinquent activity.

Analyses of variance (ANOVAs) revealed significant and substantial differences among crowds on mean scores for each of these measures (see Table 9.1). Indeed, crowd affiliation accounted for between 13% (for delinquency) and 40% (for drug use) of the variation in these measures. *Brains* displayed consistently adaptive outcomes on these measures, whereas *druggies* manifested consistently maladaptive outcomes; the outcomes of *floaters* were consistently normative, which seemed sensible in view of their lack of attachment to any particular crowd. The profile for other groups was more mixed. Generally, however, various crowds had clearly distinctive profiles on this set of measures, validating other investigators' contentions that crowds provide disparate peer social contexts for adolescents (i.e., members do seem to reflect the normative characteristics associated with their particular crowd).

Parental Influences Among Different Peer Contexts

Our primary interest was in how peer social contexts moderated parental influences on adolescent behavior patterns. For this set of analyses, we turned to a larger and more diverse sample drawn from six public high schools (Grades 9–12)—three in the Midwest and three in California. The schools varied substantially in size, socioeconomic status (SES), and ethnic distribution. Two of the midwestern schools had almost exclusively Euro-American student bodies. One was a small, rural school serving a predominantly working-class population; the other was located in a wealthy suburb

TABLE 9.1
Crowd Differences in Mean Scores on Outcomes in Preliminary Study

Outcome	Total	Jock	Popular	Druggie	Outcast	Brain	Normal	Floater	Outsider
GPA	3.06	3.26	3.18	2.82	2.87	3.61	3.19	3.13	2.65
Importance of schooling	3.86	4.22	3.95	3.34	3.84	4.23	4.10	4.02	3.42
Drug use	1.62	1.33	1.43	2.61	1.28	1.11	1.27	1.34	2.02
Minor delinquency	1.41	1.33	1.34	1.77	1.31	1.15	1.21	1.29	1.64

Note. Values are adjusted for the effects of gender and grade level. Higher scores indicate higher levels of the construct described by the scale.

of a major city. The other schools were more ethnically mixed, with 40%–70% Euro-American students and substantial numbers of at least two other racial/ethnic groups. One was an inner-city school with a diverse socioeconomic mix of students; another drew from primarily working-class sections of a mid-sized California city. The other two were in predominantly middle- and upper-middle-class cities in the San Francisco Bay area, but included a large number of minority students from neighboring cities.

Sample

Collectively, 5,497 students participated in the study, but analyses here are confined to a subsample of 2,947 students, for whom peer ratings of crowd affiliation were conducted and who fit into 1 of 10 major peer-crowd categories: *jocks, populars, brains, normals, druggies, nerds, Blacks, Hispanics, floaters,* or *unknowns.* These were the major crowd contexts among respondents (i.e., ones that could be found in a number of the schools). As before, crowd assignments were based on peer nominations, using a somewhat more sophisticated version of the STR technique employed in the first study (see Brown, 1989; Brown et al., 1993, for a full description). Because of budget and time constraints, STR ratings were not conducted for upperclassmen in the West Coast schools, but they were available for students in all four grades in the midwestern schools.

Understandably, then, compared with the 2,550 students excluded from analyses, our study sample was skewed toward underclassmen and had a disproportionate share (73%) of the African Americans in the entire sample (because most members of this ethnic group attended the midwestern schools) and a low share (35%) of the Asian Americans (most of whom attended the West Coast schools). The group selected for analyses did have significantly lower levels of SES (as measured by parents' education level), $t = 2.96$, $p < .01$; drug use, $t = 5.19$, $p < .001$; and psychosomatic symptomatology, $t = 3.35, p < .001$. However, the two groups did not differ significantly by sex, family structure, GPA, or level of self-esteem.

The sample was rather evenly split by sex (51% were girls); 38% were freshmen and 37% were sophomores, with the remainder quite evenly divided between juniors and seniors. A majority (59%) were Euro-American; 15% were African American, 15% were Hispanic American, and 9% were Asian American. The remainder were from other ethnic groups.

Procedure and Measures

All students in each participating school were asked to complete a self-report questionnaire, from which all of the measures employed in this study (outside of crowd affiliation) were derived. Because the questionnaire was too long to be completed in one class period it was split into two parts that were administered on separate days. Refusal rates were very low (less than 5% of each school's student body), but a number of students were absent on one or both days that the questionnaires were administered (about 25% of the student bodies) and were thereby eliminated from the sample.

For these analyses, we focused on three sets of measures from the questionnaire: background characteristics, family structure and parenting practices, and various behavioral outcomes measures. The background characteristics included sex, grade level, ethnicity, and SES (based on the average level of schooling completed by both parents). The other two sets of measures are described next.

Parenting Measures. The questionnaire included measures of respondents' perceptions of four dimensions of parenting practices. The first three—*warmth, demandingness,* and *psychological autonomy granting*—are the major dimensions by which parenting styles are commonly identified (Steinberg et al., 1992). The fourth, *parental encouragement of education,* represented a domain-specific measure of particular relevance to this study because two of the three prosocial outcome measures were academically related. All of the measures were based on Likert-type scale items. Where appropriate, items were reverse coded and/or standardized (if the scale combined items with different numbers of response categories) before calculating scale scores. Except where indicated, scale scores represented the mean of item responses.

The first dimension, parental warmth, was addressed with three specific measures. A 15-item *parental involvement* scale ($\alpha = .72$) assessed respondents' perceptions of how loving, responsive, and involved their parents were. Sample items were: "I can count on my mother (father) to help me out if I have some kind of problem"; "She (he) keeps pushing me to do my best in whatever I do." A 4-item index of *family time* ($\alpha = .71$) evaluated parents' efforts to engage family members in joint activities. Students were asked how often: "my parents spend time just talking with me," "my parents eat the evening meal with me," "my family does something fun together," and "my parents are home in the evening with me." Also, a 5-item *family organization* scale ($\alpha = .79$) evaluated the family's tendency to follow routines and display collective patterns of organized behavior. Students indicated their agreement or disagreement with items such as: "In my family, we check in or out with each other when someone leaves or comes home," and "My family has certain routines that help our household run smoothly."

There were also three measures of parental demandingness. One was a 9-item measure of *behavioral control* ($\alpha = .76$), which assessed parental efforts to provide limits for or impose restrictions on their child's behavior. Scale items inquired about parents' efforts to establish curfews, track the child's spending patterns and use of free time, and the like. Another was a 5-item *parental monitoring* scale (α = .80) similar to ones that have been used in previous studies (Dishion, 1990; Dornbusch et al., 1985; Patterson & Strothamer-Loeber, 1984). On a 3-point scale (*don't know, know a little, know a lot*), they indicated how much their parents really knew about who their friends were, how they spent their money, where they were after school, where they went at night, and what they did with their free time. A third scale indicated the degree to which parents engaged their child in *joint decision making*. Respondents rated 13 items, using a 5-point scale (from *My parents decide this without discussing it with me* to *I decide this without discussing it with my parents*), to indicate how they and their parents arrived at a decision about such issues as choice of school classes, curfew times, spending patterns, and use of alcohol (Dornbusch et al., 1985; Steinberg, 1987). The scale's alpha was .82. Scale scores indicated the proportion of items on which decisions were derived jointly as opposed to unilaterally (by parents only or the adolescent only).

A 12-item scale assessed the third dimension, parental encouragement of autonomy, or the extent to which parents employed democratic discipline techniques and encouraged the adolescent to express individuality within the family. Two sample items, both reverse coded, were: "How often do your parents tell you that their ideas are correct and you should not question them?"; "How often do your parents say that you should give in on arguments rather than make other people angry?" The scale's alpha was .74.

The final dimension, parental emphasis on achievement, was examined with a 15-item measure with questions about achievement levels that parents expected and parental participation in school-related efforts: checking homework, giving advice on class selections, and so on (see Brown et al., 1993). The scale's internal consistency alpha was .84.

To affirm the dimensionality of these variables, we submitted all eight measures to a factor analyses, using an oblique rotation because we expected dimensions to be moderately intercorrelated. Three factors emerged, with the variables arranged as specified earlier, except that parental emphasis on achievement had moderate loadings on both the warmth and demandingness factors; removing this variable from analyses did not alter the factor structure of the remaining measures. The three factors accounted for 74% of the variance in the seven variables (excluding parental emphasis on achievement).

Outcome Measures. Six outcomes were selected. Three reflected prosocial behaviors: (a) *academic achievement*—the student's self-reported, cumulative GPA in all high school classes (which was again converted to the standard 4-point rating system); (b) *academic effort*—the average number of hours per week devoted to homework across all subjects that the student was taking; and (c) *constructive use of leisure time*—the average number of hours per week spent in organized activities (excluding extra-curricular school activities), such as club meetings, private lessons, or religious groups. The other three measured antisocial or problem behavior: (d) frequency (in the past 6 months) of *drug use*; (e) frequency of *minor delinquency* (petty theft, use of a phony ID, purposely damaging property, etc.); and (f) average number of hours per week devoted to *socializing with peers* (e.g., time spent partying, hanging out with friends, being with a boyfriend or girlfriend, etc.), which has been linked to deviant activity in previous research. The drug use and delinquency scales had internal consistency alphas of .86 and .82, respectively.

Academic achievement and effort were moderately intercorrelated ($r = .35$), but had lower correlations with constructive use of free time (.13 and .10, respectively). Drug use was fairly strongly correlated with both deviance (.52) and time socializing with peers (.48), which in turn displayed a moderate correlation (.21) with each other. The two sets of outcomes had small, negative intercorrelations ($rs = -.05$ to $-.24$), except for the two measures of use of free time ($r = .01$).

Identifying Peer Contexts and Parenting Categories

As in the preliminary study, ANOVAs revealed that crowds differed significantly on each of the outcome measures (see Table 9.2). Once again, *brains* displayed the most consistently positive and *druggies* the most consistently negative set of scores. *Floaters*, along with *normals*, were remarkably normative—scoring close to the sample average on each of the outcomes. However, because our interest was in different peer contexts, rather than in specific crowds, we decided to collapse the crowds into four distinct groups. Two crowds, *brains* and *nerds*, offered adaptive contexts for adolescent development; that is, members scored at least one tenth of a standard deviation above the mean (*above* meaning in the prosocial direction) on most of the outcomes (and close to the mean on the rest). Four other groups—*druggies, Blacks, Hispanics*, and *outsiders*—displayed the reverse pattern of scores, providing a maladaptive context. Two crowds, *normals* and *floaters*, furnished a neutral context (members scored close to the sample average on all outcomes). The remaining two groups, *jocks* and *populars*, supplied an ambivalent context, with members displaying comparatively adaptive scores on some variables and comparatively maladaptive scores on others. Nineteen percent of respondents were in an adaptive crowd context, 31% were in a maladaptive context, 37% were in a neutral context, and 13% were in an ambivalent context. This grouping of variables was used for subsequent analyses.

It would have been possible to use scores on the parenting measures to group families according to their family's parenting style: authoritative, authoritarian, indulgent, and neglectful. There were two problems with this

TABLE 9.2
Crowd Differences in Mean Scores on Outcome Measures

Outcome	Total	Jock	Popular	Druggie	Nerd	Brain	Normal	Black	Hispanic	Floater	Unknown
GPA	2.83	2.88	2.95	2.19	2.89	3.62	2.92	2.60	2.52	2.90	2.56
Time on homework	3.63	3.56	3.94	2.85	3.67	4.26	3.67	3.40	3.25	3.74	3.44
Time in organized activities	2.88	2.24	3.19	2.13	3.20	5.05	3.11	3.04	1.22	3.09	2.13
Drug use	1.54	1.36	1.71	2.52	1.22	1.05	1.41	1.73	1.52	1.57	1.71
Delinquent acts	1.20	1.06	1.14	1.39	1.12	1.08	1.13	1.37	1.24	1.20	1.35
Time socializing with peers	12.08	11.31	15.51	26.05	8.76	6.58	12.68	14.37	11.64	12.47	10.37

Note. Mean scores are adjusted for the effects of gender, grade level, and ethnicity.

161

approach, however. First, only those with extreme scores on the variables are assigned to parenting categories, so that the majority of the sample is lost for analyses. Second, the parenting styles cannot be easily ordered from most to least adaptive, so such a categorizing scheme did not fit our purposes. Instead, we used scores on the four parenting dimensions to assign respondents to one of four parenting contexts.[1] A third of the respondents were placed in the *facilitative* category; they scored at least one standard deviation above the sample mean on at least one dimension, and within a standard deviation of the mean on the rest. Thirty percent were in the *inhibitive* group category; they scored at least one standard deviation below the sample mean on at least one dimension, and within a standard deviation of the mean on the rest. The 26% in the *normative* group reported scores within a standard deviation of the sample mean on all four dimensions. The *ambivalent* category included 11% of respondents who scored at least one standard deviation above the mean on one dimension, and at least one standard deviation below the mean on another.

Except for grade level, there were notable differences in the demographic distribution of respondents on these two grouping variables (see Table 9.3). Lower and working-class youth were overrepresented in the more problematic categories (maladaptive crowds and inhibitive parenting) and underrepresented in the more positive environments. This was also the case for African-American and Hispanic-American youth, although more so with regard to crowd context than parenting. Euro-American respondents dominated the facilitative parenting group, as well as the adaptive and ambivalent crowds. Boys were moderately overrepresented in adaptive crowd contexts and the ambivalent parenting group; obviously, the opposite was true for girls.

**Differences Among Parenting Categories
on Outcome Variables**

We hypothesized that, despite the ostensibly competing influence of peers, parenting practices would still affect children's attitudes and behaviors in adolescence. Thus, we expected to find significant linear trends on all outcomes when respondents were grouped by parenting category, such that adolescents exposed to facilitative parenting would display more adaptive scores than those who encountered normative parenting, who in turn would outscore teenagers who reported inhibitive parenting. Linear trend analyses

---

[1]Before creating the categorical summary parenting variable, we regressed each of the outcomes on the four parenting dimension scores to determine if there were one or two superordinate parenting dimensions that had strong and significant associations with all of the outcomes. This was not the case. Instead, the effects of each dimension varied substantially (from nonsignificance to strong significance) from one outcome to the next, and virtually all of the outcomes were significantly affected by several dimensions. This lent credibility to creating a summary variable.

TABLE 9.3
Demographic Distribution of Respondents Among Parenting Categories and Peer Crowd Contexts

Demographic Group	Peer Crowd Context				Parenting Category			
	Adaptive	Neutral	Maladaptive	Ambivalent	Facilitative	Normative	Inhibitive	Ambivalent
SES								
Lower/working	48	54	73	45	40	56	62	48
Middle/upper	52	46	27	55	60	44	38	52
Gender								
Boys	60	44	49	44	43	46	46	53
Girls	40	56	51	56	57	54	54	47
Ethnicity								
African American	4	14	28	5	9	13	14	16
Asian American	12	10	8	5	7	10	7	7
Euro-American	78	66	31	82	76	66	62	61
Hispanic American	4	10	32	7	8	10	14	15
Other	1	1	1	1	0	1	2	1

corroborated these expectations for each outcome variable (see Table 9.4). Planned comparisons revealed that, with one exception, each parenting group was significantly different from both others for the three prosocial outcome variables. On the antisocial variables, however, those in the facilitative and normative groups were not significantly different in drug use or delinquent activity, and those in the normative and inhibitive groups were not significantly different in time spent with peers. In essence, inhibitive parenting hurt more than facilitative parenting helped in curbing deviant behavior, and facilitative parenting helped more than inhibitive parenting hurt in minimizing inclinations to spend excessive free time with peers.

Effects of Crowd Context

The pattern of findings was expected to grow more complex when the sample was examined within crowd contexts. Simple linear trends should remain among those in neutral peer groups, but we postulated that association with adaptive or maladaptive crowds would either enhance the positive effects or exacerbate the negative effects of particular parenting practices. The analytical strategy was the same as in the previous set of analyses, except that analyses were repeated within each crowd context. The results essentially conformed to expectations with regard to prosocial outcomes (see Table 9.5). Linear trends remained strong in neutral crowd contexts, whereas members of adaptive crowd contexts seemed to be buffered against the deficits of inhibitive parenting while still profiting from the positive effects of facilitative parenting. Results were less consistent for those in maladaptive crowds. However, for the most part, inhibitive parenting hurt respondents more than facilitative parenting helped them. In short, adaptive crowd contexts had an enhancing effect, magnifying the benefits of facilitative parenting, whereas maladaptive peer contexts had a debilitating effect, magnifying the drawbacks of inhibitive parenting.

Surprisingly, crowd contexts failed to differentiate the pattern of associations between parenting group and antisocial outcomes (see Table 9.5). Across

TABLE 9.4
Differences Among Parenting Categories
in Mean Scores on Outcome Variables

Outcome	Facilitative	Normative	Inhibitive
GPA	3.22^a	2.29^b	2.67^c
Time on homework	4.03^a	3.74^b	3.36^c
Time in activities	3.85^a	3.00^b	2.48^b
Drug use	1.36^a	1.46^a	1.75^b
Delinquent acts	1.10^a	1.14^a	1.25^b
Time with peers	11.11^a	13.39^b	15.76^b

Note. All linear trends are significant at $p < .0001$. For each outcome, parenting groups with different superscript letters have significantly different scores at $p < .006$.

TABLE 9.5

Differences Among Parenting Categories on Outcome Scores Within Crowd Contexts

Outcome	Adaptive Crowds			Neutral Crowds			Maladaptive Crowds		
	Facilitative	Normative	Inhibitive	Facilitative	Normative	Inhibitive	Facilitative	Normative	Inhibitive
GPA	3.39[a]	3.02[b]	2.92[b]	3.22[a]	3.03[b]	2.76[c]	2.69[a]	2.55	2.38[b]
Time on homework	4.13[a]	3.76[b]	3.78[b]	4.06[a]	3.77[b]	3.47[c]	3.69[a]	3.54[a]	2.86[b]
Time in activities	4.72[a]	3.66	2.58[b]	3.99[a]	2.92[b]	2.51[b]	2.35	2.26	2.35
Drug use	1.11[a]	1.17[a]	1.47[b]	1.42[a]	1.48[a]	1.67[b]	1.49[a]	1.56[a]	1.93[b]
Delinquent acts	1.06[a]	1.11[a]	1.24[b]	1.11[a]	1.14[b]	1.20[b]	1.21[a]	1.17[a]	1.36[b]
Time with peers	8.16[a]	8.86	11.52[b]	11.06[a]	13.83[b]	16.54[c]	13.48	14.90	17.17

Note. Within each crowd context, mean scores on a particular outcome are significantly different between parenting groups with different superscript letters.

165

different types of crowds, inhibitive parenting was more strongly associated with high levels of deviance than facilitative parenting was associated with low levels of deviance. Time socializing with peers followed more of a linear trend. In short, all crowd contexts displayed what we would term an *exacerbating effect*: Inhibitive parenting promoted deviance, whereas normative and facilitative parenting were relatively equivalent in minimizing it. The contrast between crowd effects on prosocial and antisocial outcomes is illustrated in Fig. 9.1, with reference to academic effort (time on homework) as a prosocial variable and drug use as an antisocial outcome.

Consistency of Contextual Effects

We postulated that the effects of crowd context would not be entirely consistent across different demographic niches—that the effects would be stronger among girls and underclassmen than among boys and upperclassmen. To examine these expectations, the analyses were repeated, but sepa-

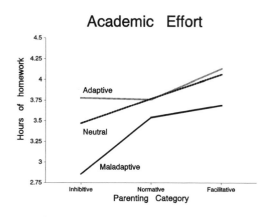

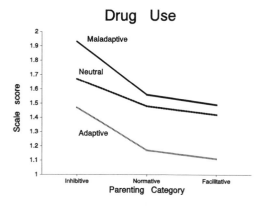

FIG. 9.1. Differences among adaptive, maladaptive, and neutral crowd contexts in associations between parenting category and academic effort and drug use.

rately for boys and girls and for underclassmen (freshmen and sophomores) and upperclassmen (juniors and seniors). Also, because those in various crowd contexts differed significantly in SES, separate analyses were conducted on respondents in lower and working-class homes (low SES) and those in middle- and upper-middle-class households (high SES). Figure 9.2 illustrates results of analyses of prosocial outcomes (time spent on homework), and Fig. 9.3 depicts findings related to antisocial outcomes (drug use).

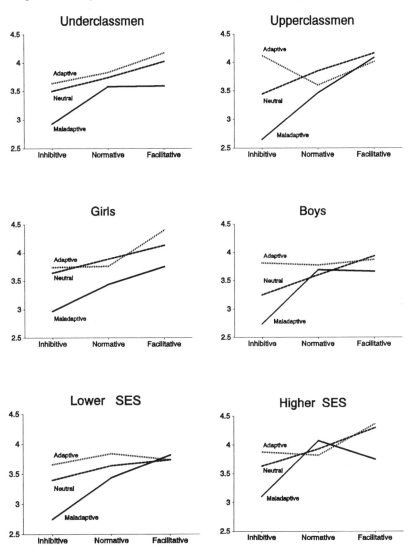

FIG. 9.2. Consistency across demographic niches in crowd differences in associations between parenting category and academic effort.

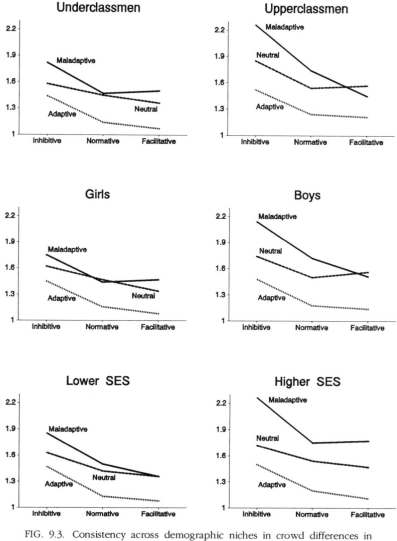

FIG. 9.3. Consistency across demographic niches in crowd differences in associations between parenting category and drug use.

Prosocial Outcomes. In neutral crowd contexts, associations between parenting and time spent on homework traced an essentially linear function in all demographic niches, replicating the general pattern of parenting effects in these contexts across the sample as a whole. As predicted, the enhancing effects of adaptive crowd contexts (in which homework time was boosted by facilitative parenting, but not diminished much below the normative group by inhibitive parenting) was observed only among girls and underclassmen, as well as respondents high in SES. The debilitating effect of participation in maladaptive crowd contexts (homework time diminished by inhibitive parenting, but not boosted by facilitative parenting past the normative group) was characteristic of underclassmen, as predicted, but also of boys, contrary to prediction, and of high-SES respondents. For maladaptive crowd members in the other three demographic niches, parenting categories traced a linear effect similar to the pattern among respondents in neutral crowd contexts. Crowd differences in time spent on homework were most distinctive among youth exposed to inhibitive parenting; this pattern was quite consistent across demographic niches.

Antisocial Outcomes. For the sample as a whole, parenting categories displayed an exacerbating effect across all types of crowd context. This pattern was absolutely consistent across demographic niches for those in adaptive crowds. In neutral crowd contexts, the pattern was more pronounced for boys and upperclassmen than for girls and underclassmen, for whom associations between parenting category and drug use were modest, but essentially linear. In maladaptive crowds, the normative and facilitative parenting groups were somewhat more distinctive among boys and upperclassmen than among girls and underclassmen. Yet all of these differences were quite subtle: There was no crowd context in any demographic niche, in which the difference in levels of drug use between inhibitive and normative parenting categories exceeded the difference between normative and facilitative parenting categories.

Looking at the data in a slightly different way, differences in levels of drug use between adaptive and neutral contexts were quite consistent across parenting categories and demographic niches. Differences between members of maladaptive crowds and those in the other two peer contexts, however, were notably stronger among boys, upperclassmen, and high-SES respondents. As in analyses of homework time, and consistently across demographic niches, members of various crowd contexts were most distinctive among youth exposed to inhibitive parenting.

A CONTEXTUAL PERSPECTIVE ON PARENTAL INFLUENCES ON ADOLESCENT TRAJECTORIES

"Well, we've done what we can to guide her. Now it's up to her to make something of her life. We just pray she doesn't 'fall in' with some crowd that will mess her up!" Some parents still carry this mindset into their relationships with adolescent offspring. Increasingly, however, evidence such as that presented in this study indicates that, with the advent of a child's adolescence, the "parenting game" is far from over. Although parents' ability to influence their offspring's life trajectory may be diminished at adolescence, it is still substantial (Steinberg, 1990).

Of course, the associations we observed between parenting practices and child outcomes are a function of several factors. They reflect the immediate impact of parents' current childrearing strategies, as well as the cumulative influence of what is most likely to have been similar parenting behavior throughout the child's first decade of life. They are also, probably, evidence of the effects of "reciprocal socialization" (Bell, 1968)—the fact that, for example, a teenager who displays an adaptive set of behaviors makes it easier for a parent to employ facilitative or authoritative parenting strategies.

Yet the main issue in our study was not the direction of effects between parenting and child outcomes, but the need for parental influences, however strong or weak they may be, to be understood in the wider context of a teenager's life. In this specific case, the findings supported the notion that parental influences are "filtered" through adolescents' experiences in peer social contexts. The degree to which positive parenting moved adolescents along a prosocial trajectory, or problematic parenting encouraged teenagers along an antisocial trajectory, was contingent on the peer-crowd context in which they were located.

Findings related to prosocial behaviors provided one image of the link between peer contexts and parental influences. Adolescents located in crowds whose behavioral profile closely paralleled the modal pattern for teenagers as a whole (i.e., crowds that were neither remarkably pro- nor antisocial) were free to be influenced by parenting practices in a simple and direct fashion: Facilitative parenting vaulted youth into an exceptionally prosocial trajectory, normative parenting kept them in an average trajectory, and inhibitive parenting constrained their progress along such a trajectory. Other adolescents, however, tended to be more sensitive to parenting practices that corresponded to the normative behavioral profile of their peer context. Those in adaptive crowds were influenced more by positive than negative parenting, whereas those in maladaptive crowds were influenced more by negative than positive parenting. In this sense, it appeared as if crowd contexts were successful in "filtering out" (countermanding or compensating for) parenting influences that ran contrary to peer-group norms. In this sense, crowds seem to function conservatively in simply reinforcing preexisting inclinations of their members. This is not surprising because adolescents tend to reflect the norms of their crowd before they enter the group (Brown, 1990; Eckert, 1989; Kinney, 1993). Yet the apparent capacity of crowds to "screen out" socializing influences that are contrary to the crowd's own orientation hints at a critical limitation in parental influences on adolescents. The pattern may be comforting for parents whose children have found a niche in an adaptive peer context, but disturbing for those with children in maladaptive peer contexts, because it suggests that facilitative parenting efforts (and, quite possibly, equally facilitative efforts on the part of school staff or other adults) may be ineffective in redirecting antisocially oriented youth onto a more positive trajectory.

The findings related to antisocial outcomes were more disturbing. Even adaptive crowd contexts did not appear to be completely successful in suppressing adolescents' movement along a problematic behavioral trajectory, nor was facilitative parenting especially successful (compared with normative parenting) in curbing drug use or delinquency. Why was there no filtering effect among peer contexts in relation to antisocial behavior? Maybe it was because low to moderate levels of deviant behavior—which was what most of our respondents reported—are so ingrained in American teenage society that they are part of the norms of all peer contexts. In other words, we expect all teenagers, even the "goody-goodies" in the *brain* crowd, to experiment with drugs and alcohol and to engage in a little troublemaking now and then. If true, then the pattern we observed would again reflect the tendency of peer contexts to magnify parental influences toward behavior that was consistent with group norms (and minimize parental influences toward non-normative behavior).

This set of modal patterns of parenting effects, however, did not display remarkable consistency across various demographic niches in the sample. Indeed, the only reasonably consistent patterns were the relatively linear relationship between parenting categories and prosocial outcomes in neutral crowd contexts and the tendency for inhibitive parenting to foster antisocial behavior more than facilitative parenting suppressed it in adaptive crowd contexts. This raises doubts about the generalizability of findings and encourages exploration of other factors that may moderate the "moderating effects" of peer context on parental influences. In this study, for example, ethnicity was not included in analyses of demographic niches because of the confound between ethnicity and crowd context (all ethnically based crowds were placed in the maladaptive category), but one can imagine other populations of teenagers in which ethnic comparisons may be more feasible. It also would be wise for investigators to consider more school- or community-specific analyses, rather than summing across several schools and communities, as was done here. Schools differ in the salience of crowd affiliations and in the separation and distinctiveness of various crowd types (Brown, 1990). Such factors may affect the capacity of crowds to form distinctive social contexts that can channel parental influences in different ways.

In this study, we examined how peer-crowd contexts moderated parental influences on adolescent behavior. Admittedly, however, other arrangements of these variables are possible and may be equally informative. For example, one might argue that parenting practices would affect a crowd's ability to influence adolescent behavior. We noticed that differences on outcome measures among members of various crowd contexts were sharpest among those who reported inhibitive parenting. Why should inhibitive parenting serve to magnify the distinctiveness of crowd contexts? Why would that not be more true of a normative set of parenting practices? One possibility is that adolescents are driven to dependence on peers when parents fail to nurture healthy social–psychological development. Others have found that parents' excessive overcontrol or undercontrol of adolescents heightens their peer orientation or susceptibility to peer pressure (Fuligni & Eccles, 1993; Steinberg, 1987). In essence, the lack of meaningful guidance from parents that underlay assignment to the inhibitive parenting category promotes a heavier dependence on peer-group norms and pressures, so that behavioral differences among members of different crowds are much sharper.

In some respects, our findings suggest that parents have more to lose than to gain in their childrearing practices during adolescence. Only those with offspring in adaptive or neutral peer contexts could hope for their children to benefit substantially from facilitative parenting—and even then, only with reference to prosocial behaviors such as academic effort or achievement. Of course, we examined only a handful of outcomes; we have no idea how consistently the patterns we observed would generalize to other prosocial or antisocial behaviors. Considering the inconsistencies of patterns across demographic niches, it would be foolish to put much faith in the generalizability of our results. Nevertheless, the findings do seem to underscore the importance of adolescents' association with particular types of peer groups. Here, too, of course, parenting plays a key role—particularly during childhood—in directing young people to certain types of peer groups or nurturing behavior patterns that will predispose youth to adaptive or maladaptive peer crowds (Brown et al., 1993; Dishion, 1990; Feldman & Wentzel, 1990; Patterson & Strothamer-Loeber, 1984). In other words, if, through their efforts prior to adolescence, parents can launch their child in a prosocial trajectory, the child's association in adolescent peer groups should enhance the possibility that parents can help maintain that trajectory through their parenting efforts in adolescence.

The major message of our findings is that, beyond the simple assertion that parenting practices continue to have an impact on children during the teenage years, there is a more complex and perhaps more pessimistic reality that parental influence in adolescence is contingent on other social contexts in teenagers' lives. Participation in peer groups seems to magnify or minimize parental influences in ways that reinforce the normative standards of a particular peer group or of the adolescent peer culture as a whole. Examining family influences in this contextual perspective gives us a more sophisticated understanding of their contributions to young people's efforts to move confidently and competently through the adolescent stage of life.

ACKNOWLEDGMENTS

The chapter is based on a paper presented at a conference entitled "Impact of Social Contexts on Adolescent Trajectories," held at the Pennsylvania State University in October 1992, and sponsored by the Program for Policy, Research, and Intervention for Development in Early Adolescence. The data examined in this chapter were gathered with the assistance of grants to B. Bradford Brown from the Spencer Foundation through the Wisconsin Center for Education Research, University of Wisconsin–Madison; to B. Bradford Brown and Laurence Steinberg from the U.S. Department of Education through the National Center on Effective Secondary Schools, Wisconsin Center for Education Research, University of Wisconsin–Madison; and to Sanford M. Dornbusch and P. Herbert Leiderman from the Spencer Foundation through the Center for the Study of Families, Youth, and Children at Stanford University. The authors gratefully acknowledge the helpful comments of Rainer Silbereisen, Laurence Steinberg, and two anonymous reviewers. The opinions expressed in this chapter are those of the authors and do not necessarily reflect the opinions of the funding agencies.

REFERENCES

Bell, R. (1968). A reinterpretation of the direction of effects in socialization. *Psychological Review, 75*, 81–95.
Berndt, T. J. (1982). The features and effects of friendship in early adolescence. *Child Development, 53*, 1447–1460.
Brittain, C. V. (1963). Adolescent choices and parent-peer cross-pressures. *American Sociological Review, 28*, 385–391.
Bronfenbrenner, U. (1970). *Two worlds of childhood.* New York: Russell Sage.
Brown, B. B. (1989). *Social Type Rating Manual.* Madison, WI: Wisconsin Center for Education Research, University of Wisconsin–Madison.
Brown, B. B. (1990). Peer groups and peer cultures. In S. S. Feldman & G. R. Elliott (Eds.), *At the threshold: The developing adolescent* (pp. 171–196). Cambridge, MA: Harvard University Press.
Brown, B. B., Eicher, S. A., & Petrie, S. (1986). The importance of peer group ("crowd") affiliation in adolescence. *Journal of Adolescence, 9*, 73–96.
Brown, B. B., Lamborn, S. D., Mounts, N. S., & Steinberg, L. (1993). Parenting practices and peer group affiliation in adolescence. *Child Development, 64*, 467–482.
Brown, B. B., Lohr, M. J., & Trujillo, C. M. (1990). Multiple crowds and multiple lifestyles: Adolescents' perceptions of peer group characteristics. In R. E. Muuss (Ed.), *Adolescent behavior and society: A book of readings* (pp. 30–36). New York: Random House.
Brown, B. B., Mory, M., & Kinney, D. (1994). Casting adolescent crowds in a relational perspective: Caricature, channel, and context. In R. Montemayor, G. R. Adams, & T. P. Gullotta (Eds.), *Advances in adolescent development: Vol. 5. Personal relationships during adolescence* (pp. 123–167). Newbury Park, CA: Sage.
Clasen, D. R., & Brown, B. B. (1985). The multidimensionality of peer pressure in adolescence. *Journal of Youth and Adolescence, 14*, 451–468.
Coleman, J. S. (1961). *The adolescent society.* New York: The Free Press.
Dishion, T. J. (1990). The peer context of troublesome child and adolescent behavior. In P. E. Leone (Ed.), *Understanding troubled and troubling youth* (pp. 128–153). Newbury Park, CA: Sage.
Dornbusch, S. M., Carlsmith, J. M., Bushwall, P. L., Ritter, P. L., Leiderman, P. H., Hastorf, A. H., & Gross, R. T. (1985). Single parents, extended households, and the control of adolescents. *Child Development, 56*, 326–341.

Eckert, P. (1989). *Jocks and burnouts: Social categories and identity in the high school*. New York: Teachers College Press.

Eder, D. (1985). The cycle of popularity: Interpersonal relations among female adolescence. *Sociology of Education, 58*, 154–165.

Entwisle, D. R. (1990). Schools and the adolescent. In S. S. Feldman & G. R. Elliott (Eds.), *At the threshold: The developing adolescent* (pp. 197–224). Cambridge, MA: Harvard University Press.

Feldman, S. S., & Wentzel, K. R. (1990). The relationship between parenting styles, son's self-restraint, and peer relations in early adolescence. *Journal of Early Adolescence, 10*, 439–454.

Freud, A. (1958). Adolescence. *Psychoanalytic Study of the Child, 13*, 255–278.

Fuligni, A. J., & Eccles, J. S. (1993). Perceived parent–child relationships and early adolescents' orientation toward peers. *Developmental Psychology, 29*, 622–632.

Furman, W., & Buhrmester, D. (1985). Children's perceptions of the personal relationships in their social networks. *Developmental Psychology, 21*, 1016–1024.

Hollingshead, A. B. (1949). *Elmtown's youth: The impact of social class on adolescents*. New York: Wiley.

Kinney, D. A. (1992, March). Coming together and going your own way: Delineating diversity and change in adolescent crowd associations. In B. Brown (Chair), *Stability and change in adolescent peer relations: Characteristics and consequences*. Symposium conducted at the biennial meetings of the Society for Research in Adolescence, Washington, DC.

Kinney, D. A. (1993). From "nerds" to "normals": Adolescent identity recovery within a changing social system. *Sociology of Education, 66*, 21–40.

Lamborn, S. D., Mounts, N. S., Steinberg, L., & Dornbusch, S. M. (1991). Patterns of competence and adjustment among adolescents from authoritative, authoritarian, indulgent, and neglectful families. *Child Development, 62*, 1049–1065.

Larkin, R. W. (1979). *Suburban youth in cultural crisis*. New York: Oxford University Press.

Larson, L. E. (1972). The influence of parents and peers during adolescence: The situation hypothesis revisited. *Journal of Marriage and the Family, 36*, 123–138.

Maccoby, E., & Martin, J. (1983). Socialization in the context of the family: Parent–child interaction. In E. M. Hetherington (Ed.) & P. H. Mussen (Series Ed.), *Handbook of child psychology: Vol. 4. Socialization, personality, and social development* (pp. 1–101). New York: Wiley.

Patterson, G. R., & Strothamer-Loeber, M. (1984). The correlation of family management practices and delinquency. *Child Development, 55*, 1299–1307.

Peshkin, A. (1991). *The color of strangers, the color of friends*. Chicago: University of Chicago Press.

Steinberg, L. (1987). Single parents, step-parents, and the susceptibility of adolescents to antisocial peer pressure. *Child Development, 57*, 269–275.

Steinberg, L. (1990). Autonomy, conflict, and harmony in the family relationship. In S. S. Feldman & G. R. Elliott (Eds.), *At the threshold: The developing adolescent* (pp. 255–276). Cambridge, MA: Harvard University Press.

Steinberg, L., Lamborn, S. D., Dornbusch, S. M., & Darling, N. (1992). Impact of parenting practices on adolescent achievement: Authoritative parenting, school involvement, and encouragement to succeed. *Child Development, 63*, 1266–1281.

Steinberg, L., Mounts, N. S., Lamborn, S. D., & Dornbusch, S. M. (1991). Authoritative parenting and adolescent adjustment across various ecological niches. *Journal of Adolescent Research, 1*, 19–36.

Whitbeck, L. B., Simons, R. L., Conger, R. D., & Lorenz, F. O. (1989). Value socialization and peer group affiliation among early adolescents. *Journal of Early Adolescence, 9*, 436–453.

CHAPTER TEN

Trajectory and Forms of Institutional Participation

Penelope Eckert
Institute for Research on Learning
and
Stanford University

For all adolescents in school, communities of practice form around the need to find a way through and around high school: to engage in common activity that gives meaning to their existence in the institution and provides them with the means to construct viable identities. In high schools across the country, these communities emerge as an apparently infinite variety of adolescent subcultures, or social categories, some of them spectacular and some of them not so spectacular. Up close, however, there is system and structure to the development of these social categories, and of the symbolic activity associated with them. The following discussion focuses on two of these categories, which appear to be structurally primary in high schools across the United States. These are two enduring, polarized communities based primarily on engagement in, and alienation from, the school institution as a whole. Although this opposition is reflected in all aspects of school participation, it focuses most clearly on the school as a social (as opposed to a curricular) institution. People from across the country recognize their names: *jocks, rahrahs, collegiates, soc's,* and *preppies* on the one hand; and *burnouts, greasers, hoods, stoners,* and *grits* on the other hand. Although the names of these categories and the specific styles that signal their opposition (e.g., clothing, musical tastes, territorial specialization, etc.) change through time and between regions and localities, the fundamental status of this opposition is virtually universal. The apparent multiplicity of subcultures masks the enduring and ubiquitous nature of the opposition between the alienated and the engaged.

This chapter is based on 3 years of intensive ethnographic work in Detroit suburban high schools: 2½ years of participant–observation in one high school, and shorter periods in each of four other high schools in the Detroit suburban area. In these all-White[1] schools, there is a clear opposition between the *jocks*, who base their lives and identities on the school's extracurricular sphere, and the *burnouts*, who reject the school as a center of social life and base their lives and identities on the neighborhood, the local community, and the margins of the school. The hegemony of this opposition in the school is underscored by the fact that virtually all students in the school who do not affiliate with one or the other category are referred to, and refer to themselves, as *in-betweens*. Because of the depth of the experience that participation in either of these categories constitutes, and because of the structural importance and universality of this opposition, participation in either of these categories can be seen as entailing a trajectory.

The notion of *trajectory* that serves as the basis of the following discussion has to do with a continual construction of the self in relation to institutions and to the communities that arise and endure within those institutions. This process of construction is embedded in participation in communities of practice, and involves the construction of kinds of knowledge that shape one's beliefs and ways of participating in institutions.

KNOWLEDGE, COMMUNITIES OF PRACTICE, AND TRAJECTORY

A community of practice[2] is an aggregate of people who come together around some enterprise. United by this common enterprise, people come to develop and share ways of doing things, ways of talking, beliefs, values—in short, practices—as a function of their joint involvement in mutual activity. Social relationships form around the activities, the activities form around relationships, and particular kinds of knowledge and expertise become part of individuals' identities and places in the community. It is not the assemblage or purpose that defines the community of practice. Rather, a community of practice is simultaneously defined by its membership and the shared practice in which that membership engages. The value of the construct *community of practice* lies not so much in the potential to identify such communities, but in the focus it affords on the mutually constitutive nature of individual, community, and practice. Among other things, it highlights the relations among these in the construction of knowledge, and the embedding of trajectory in community knowledge.

---

[1]The choice of all-White schools was dictated by the nature of the sociolinguistic research that was the primary motivation for this fieldwork.

[2]The notion *community of practice* was introduced by Lave (in preparation) and has been further developed by Lave and Wenger (1991; see also Wenger, in preparation).

Examinations of social reproduction in schools frequently focus on the direct relationship between the individual and the institution. However, the individual's institutional participation is in fact mediated by communities of practice—particularly peer communities—that arise within and around that institution. Students' forms of participation in school are embedded in peer networks and relationships, which mediate relationships with institutional personnel and resources. The opposed social categories that arise in public high schools embody very different forms of institutional participation, different forms of institutional knowledge, and different forms of identity. They are communities of practice, and it is their shared practice that constitutes trajectory.

In many cases, it is easy to identify the common endeavor that assembles a community of practice: a garage band, a day-care cooperative, a research group, or a math class. But that endeavor develops a life of its own as local practices develop around it, transforming the enterprise, the activity, and the knowledge. A community of practice arises as a response to circumstances, and it cannot be legislated. This is extremely important to recognize when considering the role of communities of practice within institutions. In an institutional setting, it is easy to confuse the common enterprise of a community of practice with the enterprise as defined by the institution. Indeed, although the membership of such a community may be brought together, or "legislated," by the institution, the practices that arise within that community develop a life of their own and cannot be predicted by institutional policy or organizational charts.

For example, although one might see a mathematics class as a community of practice based on the learning of mathematics, such a class may in fact develop a practice based on maximizing standardized test scores in mathematics, with the competitive and instrumental practices embodied in such practice. Or practices may emerge in a mathematics class that have even less to do with mathematics learning, but more to do with "outwitting" the teacher, and identities and relationships among people in that class will encompass participation in these outwitting practices. Because communities of practice arise within institutions around articulating personal and institutional goals, needs, and identities, communities of practice that are subversive to the avowed goals of the institution can develop just as easily. One could say that the success and value of the institution depends on its ability to support the development of communities of practice that provide the best articulation of personal and institutional goals, needs, and identities.

Individuals participate in a variety of communities of practice, and communities of practice may overlap or subsume others. Thus, one might see a high school as a community of practice, to the extent that those participating in it share a set of practices. Part of shared practice in the high school is the development and maintenance of the jock–burnout opposition. Indeed, the school-wide use of the term *in-between* for those who are neither jocks nor burnouts is an indication of the embedding of these categories in school-wide practice.

Community knowledge is a crucial construct to this discussion because knowledge is embedded in community practice—it is developed in the service of the community and of its shared enterprise. Learning, in turn, is the means by which participants gain, produce, and reproduce community knowledge, and the means by which they gain membership, participate, and move around in communities of practice. It is the combination of the individual's desire to participate in the community and the accessibility of the community and its practice to that individual that provides motivation and the means to learn. The possibilities for participation, therefore, have important implications for what people come to know. People strive to learn what will enhance their mobility in, and on behalf of, the community of practice, and what will enable them to make a mark on their community. At the same time, they will strive for membership in communities in which they feel the possibility of making a mark. Inasmuch as communities do not exist independently of their members, the community will continually adjust to encompass many of its members' need to make a mark and their joint need, as a community, to make a mark in the wider context. In this way, the community of practice jointly constructs its relationship to the world, constrained in this process by its place in the world.

Community knowledge, then, develops around the articulation of relationships and activities within the community, and around the community's articulation of relationships and activities in and with other communities. Community knowledge is quite particular to the community's place in the larger society, and articulates the local and larger social system. In this way, community knowledge is directly related to Bourdieu's (1972/1977) notion of the *habitus*, which ties local experience, knowledge, taste, beliefs, and so on to the larger social system. The habitus can be defined as a set of dispositions that go with a given place in society (such as determined by class) that are generative of social practice, and that are reproduced in that social practice. But the habitus as a set of generative principles is abstract, and can only be grounded and reproduced in actual practice in real-world situations and activity. The community of practice can be seen as the locus or grounding of the habitus. The continual joint construction of knowledge and perspective that takes place as participants jointly engage in community practice, and as they jointly negotiate their way in the world, is part of the process of the reproduction of the habitus. Community knowledge, as part of this joint negotiation, embodies a particular perspective on the world. The individual's knowledge—the result of a negotiation of participation in a variety of communities of practice—is not limited by participation in any one community of practice. However, community memberships tend to cluster: Working-class people tend to belong to bowling leagues rather than tennis clubs, and to unions rather than professional organizations.

For the purposes of this chapter, I focus on two aspects of learning and knowledge as they are organized in communities of practice. The first is the kind of knowledge that is embodied in the community. The place of the community of practice in the world, and its view of itself in the world, is intertwined with the nature of knowledge that will constitute that community. A janitor and a senior executive will have different understandings of the same workplace and organization. They will have different interests in relation to that organization, different social relationships with others in the organization and among themselves, different familiarity with physical and organizational locations, and so on. Neither of these people would have the knowledge required to function well in the other's communities of practice. Indeed, their ability to function in their own depends, to some extent, on their inability to function in the other. That is, community knowledge involves particular structurings of knowledge and ignorance.[3]

The second aspect of learning and knowledge that I discuss is what I call *knowledge making*.[4] The construction of knowledge and ignorance is a key component of community practice: Access to knowledge and the authority to "make" knowledge are both key parts of what characterizes practice in a community. Knowledge practices are closely intertwined with social relationships and forms of participation in a community of practice. Different forms of participation afford different kinds of access to knowledge: They may bring access to implicit instruction, to situations in which one may observe others in activity, or to explicit instruction or explanation. Forms of participation are also associated with knowledge-making rights, or authority: whether, when, and how one's ideas, suggestions, and contributions are taken up by the community. In a hierarchical community of practice, for example, knowledge may be passed down from on high, and certainly tentative constructions of knowledge will be evaluated on the basis of the hierarchical position of the actor and the reactor. The hierarchy, in turn, will be reproduced through this privilege. A key kind of knowledge to develop in a community of practice, then, is knowledge of the knowledge-making practice.

JOCKS, BURNOUTS, AND THE INSTITUTION

In previous work (Eckert, 1989), I have described the U.S. high school as a corporate institution, embodying corporate norms and values, facilitating corporate identities, and offering corporate rewards. This is nowhere more

---

[3]See Wenger (in preparation) for a detailed discussion of the interplay of visibility and invisibility in the creation of transparency.

[4]The concept of *knowledge making* is developed in detail in Eckert, Maxson, Newman, and Shethar (in preparation).

apparent than in the extracurricular sphere, and in the intimate relation between the extracurricular sphere and all other aspects of school life. The normative high school student is a corporate individual: Students are expected to base their friendships, networks, activities, and identities within the school, and indeed to mold them onto the formal structure of the institution. The institution exists in a field of like institutions, and students are expected to be motivated by loyalty to their own school and by competition with other schools. Loyalty dictates confining one's networks and activities to the school at the expense of involvement in the local community and in other communities or organizations that would take time away from school activities.

The school year is built around a relatively unchanging sequence of activities designed to enhance the social atmosphere in the school and the school's competitiveness with other schools. School personnel control resources for the development of these activities, and students organize themselves to make use of the resources. Students compete for management of the resources, and they build "careers" through the strategic use and distribution of these resources among the student body and through the organization and execution of successful activities. The distribution of resources is facilitated by a student hierarchy, in which the individual's place is a function above all of corporate roles (e.g., cheerleader, student council member or officer, varsity athlete, honor society president, etc.), relationships with teachers, and the size and breadth of the individual's student network and constituency. For the corporate individual in the high school, identity, activity, and social relations are built on the institutional structure of the school. Because the corporate success of the school depends on the participation of corporate students, these students are in a position to maintain collegial relations with school personnel.

The jock and burnout communities of practice develop around the issues of boundaries and hierarchy (i.e., of corporate practice). Students' responses to these issues are based on experiences they bring into the school, and a key aspect of these experiences is class (i.e., social class). The class differences between the jocks and the burnouts are well known in the school, and both jocks and burnouts (but more commonly burnouts) comment on these differences. However, these class differences are statistical, rather than absolute, as shown in Table 10.1. Thus, although the jock and burnout

TABLE 10.1
Socioeconomic Class Makeup of Jocks, Burnouts, and In-Betweens

Socioeconomic Status	Jocks (%)	In-Betweens (%)	Burnouts (%)
Working Class	16	16	50
Lower Middle Class	34	42	22
Upper Middle Class	50	42	23

categories constitute middle-class and working-class cultures, respectively, class does not absolutely determine category affiliation. Rather, the categories are built on social networks that extend back into childhood and that differ with the neighborhoods in which they are centered. Later, kids from other neighborhoods are attracted to these networks by virtue of affinity based on things not directly (but in some cases indirectly) related to class.

Although the following discussion focuses on class-related phenomena underlying opposing orientations to school, it does not insist that class is the only social difference that will lead to such an opposition. However, earlier studies (e.g., Coleman, 1961; Hollingshead, 1949) have shown a relation between class and participation in both the extracurricular and curricular spheres in school, suggesting that class commonly does underlie primary social divisions in the school. At the same time, it is clear that other dynamics, such as ethnic differences and conflicts, can lead students differentially to become alienated or involved in school as well. Informal reports from ethnically diverse schools suggest that, where class difference corresponds to ethnic difference, the categories are simultaneously ethnically based. Further, where class crosscuts ethnicity, there can be a complex crosscutting of categories. It remains to be established whether ethnicity alone ever underlies fundamentally opposed categories based on school orientation.

Simply (perhaps too simply) put, jocks are a middle-class response to the corporate institution of the school—to the opportunities it offers for students to develop corporate identities and corporate roles, to engage in competition for institutional status, and for entrance into similar institutions after high school. The jocks embody middle-class culture. They are college bound, and they build their social lives and identities within the school and its extracurricular sphere. As a result, their social networks are hierarchical and competitive, and limited to the school.

In the same way, burnouts are a working-class response to the corporate institution of the school—to its corporate orientation, its rejection of local community resources, its hierarchical practices, and its closed boundaries. The burnouts embody working-class culture. They are workplace-bound vocational students, and they build their lives and identities in the neighborhoods and communities outside of the school.

Burnout networks in the high school are demonstrably based in working-class neighborhood networks. These networks are built around friends, friends' siblings, siblings, and siblings' friends, and therefore are age heterogeneous. With the intensity of peer activity outside the home in the neighborhood, a peer culture develops early, in which children share information, guidance, emotional support, and material resources. This egalitarian and open flow of resources frequently compensates for a lack of parental resources, and leads to strong peer alliances. As a result, burnout social practice is built on strong loyalty, support, and egalitarianism. As burnouts approach high school, their networks become increasingly geographically heterogeneous, as older siblings go into the city to live and/or work, or bring home friends from the city. Kids from the city move into the neighborhood or the school, maintaining their connections with urban networks and incorporating them into their new friendships.

The middle-class neighborhood, home of the typical jock, contrasts sharply with this picture. The sparser child population that characterizes most affluent neighborhoods precludes the development of extensive neighborhood-based child networks. But furthermore, the orientation of the typical middle-class adult away from the neighborhood means that these children do not develop the kinds of extensive local peer networks and strong ties that are characteristic of working-class neighborhoods. Thus, the school constitutes a better locus for the development of friendship networks and activities.

FORMS OF PARTICIPATION, KNOWLEDGE, AND THE INSTITUTION

One might say that the mutual enterprise that constitutes the jocks as a community of practice is integrating their lives with the school, constructing jointly through their social relationships a corporate community and corporate identities. Burnout social networks and interests reside in the local community and its workplaces, and extend only partially into the school. The burnouts arise in school as a community of practice out of a need to find ways to exist in school that neither implicate them in corporate practice nor cost them their participation in the institution altogether, and that allow them to foster a strong sense of identity and participation in their broader community.

Thus, the jocks and burnouts emerge as communities of practice in response to the school institution, as they seek resources to pursue different lives within and without the school. The knowledge constructed within these communities of practice is intertwined with their orientation to the school, and with the articulation between their shared interests and the communities and institutions in which these interests are pursued. Functioning at the margins and the center of the school, respectively, the burnouts and jocks have very different views of the institution and its preoccupations. The forms of participation that they develop in the institution give them different understandings of the institution and its practices. At the same time, their differing orientations to the local and adjacent urban community yield different understandings of the world outside the school.

Knowledge and Institutional Identity

Because plans for after high school are a key difference in jock and burnout trajectory, college and workplace orientation seems a natural place to begin a discussion of participation and knowledge. College and vocational orientations do not spring from simple individual choice, but are built tightly into community practice. The differences in trajectories that this represents bring differences in knowledge not only about college and the workplace, but about the meaning of one's presence in school. The jocks live in a world of preparation for college. Their families, neighborhoods, friendship networks, school counselors, and teachers all form a network of assumption and information about college entrance. For the jock, high school is a pipeline to college, and corporate activity in the high school is directly linked to college entrance and activity in college. Choice of college, preparation for college boards, choice of college preparatory classes, and the significance of extracurricular activities for college admission are all daily conversational fare in jock networks—engaged in by parents, siblings, neighbors, and teachers, all of whom share the assumption that members of the jock community of practice will go on to college.

No one assumes this about burnouts. Information about college does not flow in burnout networks, as witnessed by the following burnout's account in the course of some discussion of what she was going to do after high school:[5]

I—I kind of want to be an art teacher, but you have to go through a lot to be something like that.

HAVE YOU EVER THOUGHT OF GOING TO COLLEGE?

Yeah, my parents said, "Well, you know, if you want to go to college we'll pay your way," so why not, you know.

YEAH. DO THEY WANT YOU TO?

Yeah. I'm—I'm pretty—I think, you know, if I really get my stuff together in art, you know, really get into it I—I probably will try to be an art teacher.

UM, ARE YOU TAKING COURSES AND STUFF THAT YOU HAVE TO TAKE TO GO TO COLLEGE?

Um, I re—I'm not really aware of, you know, what I have to do to be in college, but I—I think I've got a low grade—you know—grade average pretty much.

Because college is the "natural" sequel to high school for jocks, preparation for college is built into their daily practice. Their social networks map onto the classroom as well as extracurricular space, as curricular choice brings jocks into college preparatory and advanced placement classes. Jocks' social activities on weeknights are generally limited to phone conversations, building homework into their joint schedule.

---

[5]All quotes are from tape-recorded conversations with students. Speech in small caps is mine. These quotes are reproduced as uttered; they are not edited to remove such things as repetitions, hesitations, or discontinuities.

Just as knowledge about college does not flow in burnout networks, burnout activity schedules do not leave time for homework. The experience of one burnout from a middle-class family underscores the lack of fit between college and participation in the burnout community. Although this girl followed an academic curriculum and applied to college, she did so under her college-educated parents' tutelage, without discussing it with her friends. This is not because she hid the fact that she was going to college from her friends, but because college preparation was not part of their practice and, as a result, not a topic of conversation. For this girl, who had casual friends among the jocks dating back to her childhood neighborhood networks, the difference in cultures made her feel torn. The following quote shows her view of the contrast between jock and burnout approaches to the future in school:

> I can go out, and I can party with them [burnout friends], but then, either right before first hour, or during another class or something, I'm doing my homework. And I get—you know, this last report card was all A minuses and Bs. And my friends just looked at me and went, "Wait a minute, you were out with us Friday, why are you getting these good grades?" you know. They're not thinking about after they graduate. And I think, out of those friends, I'm thinking about that. And then there's my jock friends . . . they always have been looking for "What am I going to do for the rest of my life," and "What am I going to do here and there." It's—I'm torn apart again, you know.

Most burnouts who think about going to college perceive college as separate from high school, and they are encouraged to perceive it as such by the assumptions made by their parents, teachers, counselors, neighbors, and friends. The middle-class burnout quoted previously talked about her friends:

> I think that by the time they're a senior, and by the time they're faced—by the time they graduate and get their cap, and they're done, they're just going to sit down, and they're going to go "Now what do I do?" And they're going to go out, and they're going to get a job, or they're going to go out and they're going to either finish their high school or go, you know, somewhere else to get some kind of diploma or something. It's just taking them longer.

What will be continuous for burnouts will be their friendships; they expect their institutional experiences to change radically. Indeed, they see high school graduation as deliverance. By providing no clear transition to the workplace, and by assuming no interest in college, the high school leaves the burnouts to take it upon themselves to construct a path into adulthood. This construction is aided by the age-heterogeneous friendship networks that begin in the neighborhood; by the time they are in high school, burnouts already have friends who are in the work force, having either graduated or dropped out. Thus, information about the local workplace flows in burnout networks in much the same way that information about college flows in jock networks. However, this information has no particular value in school because it is not purveyed by the school. On the contrary, attention to the workplace outside of school co-op programs is regarded as reflecting a lack of interest in school.

The relation between participation in high school and perceived participation in future institutions makes high school a different place in jocks' and burnouts' lives. Burnouts perceive that, although high school graduation is a procedural requirement for future employment, they are going to have to make their own way once they are out of high school. Those who are deeply involved in vocational courses in high school recognize that the high school vocational curriculum is inadequate to qualify them for good employment, and they resent that they will have to supplement an inadequate vocational curriculum with trade school.

RELATIONSHIPS AND COMMUNITY PRACTICE

Central to community practice is the nature of relationships among community members. Jocks and burnouts enter high school with divergent values and beliefs about personal relationships, and they leave high school with these differences crystallized. These values and beliefs, in turn, are an integral—perhaps the most crucial—aspect of trajectory because they are part of the invisible matter of class-based practice.

The corporate knowledge that jocks develop in high school consists of their explicit knowledge of resources and networks, as well as a deep and implicit knowledge of corporate social relations. Success in controlling and managing corporate resources depends on the ability to find one's way around the institution—to know where resources related to the production of activities are, who controls them, what it takes to gain control of them, and so on. This requires knowledge of people and their formal roles, and of the informal relations that articulate with the formal. It is partially the need for rich social and professional information—which can only come with the regular and time-consuming servicing of networks—that makes it necessary for professionals to merge their personal and work identities. It is such a merger that is required of high school students for success in the school's extracurricular sphere.

Peer Relationships

Choice and maintenance of friendships among jocks is determined, to a great extent, by shared involvement in school activities. A friendship between two jocks whose activities are radically different is difficult to maintain, as is a friendship between two people whose hierarchical positions are radically different. Thus, friendships tend to be somewhat fluid, particularly in the early years of secondary school as the corporate hierarchy is falling into place. Furthermore, jocks see high school as a separate stage in life that leads to—but is discontinuous with—college. Thus, they talk about the importance of keeping in touch with their high school friends in college, fully recognizing that their primary relationships will change along with their institutional membership.

Constraints on jock friendships reflect the hierarchical system in which they are embedded. Friendships are constrained by the need to control the spread of personal information that might damage their corporate image. Jocks overwhelmingly say that they do not confide such information in their friends; many of them report that if they have something personal that they need to talk about, they go to friends or relatives who do not attend the same school. They perceive a need to project a well-adjusted, "happy" image in school, where personal problems can harm one's "in control" image.

Jocks' closer friendships are embedded in a broad network within the school. Jocks devote a good deal of time developing acquaintances throughout the student body because a broad constituency and broad familiarity are necessary both for election to office and the organization of good events. Thus, one jock described the importance of knowing the larger student body for garnering human resources:

> The more variety we have, the—probably the better chances of ideas and stuff, you know, to get going . . . each different group has like someone in there that's a leader anyway, you know, no matter what group they're from. And they all have some quality, you know, like some are artists, some of them give good ideas, some write good, and the more that you have the better are things going to be. Because if you have the same ideas all the time, and the same people with the same limited talents, you know, it can only be so good.

Jocks' networking explicitly involves gaining influence with, rather than joining, a wide range of groups. As in the corporate hierarchy, jocks acquire a student constituency by virtue of their apparent responsibility to the interests of the student body at large. Therefore, much of the jocks' networking is ultimately aimed at convincing a wide variety of people that they share—or at least take into account—their personal interests. One student body officer put it this way:

> You tend to overcome, and win a lot more people if you become popular, but still at the same time, not too snobby. I try to talk to a lot of people now, and like right now, you know, because—because I'm president . . . there's a lot of people that, sort of like, may know me by name or something, but

there's not like really a group of people I won't talk to. Because a lot of people, they'll say, "Well, I don't like to talk to people in the courtyard,"[6] you know. That's just the way it is. But I don't see what's wrong with it. It's not like you're becoming one . . . you know, what they do, it doesn't bother me. If they want to do what they do with their life, it's fine, and you shouldn't distinguish between certain types of people. You should just want to relate to as many people as possible.

Jocks meet new people through school activities, and their initial contacts and conversations are supported by the institutional connection. Thus, one jock boy told me about how he got to know boys from the other junior high school that ultimately merged with his own in high school:

HOW DID YOU MEET THEM?

Basketball clinic. They were there, and I was there. And I remember the last day of the clinic, we sat in the weight room talking for about some two and a half some hours just about different people from our school, different people from their school, and just, you know, talking about things we like to do and stuff, and we became really close.

Another jock talked about getting to know people at regional workshops where, once again, the institutional connection provides the means to initiate interaction:

I like to—I like to be able to go up to somebody that I know is better than me in a certain subject, and ask questions about that. Because basically, they might know something that could help me. And I went up to them, and I would talk to them because I noticed that they were so good. I would talk to them about, uh, their school.

Jock friendships are legitimated by the school because they are seen as existing in the service of corporate activity. Thus, in a real way, the jocks see themselves as embodying the school. Jocks see their hierarchical and competitive relationships as motivated by, and justified by, their corporate activity. Although they adjust their social ties to suit these corporate requirements, they do not see themselves as personally disloyal, but as appropriately building friendship and identity on shared activity in an institution that they see as primary.

The burnouts do not recognize the corporate possibilities of the school, but see high school as an institutional extension of elementary school, where the school provides resources and permits students to use them. They see the school from start to finish as a paternalistic institution that seeks to

---

[6]The courtyard is the burnouts' territory in the school.

confine and control, and they see the roles that the school offers as purely infantilizing. Thus, the understanding between the burnouts and the school is fundamentally adversary, foregrounding the school's power over the adolescent age group.

The burnouts see relationships with their own peers as purely informal, and as unfolding around the school rather than in it or as part of it. Their school networks transcend the graduating class, and, in turn, are only a partial set of their broader networks that extend into other age groups and localities. Therefore, the school walls do not define the burnouts' social groups, but divide them. These walls serve as a social facilitator for the jocks, whereas they serve as a social barrier for the burnouts. Burnout social activities, by and large, are discouraged by the school, as are their very friendships. The serious matter of life for the burnouts unfolds in the workplace, in interests not endorsed by the school (such as dirt biking), and in the family and personal problems that they commonly share. Jocks hide such problems because of their potential damage to their place in corporate networks, whereas burnouts freely share problems and other kinds of information that might be damaging for jocks. Such sharing among one's peers is part of a system of mutual support and emphasizes group solidarity. Furthermore, rather than being damaging, such information attests to burnouts' status as adults coping with real-world problems.

The burnouts' grounding in long-term and solidary neighborhood peer networks leads them to have different assumptions about friendship and network construction than the jocks. Loyalty to individuals and to the group is a primary value, thus burnouts are more likely to let their friendships determine their activities than vice versa. Burnouts neither perceive nor recognize a corporate justification for jocks' social organization, and assume a purely personal rationale for their hierarchies and competition. Above all, burnouts are suspicious of any individual's attempt to influence relative strangers. This is always seen as a means to power and ascendancy over others, which runs directly counter to the burnouts' egalitarian norms. Thus, they consider the jocks' cultivation of broad, casual relationships to be insincere, and they are extremely critical of what they term the *jock smile*. For the burnout, and many in-betweens, this broad networking can only be at the expense of the most valued kind of social relationship—close friendship:

> I just think that they're all competing to be better than each other. And trying to get as many friends as possible, and they're competing and they're great. And I don't agree with that at all. I think you should be who you are, and do what you want, and not try to impress everybody by being Joe Athlete, or Joe Float Builder. I think it's been like that for quite a long time. I don't even know when it—junior high school is really when the first pressure starts. I don't know. Because if you have a lot of friends and not very many close friends, I think you're cheating yourself, because you don't have anybody to

confide in, or anybody to really trust. Because you don't really know, you
know, if you just have a broader range of friends.

This is not to say that burnouts do not attempt to develop broad networks.
However, their networking efforts focus on developing informal relationships
and access to urban resources, both of which are shared with their existing
friendship network, rather than serving as material in network competition.
Furthermore, these networking efforts do not map onto school, but frequently move the student away from school, highlighting the limitations of
the institution with respect to burnout social life.

Corporate activity provides jocks with a pretext to initiate interactions,
whereas burnouts initiate such interactions on informal grounds. It is significant that burnouts quite commonly use burnout symbolic activities (e.g.,
cigarettes or drugs), which are structurally equivalent to jocks' corporate
activities, as their pretext for such initiations. The following two descriptions
of the beginnings of friendships are typical of burnouts' approaches to relative strangers:

CAN YOU REMEMBER THE FIRST TIME YOU MET?

Yeah, I do. Remember? You came up to me and asked me for John Day's
phone number. And she called me up and goes, "You know where I can get
a bag from?" I go, "Who is this?" She goes, "Sue."

(Both parties to the reported interaction were present during this conversation.)

* * *

HOW DID YOU MEET?

She comes up to me, "Got a smoke?" I go, "Yeah." And then, then the other
day, "You got a smoke?" And then, and one day, a couple days later, I go,
"Hey, you," because I didn't have no smokes, I go, "You, you owe me couple
smokes." She goes, she goes, "Oh, really?"

Relationships with Teachers

Because the jocks share the school's corporate view of itself, the jocks and
the school work for each other. The jocks' careers are built on—and build—
the school's extracurricular success. Thus, there is a sharing of interests—a
collegial relationship—between jocks and school personnel. To the extent
that the individual jock's identity is based on corporate activity, that identity
is part of the institution's identity. Because corporate activity cannot be
engaged in by solitary individuals, the individual jock's identity, the jock
community of practice, and the institution are all mutually constitutive.

190

3 ECKERT

As in the corporate context, the jocks strive to achieve cooperative, collegial relations with their hierarchical superiors; and as in the blue-collar workplace, the burnouts strive to protect the interests of their solidary subordinate category in the face of corporate interests. Jocks avoid confrontation with school personnel, preferring to negotiate their wishes, whereas burnouts reject negotiation with staff as the cultivation of favor at the expense of their peers. One class officer gave the following account of avoiding punishment through his handling of an incident in which he had been caught in a prank with some friends:

> If I have a chance to talk to an adult I can do good. I think that's one of the reasons I talked to [the principal]. I went down, you know, my friends got caught . . . and since they were caught I was caught, and so I went and turned myself in to him. And I talked to him for forty-five minutes. He didn't say one word. When I walked out of there he was like, "All right, no problem. We'll talk to you later." If he would have had to call me down I would have been suspended for three days, but see, since I talked to him, I told him all my views, I told him, "You know, I know your point," and I didn't say it was right, but I told him why I did it, why this, and you know. And it was great. And if I can, if I get my chance to talk with, you know, adults, I can usually do good, you know.

Because of their different understandings of the nature of the school institution and their different roles in the school, negotiation with staff has different meanings and effects for jocks and burnouts. Such negotiation underlines and strengthens jocks' collegial relations with adults, whereas burnouts have little to negotiate with because they are not engaged in corporate activity. Burnouts perceive two kinds of possible relationships with teachers: institutional and personal. Institutional relationships are, by definition, adversary, and friendly relationships with teachers are seen as potentially transcending the institutional. Although the personal may be used to manipulate the institutional, they do not perceive a direct connection between the two. Because burnouts perceive personal relationships as transcending rather than reproducing the institutional, a personal relationship with a teacher is seen as possibly overriding institutional strictures, and burnouts expect good relationships with teachers to yield special treatment or favors. But because many of the relationships with teachers that burnouts perceive as friendly are not based on institutional activity, burnouts are frequently disappointed.

Jocks value individual teachers to the extent that they have access to school resources, and to the extent to which they are responsive to student status in dispensing these resources. Teachers who are valued are incorporated as extensions of jock networks, and information about their corporate roles and their formal and informal relationships with other teachers and students becomes important corporate knowledge. Jocks know how teachers feel about each other, and they know about their formal and informal relationships, their relative power and authority, and so on. Thus, when they are seeking resources, jocks know not only the formal means to approach those resources, but the informal relationships that give life to the formal. This puts them in a position to broker, peddle influence, and manipulate—in short, to work the system.

The burnouts seek to extend their networks outside of school, gaining access to community resources, and they cultivate school-based networks insofar as those networks provide them with connections to the community. This includes connections to those school resources that facilitate their need for community participation and for the means to escape school into the community. Thus, for the burnouts, adult school personnel are valued for their usefulness to the nonschool enterprise, and to making it possible for burnouts to function in the school on their own terms. The vocational teacher who is providing guidance for the workplace, the adult who can help kids find jobs or other community resources, or simply the teacher who recognizes the burnouts' social networks is of value to burnouts. However, teachers who function in school gatekeeping roles (e.g., hall monitors, study hall teachers, vice principals, academic teachers) are of interest primarily for their usefulness in getting around that gatekeeping function. What burnouts want to know about those teachers is not what school resources they control, but how they function in their gatekeeping roles and what has to be done to move around them.

The teachers' use for the burnouts articulates well with the burnouts' use for the teachers. Because burnout cooperation does not enhance the teachers' status in the corporate hierarchy, and because their careers also depend on maintaining boundaries without and order within, teachers' relationships with burnouts center around boundary maintenance. Boundary maintenance involves keeping burnouts in school once they are there and keeping their nonschool friends out. It also involves keeping burnouts out with suspensions and expulsions, and with simply not discouraging burnouts from dropping out.

KNOWLEDGE MAKING

By virtue of their different relations to the school and the surrounding community, jocks and burnouts engage in quite different practices in relation to the acquisition of information and the construction of knowledge.

For the jock, school-based knowledge is important and school personnel are valued sources of information. The burnouts, however, do not generally consider the school to be a trusted source of relevant knowledge. One might trace the origins of this to burnouts' long-term knowledge practices. The most often quoted difficulty arising from age-heterogeneous networks is the early exposure to older behavior. As these children mature, their earlier contact with adult experiences and prerogatives (e.g., cigarettes, alcohol, drugs, sex, contact with the law, and the emotional difficulties that may accompany these) creates a need for certain kinds of information earlier than adults are willing to give it to them. Information about such things as drugs, sex, birth control, legal rights, and so on is generally not openly available from adults until they feel that children "need" (i.e., *should* need) it. This means that, from a fairly early age, adults cease to meet the most pressing informational needs of these children, and therefore these needs are being met, however inadequately, by older members of the peer group. Because of the relative autonomy and diversity of their networks, burnouts have access to a range of information from friends rather than from adults. Furthermore, with the complexity of peer relationships within a heterogeneous extended network, information does not come from a single source, and it does not come from an authority figure who can or would apply norms or strictures on the acquisition and use of that information.

Middle-class children's homogeneous network leaves its members dependent on adults for information of all kinds. But insofar as these children's developmental timetables correspond more closely (although rarely entirely) to adult norms, they will find adults to be more adequate purveyors of relevant information, and will not resent their ultimate control of it. In fact, the delivery of information may function in a system of personal rewards. In school, the teacher comes simultaneously to share the middle-class parent's role as appropriate and major source of adult-controlled information, and the working-class parent's role of arbitrary safekeeper and denier of adult information.

The right to make knowledge within the jock community of practice is related to hierarchical status—activities are organized from above, and they are given institutional meaning from above. Thus, just as curricular knowledge is handed down from above, so is extracurricular knowledge. The jock hierarchy plans and executes activities, but students who are not part of this hierarchy have little authority to initiate activities, and their access to participate in activities is a function of their access to hierarchical networks and information. Thus, for the jock and the aspiring jock, information has value within a hierarchical social system, and knowledge is made hierarchically. Not only is the value of a piece of information based on its hierarchical origin, but its use can serve the hierarchy. The rarity of a piece of information can contribute to its value because it represents hierarchical status, thus hierarchical status is enhanced by the hoarding, as well as the display and trading, of knowledge. The right to make institutionally legitimate knowledge within the school, then, resides within jock networks, and competition for the right within these networks is a fundamental component of jock practice.

For the burnout, functioning in an egalitarian network whose trademark is mutual support, information has no trading value. Rather, information, like cigarettes and personal possessions, is freely shared, and the act of sharing such information can establish both the authority and the good will of the sharer. For the burnout, an important aspect of information value is the degree to which it can provide solidarity and support within the peer network, and autonomy for the network as a whole and for its members. Information about things such as coping in the urban environment, resources for juveniles, drugs and birth control, and the legal system can provide such autonomy. The value of a particular piece of information, therefore, is not based on hierarchical origin, but on origin within a wider field of trusted sources.

The key to basing one's identity on a particular institution or community of practice is related to one's perception of the possibilities for making a mark there—for participating in the construction of community knowledge. The jocks are clearly in a position to make knowledge at the institutional level in the school. It is they who "represent" the institution, who plan and execute activities for the institution, and it is their corporate oneness that gives their knowledge the status of school knowledge. The relation between jock social hierarchies and corporate hierarchies also allows knowledge making within the jock community of practice to be institutional knowledge making.

The collegial relation between jocks and the school authority structure gives the former apparent ascendancy over the burnouts. Although jocks have no direct power over burnouts, they have a certain amount of control over the school through their access to the authority and resources necessary to affect the social and physical environments of the school. Jocks choose and organize social activities, modify the physical environment through posters and other decoration, and manipulate the daily schedule through the organization of programs that frequently affect class schedules. They also control community-level information—when they are the source (e.g., when the information concerns activities that they are organizing) or when the adults are the source (to whom they have privileged access).

TRAJECTORY

Because of the merger of the informal and the formal, daily participation in the jock sphere brings a gradual building of key knowledge about the people in corporate roles that make up the institution. As a result, jocks develop a rich and textured map of the structure and resources at the extracurricular center. This makes the corporate structure of the school quite transparent, and it affords jocks a kind of empowerment and mobility within that institution and beyond it in other institutions. However, jocks develop little knowledge of the workings of the local community or the margins of the school. The map that burnouts develop of the school is richly elaborated around the margins, and not at all elaborated at the corporate center. However, this map is an adjunct to a map of the community, and it facilitates invisibility in school and exit to the community. It does not carry much information about how the institution functions and views itself at its corporate center.

Understanding jocks and burnouts does not just tell us about school; the knowledge and forms of identity developed in these communities of practice are what constitute a long-term trajectory—the individual's knowledge of, and forms of participation in, institutions in general. These forms of participation extend from one institution to another—from high school into college on the one hand, and into the workplace on the other hand. Furthermore, what constitutes these as trajectories is the fact that they are embedded in knowledge—through engagement in social practice, people develop systems of knowledge and understanding that lead them to particular forms of participation in communities and institutions. Different understandings of such widely disparate things as what school is for, what constitutes appropriate conversation, what friendship is, and what constitutes public versus private information will result from participation in different communities. These different understandings will lead to differential success in other communities and institutions.

Both jocks and burnouts are learning corporate practice in school. The jocks are learning the practice of those engaged in the middle-class hierarchy of the workplace, whereas the burnouts are learning the practice of workers at lower echelon jobs. Marginal practice suits the purposes of those who prefer to remain unengaged in corporate practice—who prefer to develop a view of the workplace from the margins, as they have in school.

In an ethnographic study of insurance claims processors, many of whom had been burnouts in high school, Wenger (1991) found that the workplace was constituted in such a way that the claims processors could not see its larger structure or the meaning of their own work within it. According to Wenger, the opaque character of the institution limits their access to resources that would allow them to build an understanding of what their job is about within the corporation and the broader health-care system. One can see this orientation to the workplace as a continuation of the burnouts' forms of participation in the high school. The structure and meaning of the corporate workings of the workplace, like the school, is opaque to those who play marginal roles in it.

Knowledge is constructed within a social world in the process of mutual engagement in activity, and of mutual sense making in and around that activity. Identity is inseparable from the individual's opportunities to engage in activity and in the negotiation of knowledge with others. The forms of participation that one enjoys in high school are inseparable from one's knowledge of that institution and of the social world. This knowledge is inseparable from identity, and thus constitutes a powerful form of personal, group, and institutional trajectory.

REFERENCES

Bourdieu, P. (1977). *Aspects of a theory of practice.* Cambridge, England: Cambridge University Press. (Original work published in 1972)

Coleman, J. S. (1961). *The adolescent society.* New York: The Free Press.

Eckert, P. (1989). *Jocks and burnouts.* New York: Teachers College Press.

Eckert, P., Maxson, J., Newman, S., & Shethar, A. (in preparation). *The use and misuse of abstractions.*

Hollingshead, A. B. (1949). *Elmtown's youth.* New York: Wiley.

Lave, J. (in preparation). *Tailored learning: Apprenticeship and everyday practice among craftsmen in West Africa.*

Lave, J., & Wenger, E. (1991). *Situated learning: Legitimate peripheral participation.* New York: Cambridge University Press.

Wenger, E. (1991). *Towards a theory of cultural transparency.* Doctoral thesis: University of California at Irvine.

Wenger, E. (in preparation). *Communities of practice.* New York: Cambridge University Press.

CHAPTER ELEVEN

How Parenting Styles and Crowd Contexts Interact in Actualizing Potentials for Development: Commentary

Rainer K. Silbereisen
The Pennsylvania State University

Peer affiliations during adolescence tend to fall into two broad categories: peer cliques and peer crowds. Whereas the former are defined by mutual personal relationships among a small group of adolescents, most often manifested in frequent social interactions and shared activities, the latter are of a different nature. According to Brown (1990), crowds are "reputation-based collectives of similarly stereotyped individuals" (p. 177). More specifically, the affiliation among members of a crowd is not dependent on their actual interaction, but on common attitudes and behaviors ascribed by peers in school or from the neighborhood.

THE POWER OF CROWDS

Belonging to a specific crowd helps adolescents cope with a basic problem. In the views of others and in their own perception, they gain what one could call a "provisional identity." Although crowd membership may foreclose the search for authentic identity for some time, this comes at the advantage of an increased security about one's place among peers, and in relation to expectations from institutions such as the school. In Eckert's (chap. 10, this volume) view, different crowds in school even represent different "communities of practice"—meaning the totality of a group's own beliefs and actions vis-à-vis the institutional aims and constraints of schools.

I found this concept highly stimulating because it stresses that individuals within groups exert mutual influence on their behavior and development.

197

The community of practice represents an excellent instance of what one may call *codevelopment*. Furthermore, rather than simply relying on crowds as nominal categories, the concept helps to distinguish dimensions of individuals' shared beliefs and processes of joint activities within school contexts.

When contrasting the emergence of crowds, such as jocks and burnouts, as social class-based, differential reactions of the young to the middle-class-oriented schools, Eckert (chap. 10, this volume; 1989) is obviously dealing with overgeneralized, ideal types. In my view, the challenge of her approach for researchers less subscribed to hermeneutics is to translate the dimensions covered by the concept of *community of practice* into empirical assessments. This would allow one to get a handle on the differences in the features of crowds within the same social background.

Moreover, her study may help develop guidelines to improve the match between the corporate principles of schools and adolescents' needs. The latter reminds one of the Eccles et al. (1993) results concerning the gap between adolescents' growing demands for autonomy and classroom management following the transition to high school. Eckert's emphasis on groups and codevelopment seems to be a necessary complement to more individual-oriented approaches.

Brown and Huang (chap. 9, this volume) enriched the picture of crowds as potent contexts of adolescent development with a provocative new perspective. In their view, crowds have the capacity to "filter out" parenting influences that do not match the former's developmental agendas. If this were true, parents who want to counterbalance negative crowd influences would have little chance to succeed.

In the remainder of this chapter, I analyze this concept and the empirical evidence, I outline an alternative interpretation, and I suggest issues for future research. The following remarks on the mutual relationships among community, family, and school in the formation of crowds provide a backdrop for the discussion.

THE ROLE OF FAMILY AND SCHOOL IN CROWD FORMATION

To some extent, the membership of crowds cuts across all kinds of sociodemographic clusters. However, depending on the community, there are some major differences with regard to the relationships among crowds, families, and schools (Ianni, 1989). First, crowds tend to emerge around perceived social distinctions. In impoverished communities where differences in ethnicity or social class are the most salient organizers of life, students bring crowd affiliations tied to these social categories with them to school. In part due to teachers who presume a correlation between social background and school behavior, they are often assigned to the same slow tracks and they experience similar achievement histories. Given such conditions, crowd affiliations that originally evolved in the neighborhood as a response to the dire living circumstances have a good chance of being reinforced during the school day. However, shared neighborhood backgrounds and related activities foster their identities, not attitudes and behaviors that are supportive of the academic agenda of school.

In contrast, in mainstream communities that are relatively homogeneous with regard to social distinctions, crowd affiliations tend to emerge in school and, consequently, are more likely to be organized around school-related issues. Neighborhood-based crowds may be dominated by issues of survival in a hostile environment, such as protection against violence, whereas school-based crowds may be dominated by activities directly associated with educational success, quite often pursued under the supervision of adults. The fact that school plays a major role in their activities, however, should not imply that all such crowds are in favor of school.

Second, in their attitudes and behaviors toward academic achievement, neighborhood-based—compared with school-related—crowds tend to reflect different types of alignment between family and school. Families from mainstream communities raise their children with the belief that school success puts one on a trajectory toward a decent career and a fulfilled life. This orientation meets the institutionalized objectives and the traditional self-understanding of high schools. In contrast, families in socially divided and impoverished communities cannot empower their children with trust in the promises of education and the import of scholastic values. Consequently, a mismatch emerges between the beliefs held at home and the priorities of schools.

There is evidence from qualitative and quantitative studies that crowds represent a genuine context for the promotion of adolescent development (Brown, 1990). However, as the juxtaposition of the two family–community patterns and their particular types of crowd affiliations demonstrated, rather than standing alone, crowds interact with other contexts of development. More specifically, their influence on adolescents' positive or negative developmental outcomes may be counterbalanced or, alternatively, reinforced by experiences originating in other contexts, such as the family.[1]

FILTERING OUT—THE WAY CROWDS WORK

The prime aim of the Brown and Huang (chap. 9, this volume) chapter is to better understand this interplay between crowd affiliation and home. Their basic assumption is that parental influences on development, when in mismatch with the attitudes and behaviors of crowds, would be overridden by the crowds' impact. In other words, crowds were expected to "filter out" incongruent influences from parent–adolescent interaction.

---

[1]To avoid confusion between *adaptive* and *maladaptive* as labels for crowd contexts, I use *positive* and *negative* to characterize the quality of developmental outcomes.

To characterize differences in family contexts, they chose the quality of parenting styles. Drawing primarily on the dimensions of *parental warmth, demandingness,* and *encouragement of psychological autonomy* (Steinberg, Lamborn, Dornbusch, & Darling, 1992), parenting styles are classified as *facilitative,* reminiscent of Baumrind's (1991) authoritative parenting, *inhibitive,* and *normative.*

Concerning the likely impact of crowds, Brown and Huang categorize crowds in terms of their known affinity to conventional adult values and expectations as manifested in, for instance, their attitudes and behaviors toward school. This leads to the distinction among adaptive, neutral, and maladaptive crowd contexts. However, it should be noted that the maladaptive context, in particular, looks quite heterogeneous, lumping together ethnically defined crowds with crowds characterized by their proneness for problem behaviors. Thus, in light of my earlier remarks on the origins of crowd formation, rather different social backgrounds and life experiences seem to be represented in this group.

The Model Case

To better understand what the filtering function of peer contexts vis-à-vis parenting styles is meant to accomplish, I found it helpful to refer to the fictional data shown in Fig. 11.1, depicting differences in the crowd-specific relationships between parenting and outcome. The latter should represent increasing levels of the positive developmental outcomes studied, such as grade point average (GPA), the hours per week devoted to homework, or adolescents' achievement-oriented leisure activities.

Concerning neutral crowd contexts, Brown and Huang expect that "adaptive behaviors will vary directly with the degree to which parenting practices promote such behaviors." Consequently, a linear function is shown for the relationship between the levels of parenting and the amount of positive outcome. This neutral context serves as a frame of reference for the description of the other crowd-specific functions given later.[2]

---

[2]The definition of the parenting styles refers to individuals' levels on the dimensions of *parental warmth, demandingness,* and *encouragement of psychological autonomy.* With regard to likely developmental outcomes, facilitative parenting (one standard deviation above the sample mean in at least one aspect) was distinguished from inhibitive parenting (as before, but below the mean) and normative parenting (within one standard deviation of the mean). The functional relationships shown in the figure may not exactly correspond to what Brown and Huang had in mind. However, they should be close, and the authors are not very specific. I do not see why a curvilinear relationship among the neutral crowd would change the argument. Furthermore, I read their description of the interaction between crowds and parenting as expecting an asymmetry between, for instance, the enhancing effect of adaptive crowds with regard to facilitative parenting and their buffering effect with regard to inhibitive parenting (the latter effect is smaller).

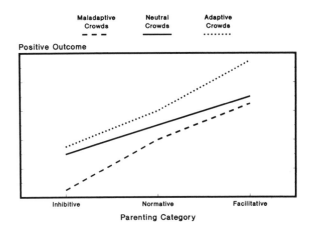

FIG. 11.1. Schematic representation of the "filtering-out" effect of peer crowds with regard to the influence of parenting styles. Shown is the (fictitious) level of positive developmental outcome as a function of the interaction between categories of parenting and types of crowds.

Following Fig. 11.1, adolescents affiliated with adaptive crowds, on average, show higher levels of positive outcome. This advantage is especially pronounced for adolescents experiencing facilitative parenting. Compared with the neutral crowds, however, the two other styles show only a slight benefit, with normative parenting still a bit better than inhibitive parenting. For adolescents affiliated with maladaptive crowds, the relationship between parenting styles and positive outcome is quite the opposite. Their average level of positive outcome is lower than among the neutral crowds. The disadvantage is especially pronounced for inhibitive parenting, whereas normative parenting is better, but still a bit worse than facilitative parenting. In summary, filtering out means that peer contexts have a salient effect above and beyond what is shown in neutral contexts if the kind of parenting and the quality of the context are in accord.

What about negative outcomes? In their theoretical formulations, Brown and Huang obviously refer more to positive than to negative developmental outcomes, such as drug use, delinquency, or time spent socializing with peers. However, by definition, the filtering principle should apply to these outcomes as well. For obvious reasons, one expects negative relationships between the level of negative outcome and the quality of parenting. Otherwise, the relationships are just a mirror image of those for positive outcomes.

Discrepant Results

According to Brown and Huang, the empirical evidence on their sample of almost 3,000 adolescents reveals that "contexts were successful in 'filtering out' . . . parenting influences that ran contrary to peer-group norms." Indeed, as shown in Fig. 9.1, for instance, adolescents affiliated with maladaptive crowds who experienced inhibitive parenting showed the lowest positive and the highest negative outcomes, and neither normative nor facilitative parenting could actually outweigh the effects of the crowd contexts.

However, the expected effect of the combination of facilitative parenting with adaptive crowds did not show up. More specifically, adaptive crowds did not reveal higher positive outcomes than in the neutral context, and the protective effect against negative outcomes was less pronounced than expected.

Because the results seem not to confirm expectations, conceptual issues need to be addressed. Beyond providing a label for a specific form of a statistical interaction, the notion of *contexts that work like filters* seems to be more of a metaphor than a substantive model of the processes of mutual influence between parenting and peer crowds. This is not to say that specifying such processes would be impossible or even difficult, but it needs to be done in substantive terms.

TOWARD AN ALTERNATIVE INTERPRETATION

The recent debate on the role that individuals—and in particular their genetic endowment—play in their own development has also led to a better understanding of the role of contexts (Bronfenbrenner, Lenzenweger, & Ceci, 1993; Scarr, 1993). In a nutshell, contexts provide opportunities for developmentally instigative experiences for those who can make use of them. Even the best contextual potential remains latent, however, if the individual either has no access at all or is otherwise not capable of actualizing the opportunities.

In this regard, many of the social interactions that parenting styles encompass share a special feature. Rather than representing simply one of many equivalent aspects by which family contexts can be characterized, parenting dimensions—such as efforts to engage family members in joint activities or to promote communication about experiences—exemplify what Bronfenbrenner, Ceci, and Lenzenweger (1993) called "proximal processes" (i.e., fairly regular, progressively more complex, reciprocal interactions occurring over extended periods of time between the individual and the persons, things, and symbols in the immediate environment).

Such activities, initiated by the individual, help to actualize the latent potential for the stimulation of positive development provided in contexts such as the school or peer groups. For the following predictions, Bronfenbrenner, Ceci, and Lenzenweger (1993) provided empirical examples from recent studies on children and adolescents. The relationship between levels of proximal processes and positive developmental outcomes is seen as negatively accelerated, not linear. An increase in levels of proximal processes at the lower end corresponds to a relatively large increase in outcome level, whereas the gain in outcome at the upper end tends to level off. Further, other circumstances being equal, the effect of proximal processes for positive developmental outcomes as described should be more pronounced in environments potentially advantageous for positive development. This is so because these environments offer more opportunities for academic achievement (or other positive outcomes), and thus a given level of proximal processes is likely to elicit more stimulating experiences compared with less advantageous contexts.

Parenting and Positive Outcomes

How can this view of the role of proximal processes be applied to the interplay between parenting styles and peer crowds, as studied by Brown and Huang (chap. 9, this volume)? Adolescents who consistently experienced facilitative parenting should be better suited than age mates to actualize the latent developmental potential for positive outcomes provided by the people, things, and symbols in their peer crowds; one only needs to think of the particular role models, accessories, and symbols that affiliation with a crowd implies, and that can convey particular experiences for the promotion of development. For the adaptive crowds, for instance, one would expect a gain in adaptive outcome with increasing levels of proximal processes. For lower levels, the gain should be steeper than for higher levels. Further, because the experiences provided by the other crowds are presumably less instigative for adaptive outcomes, adolescents affiliated with these contexts should also gain with increased proximal processes, but on a lower overall level, and the relationship with outcome should be less accelerated. Finally, all of this taken together, one would also predict an increase in the variance of outcome across levels of proximal processes.

   To compare these expectations with the results reported by Brown and Huang, I simply averaged their three variables measuring adaptive outcomes (see Fig. 11.2). As can be seen in the figure, there was increase in all crowd contexts, with gains a bit more pronounced in the adaptive crowd. Furthermore, as predicted, the variance in outcome among the crowds increased. However, the slope seems to be positively accelerated, with a steeper increase (especially for the adaptive peer crowds) toward higher levels, rather than at the lower end as postulated. This major deviation from the expected gives rise to further considerations concerning the parenting variables and their levels as assessed.

   First, the degree to which the parenting scales reveal differences in proximal processes varies. Concerning the dimension of parental warmth, for instance, the scale addressing parents' efforts to engage family members in joint activities addresses proximal processes, whereas the parental involvement

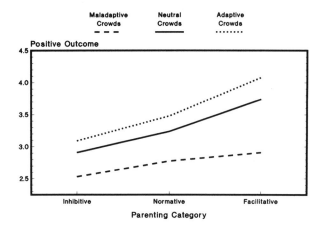

FIG. 11.2. A summary of Brown and Huang's (chap. 9, this volume) results
for positive developmental outcomes (see text for details).

scale is not particularly relevant. With regard to parental demandingness, the
monitoring scale assesses whether adolescents communicate with parents
about their friends and whereabouts, certainly an aspect of proximal processes; and the measure for joint decision making also refers to communication
about shared issues. The behavioral control scale, however, appears to be less
relevant. The items aimed at encouragement of autonomy, in turn, seem to be
only indirectly related to the actual interaction between adolescents and their
environment. Thus, the actual stimulation of proximal processes may have
been somewhat clouded by pulling together aspects of parenting that differ
in the degree to which they are conducive to the encouragement of reciprocal
interactions with people, things, and symbols.

Second, the categories of parenting were formed in such a way as to
keep enough subjects in each. Thus, facilitative compared with normative
parenting does not represent the extreme difference one would like to study
to understand the role of parenting in actualizing the potential for development. Consequently, it may be that the expected functional relationships
would have turned up at higher levels (and when utilizing more intermediate
levels) of facilitative parenting. Moreover, it is not quite clear whether the
category of inhibitive parenting represents the low end of the proximal
processes addressed, or whether it stands for a qualitatively different style.
This distinction turns out to be important in the following discussion of
negative outcomes as well.

Parenting and Negative Outcomes

Figure 11.3 shows the overall tendencies found for negative outcomes, again
formed by simply averaging the three variables for negative outcomes. According to the data, there was an increase in negative outcome in all crowd

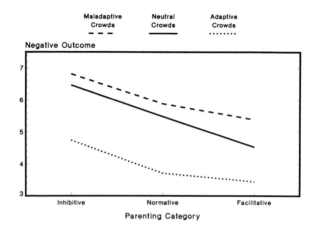

FIG. 11.3. A summary of Brown and Huang's (chap. 9, this volume) results for negative developmental outcomes (see text for details).

contexts as expected, but no particular acceleration among the maladaptive crowds could be observed. Furthermore, the variance did not increase with increasing levels of inhibitive parenting. Although this could be because the adaptive crowds were extremely low in maladaptation to begin with, another problem with the conceptualization of the parenting styles in regard to their interplay with crowds is probably relevant here.

In line with Bronfenbrenner, Ceci, and Lenzenweger (1993), interactions between adolescents and their environment that promote negative developmental outcomes are not simply characterized by low levels of proximal processes. Rather, what provokes the potential for problem behavior to become actualized are parenting styles that represent the opposite of proximal processes—the continued lack of reciprocal interactions with people, things, and symbols in adolescents' immediate environment. Examples include coercive and inconsistent parenting, which are experiences that rank prominently among the risk factors for delinquency described by Snyder, Dishion, and Patterson (1986).

In comparison, inhibitive parenting, as assessed by Brown and Huang, certainly does not cover the extreme of such experiences. Consequently, the predicted increase among the maladaptive crowds with inhibitive parenting was not present, and this is also why, in my view, the expected increase in the variance did not appear.

CONCLUSIONS

Crowds are powerful shapers of adolescents' experiences and development. Belonging to a crowd provides the security of a provisional identity. Furthermore, as a community of practice, crowds often provide adolescents

with opportunities to gain knowledge about the relationship between themselves and the institution of school—one of the most important developmental contexts for the development of a perspective on adult life (Eckert,
chap. 10, this volume).

However, crowds do not stand alone. They are intertwined with other
contexts, such as family and community. The chapter by Brown and Huang
is important because it addresses effects of interacting contexts—a line of
research central to ecological approaches on human development, and yet
only in its beginnings (Silbereisen & Todt, 1994). The proposed filtering
function of peer crowds with regard to parenting influences is a stimulating
concept, despite that it seems more descriptive than explicative, and despite
that the data do not confirm some major predictions.

In the latter respect, the alternative view of the interplay between parenting styles and crowd contexts is no better with the present data. However,
it helped to make a case as to why the data may not have complied with
expectations. What are the main propositions of the approach?

More important, it ascribes to peer crowds a role different from that which
Brown and Huang (chap. 9, this volume) seem to prefer. Accordingly, crowds
do not filter (reinforce or diminish, respectively) the effects of parenting
styles as a function of their match with the agenda of crowds. Rather, parenting styles indirectly help to actualize the potential for positive or negative
developmental outcomes, resting in the beliefs and activity patterns of the
different peer contexts.

Seen in this framework, the categories of facilitative and inhibitive parenting confounded processes of adolescents' interactions with their immediate environment with other less relevant aspects of parenting. Furthermore,
they represented too narrow a range of the respective styles. Consequently,
for positive outcomes, the extra benefit of facilitative parenting within adaptive crowds was less pronounced than predicted, compared with other crowd
contexts. A similar argument was made for inhibitive parenting in regard to
maladaptive crowds.

The view presented in this chapter implies some straightforward suggestions for future research. Measures of reciprocal processes of interaction
between adolescents and the people, things, and symbols of their immediate
environment need to be assessed in a way that represents the full range of
intensity and/or frequency. Instead of averaging across various parenting
dimensions when comparing the interplay between crowds and family, one
may want to analyze more content-specific, single aspects of interactions
between parents and adolescents.

The actualization of the developmental potential provided by contexts is
also a function of individual differences in adolescents' propensities, which
I could not discuss in this chapter. Although Brown and Huang take the
first step by comparing results across age groups and sex roles, an important

aim of future research would be to study the impact of person variables, such as locus of control or sensation seeking, which are known to influence how individuals approach contexts.

ACKNOWLEDGMENTS

This chapter is based on comments presented at a conference entitled, "Impact of Social Context on Adolescent Trajectories," held at the Pennsylvania State University in October 1992, and sponsored by the Program for Policy, Research, and Intervention for Development in Early Adolescence. The work on this chapter was supported, in part, by a grant from the German Research Council (Si 296/14-1,2).

REFERENCES

Baumrind, D. (1991). The influence of parenting style on adolescent competence and substance use. *Journal of Early Adolescence, 11,* 56–95.
Bronfenbrenner, U., Ceci, S. J., & Lenzenweger, M. F. (1993). *Nature–nurture reconceptualized in developmental perspective: Toward a new theoretical and operational model.* Unpublished manuscript, Cornell University, Ithaca, NY.
Bronfenbrenner, U., Lenzenweger, M. F., & Ceci, S. J. (1993). Heredity, environment, and the question: *"How?"* In R. Plomin & J. McClearn (Eds.), *Nature, nurture, and psychology* (pp. 313–324). Washington, DC: American Psychological Association.
Brown, B. B. (1990). Peer groups and peer cultures. In S. S. Feldman & G. R. Elliott (Eds.), *At the threshold: The developing adolescent* (pp. 171–196). Cambridge, MA: Harvard University Press.
Eccles, J. S., Midgley, C., Wigfield, A., Buchanan, C. M., Reuman, D., Flanagan, C., & Mac Iver, D. (1993). Development during Adolescence: The impact of stage-environment fit on young adolescents' experiences in schools and families. *American Psychologist, 48,* 90–101.
Eckert, P. (1989). *Jocks and burnouts: Social categories and identity in the high school.* New York: Teachers College Press.
Ianni, F. A. J. (1989). *The search for structure: A report on American youth today.* New York: Free Press.
Scarr, S. (1993). Biological and cultural diversity: The legacy of Darwin for development. *Child Development, 64,* 1333–1353.
Silbereisen, R. K., & Todt, E. (1994). Adolescence—A matter of context. In R. K. Silbereisen & E. Todt (Eds.), *Adolescence in context: The interplay of family, school, peers, and work in adjustment* (pp. 3–21). New York: Springer.
Snyder, J., Dishion, T. J., & Patterson, G. R. (1986). Determinants and consequences of associating with deviant peers during preadolescence and adolescence. *Journal of Early Adolescence, 6,* 29–43.
Steinberg, L., Lamborn, S. D., Dornbusch, S. M., & Darling, N. (1992). Impact of parenting practices on adolescent achievement: Authoritative parenting, school involvement, and encouragement to succeed. *Child Development, 63,* 1266–1281.

PART FOUR

APPROACHES TO INTERVENTION

Enhancing Contexts of Adolescent Development: The Role of Community-Based Action Research

Stephen A. Small
University of Wisconsin–Madison

My aims for this chapter are perhaps a bit different from the other chapter authors in this volume. I am interested in understanding how social context can impact adolescent trajectories, as well as how the research process can impact adolescent development. I present a model and program of research on adolescents that I have developed and implemented over the past 5 years in over 140 communities in Wisconsin and around the nation. I demonstrate how this research provides insight into the contexts and processes affecting adolescent development, as well as how the research process can bring about community change and actually impact adolescent development. The chapter is divided into two parts. First, I challenge traditional thinking about how research can and should be conducted, and the relationship between research and action in the area of adolescent development. To do this, I present an evolving model of research on adolescence that I have been developing over the past 5 years. Second, I present some findings that are based on data collected from this program of research. I demonstrate how such data can contribute to our current scientific knowledge base while also leading to actual, lasting impacts in a community.

A HISTORY AND OVERVIEW: COLLABORATIVE RESEARCH ON ADOLESCENCE

My role at the University of Wisconsin–Madison involves a significant amount of time devoted to outreach. In addition to my responsibilities as a researcher and on-campus teacher, my role as an extension specialist for the University

211

of Wisconsin Cooperative Extension Service involves educating the citizens of the state in the area of human development. The role of outreach and extension has a long and distinguished history at Wisconsin, having its roots in what is known as the "Wisconsin Idea"—the belief that the boundaries of the university are the boundaries of the state (Watkins, 1991).

Fairly early in my work with parents, professionals, and policymakers, I discovered a curious thing: Local citizens often did not give much weight to research findings, especially those related to social problems. For example, in my work on adolescent sexuality, many adults refused to believe that a majority of adolescents in their community were sexually active, and thus at risk for pregnancy and a variety of sexually transmitted diseases. Similarly, based on what they read in the media, most parents were more concerned about their children becoming crack addicts than them becoming alcoholics or injured in a alcohol-related automobile accident. Like any good academician, I sought out the research data to support my assertions. I shared with parents the growing body of research studies showing that teens are becoming sexually active at younger and younger ages, and that by the time the typical adolescent reaches middle adolescence, he or she is likely to be sexually experienced (e.g., Centers for Disease Control, 1991a, 1991b, 1992). I also shared the results of national studies showing that, among adolescents, the use of most illicit drugs was on the decline, but that alcohol was the drug of choice (e.g., Irwin, Bundis, Brodt, Bennett, & Rodriguez, 1991; Johnston, O'Malley, & Bachman, 1989). Surprisingly, I discovered that these findings were not very convincing to nonscholars. Local citizens often responded to the research findings with skepticism: "Those findings don't hold true here, our town is different"; "That may be true for some children, but not my kid." As a result, it was often difficult to get citizens to recognize, much less to motivate them to do anything about, the problems and challenges facing their young people.

These initial efforts at addressing adolescent issues were based on a traditional model of research and knowledge dissemination. In the traditional research and dissemination model, research knowledge is generated through empirical studies designed and implemented by researchers. Citizens are rarely involved in the process, except as objects of research and occasionally as recipients of the research information (see Fig. 12.1). This model suggests that there is a central body of knowledge that can be applied to most adolescents, regardless of their personal history, family context, socioeconomic status (SES), racial/ethnic background, or community context. Furthermore, it implies that this knowledge resides in some central place with those "who know," and that it is the responsibility of these knowledge brokers to funnel or distribute this information to those "who don't know." It suggests that all or most scientific knowledge resides with the researcher, and that he or she is responsible for both generating and disseminating it.

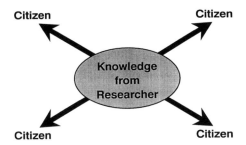

FIG. 12.1. Traditional research dissemination model: Knowledge resides centrally with the research expert.

Although this traditional method of research and knowledge dissemination is a relevant and useful approach for many situations, it also has significant drawbacks when one is trying to inform local policy and program development and educate citizens who are nonresearchers.

First, as previously noted, local citizens may not see the relevance of the research to their own community or situation if it has been conducted elsewhere. When research is based on samples that are not perceived as representative or equivalent in the eyes of the community, it is more likely to be viewed as irrelevant and not useful. In the language of social science, local citizens often question the external validity of research conducted elsewhere.

Second, a great deal of current social-science research is not meeting the needs of the nonresearch community. This is partly because the vast majority of research studies are designed and conducted for the benefit of other research scholars. Most empirical studies address issues that are of current interest to funding agencies or a small community of scholars. What is considered ground-breaking research is most likely an extension of recently conducted research, a test of a current theoretical model, or a methodological innovation. Such "cutting-edge" research may have little relevance to local policymakers, professionals, and other nonresearchers. The questions that nonresearchers want answers to are often different from the ones being asked by researchers.

Finally, little empirically based knowledge on adolescent development reaches nonscholars, such as parents, practitioners, and local policymakers, who could benefit from it. The primary (and often only) audience for social-science research is other scholars who are studying similar issues. Social scientists rarely make an effort to share their findings with the public, including the communities from which their samples are drawn. This situation is further exacerbated by the reward system in academia, which has become increasingly narrow, valuing basic research over all other types of scholarly activity (Boyer, 1990). Even when an effort is made to link research to action, it is often only a token overture. The findings are rarely put into a format that is meaningful to the nonresearcher (Rapoport, 1985; Small, 1990).

Toward a New Model of Research and Knowledge Dissemination

Although my experience working with communities (i.e., trying to help them understand the implications of relevant research) was initially frustrating, it eventually led to a new approach that has been surprisingly effective. I developed a program in which my students and I work with communities to help them conduct their own research on the needs and problems faced by local adolescents and their families. This program, known as the 77Teen Assessment Project (TAP), is based on a model of research and knowledge dissemination that I call the *collaborative research model*, or *community-based action research* (see Fig. 12.2). The roots of this approach can be found in the action-research programs carried out in the last two decades by a number of community and organizational psychologists (e.g., Argyris, Putnam, & Smith, 1985; Price & Polister, 1980; Rapoport, 1985), and in Bronfenbrenner's (1979, 1989) ecological model of human development. The aim of this collaborative research model is to contribute to both the practical concerns of local citizens and to the more scholarly goals of social science through collaboration.

The collaborative, ecological model of research, on which my work is built, is based on a number of assumptions. These assumptions address issues of both science and practice. First, the collaborative model assumes that there are benefits for both science and practice in gathering local data, rather than relying only on an existing empirical knowledge base. From the perspective of practice, local data are more generalizable to the community, and thus are more useful and relevant to local practitioners and policymakers. Moreover, as noted earlier, locally collected data are more likely to be perceived by citizens as having high relevance, and thus are more likely to be attended to and acted on by the citizens. From the perspective of science,

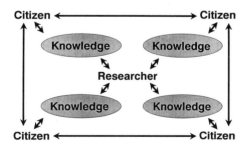

FIG. 12.2. Collaborative research model: The citizen and researcher work together to create knowledge.

locally collected data are valuable because it acknowledges that the human ecology of a particular community differs from the human ecology of other communities. Although there are certainly common processes that affect adolescent development across most community contexts, the ethnic, social, economic, and cultural histories of any particular community make it unique.

Second, the collaborative model assumes that there is value in conducting research that involves a collaboration between local citizens and academic researchers. In this approach, the research that is conducted is a partnership between the local citizens and the researchers from the university. Pursuing a collaborative relationship redefines the research relationship from one of *expert* and *learner*, or *researcher and subject*, to one of two partners developing a shared agenda. Citizens are no longer merely the objects of study, but partners in the process of defining the research. As a result, local citizens come to see themselves as partners in the process of acquiring knowledge, rather than just recipients of research knowledge. They are involved in choosing the questions that are asked, thus helping to ensure their relevance. In learning how to conduct research, they also come to better appreciate and understand the scientific process.

Finally, this collaborative approach assumes that studying adolescents from within the context of the community is both good science and good practice. From the perspective of research, studying adolescents in context is good science because these are the contexts in which adolescents actually live their lives. From the perspective of policy, studying adolescents in context is good practice because local policymakers (including parents who make policies in the home and influence community policies) are more likely to believe, and consequently use, information when they see it as reflecting their own reality. From the perspective of programs, studying adolescents in context is valuable because these are the contexts to which we hope our work will apply, and people are most likely to benefit from programs specifically tailored to local needs.

The Teen Assessment Project

The collaborative research project that I developed is known as the Teen Assessment Project (TAP). TAP is a community-based research and education program designed to help communities help local adolescents and their families. It does this by using a survey administered to local adolescents that "taps in" to their behavior and concerns, and the processes that can affect them. This information is then made available to local citizens who can solve the problems that the survey reveals. TAP empowers parents, policymakers, and youth-serving task forces and organizations with localized research-based information on which to develop community-based strategies, which enhance the contexts that support adolescent development.

In each community participating in TAP, a steering committee of local leaders is formed. The work of the steering committee is facilitated by county Cooperative Extension faculty. Typical steering committee members include school administrators and guidance counselors, health professionals, social-service administrators, local students, law-enforcement officers, parent-group representatives, youth educators, clergy, and representatives from youth-related task forces or committees. Sometimes the TAP survey is sponsored by an existing organization or coalition group.

Each steering committee begins by generating questions about their young people that they would like to have answered by a survey. Working with researchers from the university, survey questions are then either located or developed. This process results in a localized survey that reflects the interests, concerns, and needs of the community. Although every survey is unique, most share a common core. This core typically covers a range of issues relevant to adolescent health and development, including: sexuality, drug use, mental health, family relationships, perceptions of school and community, academic achievement, future aspirations, interactions with peers, and race relations. In addition to gathering information on the incidence of various adolescent behaviors, attitudes, and beliefs, the survey also examines possible risk and protective factors that may undermine or support adolescent development and well-being. Like scholars of adolescent development, local citizens who are concerned about young people want to know more than simply the incidence of certain behaviors; they also desire information that will help them identify contextual factors that may affect development, as well as knowledge about subgroups of adolescents who may be especially vulnerable.

The survey is administered to students in school by trained administrators who are often members of the TAP steering committee. In small school districts, we survey all students who are present on the day the survey is administered. In many cases, every student in all the school districts in a given county are included in the final sample. After the data are collected, they are sent back to the TAP project office at the university for analysis. The results are then returned to the local steering committee, which is responsible for disseminating the findings to the community.

SAMPLE IMPACTS AND RESULTS FROM TAP

A report and brief fact sheets featuring key findings from the survey are jointly written by the county extension agent, the local steering committee, and the university research staff. These materials are then distributed throughout the community. Much of the information is supplemented with findings from past research, as well as state and national norms for certain behaviors. The report features simple graphs and key findings, making it easy for nonresearchers to read, understand, and use. One of the most important aspects of TAP is that survey findings are shared with community leaders, educators, parents, and the general public (i.e., the findings rarely end up sitting on a shelf). Following each survey, the community-based steering committee disseminates the findings through a wide variety of methods, typically including a town meeting, forum, or press conference, as well as through presentations to various government, civic, professional, and parent groups. In addition, news releases are sent to the local media, where they are almost always used. It is our experience that local research findings featuring the concerns of community youth are always news.

A newsletter series entitled "Whose Kids? . . . Our Kids!" is sent to the parents of the teens surveyed. The newsletters feature data from the local survey, discuss current research-based knowledge about youth, provide suggestions on how parents and other adults can more effectively promote the development of young people, and include information on local services and resources that parents can access if they need additional support or information. Examples of newsletter topics include adolescent sexuality, mental health issues, alcohol and other drugs, and parent–teen relationships. Although the newsletter series has not yet been formally evaluated, we have heard numerous reports of how the newsletters have led parents to initiate discussions with their adolescents about the issues addressed in the newsletters. I plan to evaluate the newsletter in the future, examining whether the use of local data is more meaningful to parents, and whether it results in greater impact than newsletters based on data from national surveys or studies conducted elsewhere.

The survey findings are also shared with existing coalition groups, public and private agencies, and county or community task forces interested in the health and safety of children and adolescents. These groups often use the data to direct their planning and to convince policymakers, community leaders, and citizens of particular policy and program needs. To help communities fully use the results of the survey, we have developed a follow-up program entitled "Youth Futures." Youth Futures helps community leaders, including adolescents, design and implement a comprehensive community action plan based on the survey findings.

We try to share with each community the most important and interesting findings from the survey. Guidance about exactly which results are most relevant is often obtained from the steering committee, which is generally attuned to local issues and current policy concerns. Although many findings are similar across communities, there are often unique findings or anomalies that distinguish a community. Such findings would be highlighted in the dissemination. We try to keep the statistical analyses simple, generally providing descriptive statistics such as frequencies, cross-tabulations by grade and sex, and simple relationships between possible risk factors and specific behavioral outcomes. Most of the findings are presented in graphs and tables to help visualize the results. Figure 12.3 displays some types of information that are shared with the community via reports, presentations, and fact sheets. Figure 12.3a shows the rate of alcohol binge drinking in one county by grade and sex. The relatively high rate of binge drinking in this community led to the formation of a parent network, and resulted in pressure being put on the police department to enforce underage drinking laws and to be more vigilant about sales of liquor to minors. The data also served as the cornerstone of a grant proposal that resulted in new funds for a school-based alcohol-prevention program.

Figure 12.3b displays the percentage of students reporting thoughts of suicide in the past month in another county. The high rates of suicidal ideation in 9th-grade females, coupled with equally high rates of depressive symptoms, led the community group sponsoring TAP to further examine why depression and suicidal ideation were so common in this group of females. As a result, a national expert on teenage suicide and depression was brought in to lead a series of workshops for parents, teachers, and professionals. A peer-run student-assistance program was also developed in the schools.

Another community was concerned about racism. Figure 12.3c shows the percentage of students by racial/ethnic group who feel they are discriminated against by teachers. Note that one in three Native Americans and more than one in four African Americans feel that teachers expect less of them because of their race. Because these data come from a recently completed survey, no community action has occurred yet, but these findings were quite disturbing to many community leaders and parents.

Program Impacts

The previous examples are only a small sample of the kinds of findings that are shared with communities and the types of local action that occur as a result. As of May 1994, we have surveyed approximately 75,000 adolescents in more than 160 communities across Wisconsin and in more than a dozen communities in other states.

In the spring of 1994, an evaluation was undertaken to assess how the TAP program and the data it generated had been used. The evaluation plan involved contacting county extension agents in the 36 Wisconsin counties that had conducted the TAP project in the preceding 4 years. We also interviewed members of the local TAP steering committee, as well as agencies and individuals who had received a TAP final report or who requested a formal presentation of the survey findings. These individuals or organizations were

Had 5+ Alcoholic Drinks in a Row

(a)

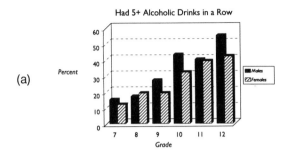

Thoughts of Suicide in Past Month

(b)

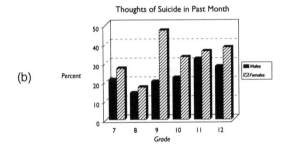

"Teachers Expect Less of Me
Because of My Race"

(c)

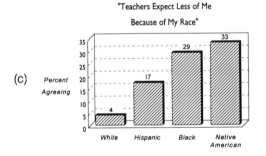

FIG. 12.3. Examples of Teen Assessment Project (TAP) findings.

then asked about the various ways they or their organizations used the TAP survey results, and whether they would attribute any personnel, program, or policy changes to the survey findings. The evaluation results reveal the innovative ways that local data about adolescents are used, and how they can lead to organizational and community change on behalf of youth.

I summarize the scope of our work to date, and then highlight some of the more interesting findings from the evaluation. I conclude by discussing some of the ways TAP has affected the role of county Cooperative Extension agents, and its potential for providing a new model for meeting the land-grant university/extension mission.

Scope of the Program

Information about survey findings has directly reached over 225,000 families via newsletters and fact sheets. Tens of thousands of others have learned about the concerns of and issues affecting local adolescents through the more than 500 published newspaper articles, the 275 radio and TV features, and the more than 425 face-to-face presentations given by county extension agents and steering committee members. These presentations have been given to a wide variety of professional, service, policymaking, and parent groups such as city councils, county boards, school boards, Optimist and Kiwanis clubs, teachers, drug-prevention coalitions, clergy associations, and parent–teacher organizations.

Organizational and Community Impacts

TAP results have been directly linked to at least 40 new school or community policies being enacted. For example, in several communities, respondents reported that curfew ordinances were enacted as a result of the data showing a link between parental monitoring and adolescent problem behavior. Several communities reported that the TAP findings led various community groups to pressure police to more strictly enforce underage drinking laws.

Thus far, the development of 37 new programs has been linked to the TAP survey. Examples include the development of school curricula to address issues such as sexual coercion and date rape, alcohol use, sexuality, and teen depression and suicide, as well as programs that provide support and education to parents. It has become commonplace for local parent-education programs to begin with an overview featuring local TAP findings. In addition, we have information from a number of school administrators indicating that the TAP findings helped them convince school boards of the need for personnel changes. For example, in one community, the principal reported that he was able to convince his school board to hire an additional, female guidance counselor after the TAP survey revealed that a majority of female students did not feel comfortable talking with the exclusively male school guidance staff. Data also show that over 112 grants have been funded, for a total of more than $750,000 using TAP data as evidence to support the need for the funding.

In addition, the TAP process has led to the formation of over three dozen community coalitions or task forces concerned with addressing some of the issues uncovered by the TAP survey. It is worth noting that, in a number of counties, the local steering committee brought together to direct the TAP project has remained in place after the survey was completed, transforming itself into a youth-at-risk or prevention task force.

The evaluation results are far from complete because we were only able to obtain information from a small number of potential data users. For instance, we did not assess the impact of the survey findings on the tens of thousands of citizens who were exposed to the findings via the thousands of newsletters, hundreds of newspaper articles, and dozens of radio and TV programs. We know the media have had an impact by the anecdotal stories we have heard over the years. For example, I discovered through a mutual acquaintance that a pastor in a small rural church had developed a series of Sunday sermons based on several newspaper articles on the TAP survey findings that had appeared in his local newspaper. Parents whom I have met at speaking engagements around the state have informed me that the TAP newsletter series has led them to take a variety of actions, such as becoming more involved in their parent–teacher organization, joining a parent group, and initiating meaningful discussions with their adolescent sons and daughters. Although these impacts come from anecdotal sources, and are difficult to assess in more systematic ways, they provide additional insight into the variety of ways local survey findings can impact the lives of citizens.

Effect of TAP on Cooperative Extension and the Land-Grant/Extension System

In Wisconsin, the TAP program has strengthened the role of county Extension agents, expanded their support base, and increased cross-program collaboration. County agents have indicated that the data obtained from the TAP survey have enhanced their leadership role in the community—by enabling them to identify local concerns and program needs, and by providing a valuable source of information sought by local and state leaders. Because agents are directly involved in the research process, they have been able to ask questions they deem important to their work and their constituents, thus giving new meaning to the Extension mission of providing research-based information. Agents also report that their involvement in conducting research has raised their status in the eyes of constituents and campus faculty, and has led them to become more equal partners in the tripartite land-grant mission of research, teaching, and service. The TAP program has also enabled agents to expand their audience from individuals and families to professionals, government, and community leaders, thereby strengthening their support base. Finally, in Wisconsin, local leadership for TAP has almost always been a team effort involving both the county Extension home economist and the 4-H youth agent. In some counties, the community resource-development agent has also been an active player.

At the state level, TAP has provided a way to involve the state land-grant university in applied research, which has direct benefits to the people of the state. For example, in Wisconsin, TAP has identified statewide concerns, provided research opportunities to university researchers who are often removed from the people of the state, and contributed to a statewide database on youth. As the TAP database grows, it becomes increasingly sought after as a source of information by state legislators, state agencies, and media professionals. For example, TAP data have been included in at least five legislative testimonies or bills initiated by state legislators.

The TAP program has been recognized as a potential new model for the execution of the land-grant/extension mission. Given TAP's use of the existing land-grant/extension system, its ability to integrate the extension and research missions of land-grant universities, its focus on important current issues, and its potential for community-wide impact, TAP has the potential to be a new prototype for how extension and land-grant universities can meet the needs of state citizens. The U.S. Department of Agriculture—Extension has recognized this potential by awarding the TAP program one of its 1992 Impact 2000 Awards for program impact, and by providing funds to nationally replicate the program. Currently, the TAP program is being replicated in 15 states.

ADOLESCENT DEVELOPMENT AND THE PROCESS–PERSON–CONTEXT MODEL

In this section, I present some research findings collected as part of a recently conducted TAP survey. I demonstrate that a community-based action-research program like TAP can produce data that benefit a community, as well as contribute to our scholarly body of knowledge about human development.

A central question for ecologically oriented scholars is whether a particular process operates the same for adolescents growing up in one set of circumstances as it does for adolescents growing up in another (Steinberg & Darling, 1991). Such a notion is consistent with Bronfenbrenner's (1989) process–person–context model. According to Bronfenbrenner, a developmental outcome is a joint function of the characteristics of process, person, and context. Developmental processes may operate differently in different environments or contexts. For example, as Steinberg, Dornbusch, and Brown (1992) recently demonstrated, childrearing strategies such as authoritative parenting appear to have different effects on school achievement for students of different races and for those residing in different racial/ethnic neighborhoods. Moreover, characteristics of the individual, such as intelligence, age, sex, and temperament, may also influence the operation of these processes.

Policymakers and practitioners are also interested in processes that may help explain a particular behavior, as well as subgroups of adolescents that may be particularly vulnerable. In an era of limited resources, policymakers and practitioners want to target their efforts toward individuals and families who are most in need and who are most likely to benefit. Like scholars of adolescent development, concerned citizens are interested in understanding the specific contexts and processes that can promote or undermine adolescent development.

The data to be presented in this section come from a TAP survey administered to a racially/ethnically diverse sample of adolescents (39% Hispanic, 51% non-Hispanic White, 8% African American, 2% Native American) who reside in a moderately sized city in the southwestern United States. The sample is composed of 2,218 adolescents who represent almost the entire population of students enrolled in Grades 7, 9, and 11.

Adolescent alcohol use and abuse has become a major concern for parents, educators, law-enforcement officials, and others interested in adolescents' well-being. Alcohol has clearly become the drug of choice among today's youth (see Comerci & McDonald, 1990). Adolescents' alcohol use can have short- and long-term consequences. While under the influence of alcohol, individuals are at greater risk for automobile and other types of accidents—one of the major sources of injury and death during adolescence (see Rosen, Xiangdon, & Blum, 1990). Frequent use of alcohol has been found to be related to a host of problematic outcomes, including: poor school performance, depression, school misconduct, delinquency, impaired interpersonal relationships, and early sexual activity (Barnes & Welte, 1986; Newcomb & Bentler, 1988; Office of Substance Abuse Prevention, 1987).

Although experimentation and occasional use of alcohol can sometimes be problematic, a bigger concern is with adolescents who use alcohol frequently and heavily. Binge drinking can affect adolescents' physical health and impair their everyday functioning, as well as lead to the host of problems noted previously.

Recent studies have indicated that unsupervised adolescents are more likely to use alcohol and other drugs (Richardson et al., 1989), as well as engage in other types of delinquent behaviors (Galambos & Mags, 1991). These studies have concerned themselves with the physical presence or absence of a parent or other adult, whereas a number of researchers have emphasized the importance of parental monitoring for the development of responsible behavior and the deterrence of potentially problematic behavior among adolescents (e.g., Patterson & Strouthamer-Loeber, 1984; Small & Eastman, 1991; Steinberg, 1986). Parental monitoring involves an awareness of a child's whereabouts, friends, and activities when the parent is not present. Monitoring does not require a parent to be with the child constantly, nor does it imply intrusiveness. Rather, parental monitoring entails an active interest, awareness, and involvement in a youngster's day-to-day life (Small & Eastman, 1991).

In our research, we assess parental monitoring by asking adolescents a series of eight questions about their parents' expectations and rules regarding their activities and whereabouts. Specifically, we ask about the extent to which parents (a) know the whereabouts of their youngster after school and at night, (b) show an interest in who the teen spends time with, and (c) discuss their child's social plans. Sample questions include: "I talk to my parent(s) about the plans I have with my friends"; "My parent(s) know who my friends are"; "If I am going to be home late, I am expected to call my parent(s) to let them know." Responses for each question range from *strongly agree* to *strongly disagree*.

In our research, we also assess the role of neighbors in monitoring adolescents' activities. Neighborhood monitoring involves the degree to which adults in the neighborhood or community are vigilant of adolescent behavior, and whether they are willing to report problematic, delinquent, or unacceptable behavior to parents (Small & Luster, 1994). Although there are limited empirical data on neighborhood monitoring, we would expect adolescents who live in neighborhoods where nonparental adults monitor the former's behavior more closely to be less likely to engage in delinquent and dangerous activities like binge drinking.

We assess neighborhood monitoring by asking teens a series of three questions about the extent to which they perceive adults in their neighborhood or community as vigilant of adolescent behavior and liable to report delinquent or unacceptable behavior to parents. Sample questions include: "Adults in my neighborhood keep an eye on what teens are up to"; "If I were to do something wrong, adults in my neighborhood would probably tell my parents." Like the parental monitoring measure, responses for the neighborhood monitoring questions range from *strongly agree* to *strongly disagree*.

For the present analyses, *adolescent binge drinking* is defined as having had five or more drinks in a row at least once during the past month. Following an ecological orientation, I employ a process–person–context analysis (see Bronfenbrenner, 1989). Specifically, I report on findings that address four questions:

1. Are parental and neighborhood monitoring related to the incidence of adolescent binge drinking?
2. Does the amount of parental and neighborhood monitoring vary across different contexts and by such person factors as the adolescent's age?
3. Are these proximal processes equally effective for adolescents of different ages?
4. Does the process of parental monitoring operate the same way—that is, is it equally effective—in different neighborhood contexts?

I begin by examining the simple relationships between parental and neighborhood monitoring and adolescent binge drinking. The first question is whether either of these process variables inhibits adolescent binge drink-

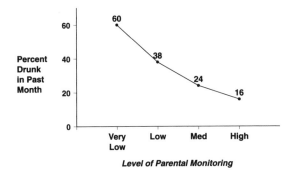

FIG. 12.4. Parental monitoring and adolescent binge drinking.

ing. For the present analysis, I divided the parental monitoring scale into quartiles, representing four levels of monitoring, and I divided the neighborhood monitoring scale into triads, representing three levels. The results of the analysis regarding parental monitoring are displayed in Fig. 12.4.

As Fig. 12.4 shows, parental monitoring is quite strongly related to adolescent binge drinking. Adolescents who fall into the bottom quartile are nearly four times as likely to report having been drunk as their peers whose parents are in the highest monitoring group. The greatest difference is between those adolescents reporting very low monitoring and those reporting low parental monitoring.

A similar, although slightly weaker, relationship is found between neighborhood monitoring and adolescent binge drinking (see Fig. 12.5). Adolescents who reside in neighborhoods where there is a high level of neighborhood monitoring are about half as likely as those living in neighborhoods with low neighborhood monitoring to report that they had gotten drunk in the past month.

As the previous analyses showed, both parental and neighborhood monitoring appear to be important processes in deterring adolescent binge drinking. But are these processes equally important for adolescents of all ages, or are they more critical for younger adolescents than older adolescents? This was tested by examining the two-way interaction between parental monitoring and grade as regressed on adolescent binge drinking while controlling for the main effects of monitoring and grade.[1] This interaction was significant ($\beta = -.216$, $t = -3.46$, $p < .001$), and reflects that parental monitoring is most effective in reducing adolescent binge drinking in the 9th grade and less effective in the 7th and 11th grades. Figure 12.6 graphically presents this relationship. Notice that the drop in slope is greatest for ninth graders. Similarly, the simple correlation between parental monitoring and binge drinking is highest for 9th graders ($r = -.47$) and lower for 11th ($r = -.36$)

---

[1] All other two-way interactions discussed in this chapter were tested in the same manner.

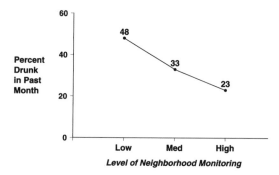

FIG. 12.5. Neighborhood monitoring and adolescent binge drinking.

and 7th graders ($r = -.31$). Using an r–z transformation to test whether these correlations differ from one another, we find that the correlation for 9th graders is significantly different from the correlations for 7th ($z = 2.62$, $p <$ .01) and 11th graders ($z = 3.50$, $p < .01$).[2] Put differently, these findings indicate that parental monitoring provides "more bang for the buck" during ninth grade than it does at the other grade levels.

A separate analysis was conducted to examine whether parental monitoring and binge drinking vary by grade level. Both parental monitoring and binge drinking were strongly related to grade. As grade level increases, there is a corresponding decrease in how closely parents monitor their children's behavior ($M = 3.11$ for 7th graders; $M = 3.01$ for 9th graders; $M = 2.91$ for 11th graders) and an increase in the amount of binge drinking exhibited (29% of 7th graders; 34% of 9th graders; 42% of 11th graders; see Fig. 12.6).

An analysis similar to the one run for parental monitoring was conducted to examine the relationship between neighborhood monitoring and binge drinking as a function of grade level. Once again, there was a significant interaction between grade level and monitoring ($\beta = -.236$, $t = -3.30$, $p < .001$), suggesting that neighborhood monitoring operates differently at different grade levels. Figure 12.7 graphically displays this relationship. Notice that the greatest drop in slope occurs for 7th graders and the smallest drop in slope for 11th graders, with 9th graders falling in-between. Correlations between neighborhood monitoring and binge drinking also support that effectiveness of neighborhood monitoring as a deterrent of adolescent binge drinking decreases with age (7th grade, $r = -.31$; 9th grade, $r = -.28$; 11th grade, $r = -.11$). The correlation for 11th graders differs significantly from the correlations for 7th ($z = 3.93$, $p < .01$) and 9th graders ($z = 3.34$, $p < .01$).

As with parental monitoring, neighborhood monitoring was also related to grade level. Adolescents in upper grades ($M = 1.66$ for 11th graders)

---

[2]All other comparisons between correlations discussed in this chapter are tested in the same manner using an r–z transformation.

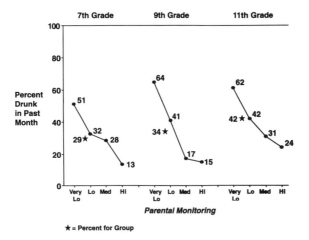

FIG. 12.6.　Parental monitoring and adolescent binge drinking by grade level.

reported less monitoring by neighbors than did adolescents in lower grades (M = 1.73 for 9th graders; M = 1.92 for 7th graders).

Thus far, neighborhood monitoring has been conceptualized as a process. However, this process can be thought of as defining a context. Neighborhoods where adults rarely monitor adolescents' behavior can be considered distinctly different contexts from neighborhoods where adults regularly monitor adolescents. The next analysis examines the relationship between neighborhood monitoring and parental monitoring. Specifically, does the importance of parental monitoring vary as a function of the level of neighborhood monitoring? On the one hand, it might be that parental monitoring

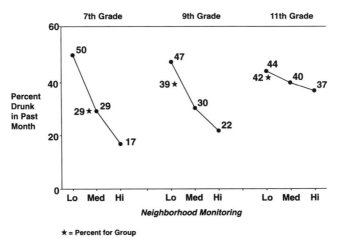

FIG. 12.7.　Neighborhood monitoring and adolescent binge drinking by grade level.

is more important in neighborhoods where neighbors do not keep a close watch on its adolescents. On the other hand, the positive effects of parental monitoring might be further enhanced in neighborhoods where other adults are also vigilant of teen behavior. For the analyses that follow, I only include ninth graders because we now know that the processes of parental and neighborhood monitoring work somewhat differently at different ages.

Figure 12.8 suggests that the process of parental monitoring may operate differently depending on the neighborhood context. The highest correlation between parental monitoring and binge drinking was found for those in the low neighborhood monitoring group ($r = -.35$), followed by those in the medium neighborhood monitoring group ($r = -.32$) and the high neighborhood monitoring group ($r = -.25$). However, the correlations were not found to differ significantly from one another. Nonetheless, the interaction between parental and neighborhood monitoring did approach significance ($\beta = .20$, $t = 1.65$, $p < .11$).

Breaking down the findings in Fig. 12.8 further, it can be seen that, for ninth graders, high parental monitoring is equally important regardless of the level of neighborhood monitoring, but that very low parental monitoring is more problematic in neighborhoods where nonparental adults are not vigilant. A chi-square analysis supports this conclusion [$\chi^2(2, N = 227) = 2.82$, n.s., for the high parental monitoring group; $\chi^2(2, N = 237) = 11.65$, $p < .01$, for the very low parental monitoring group]. The data show that, for ninth graders, very low parental monitoring is most detrimental in neighborhoods where nonparental adults do not monitor adolescent behavior closely. In contrast, in those neighborhoods where nonparental adults are

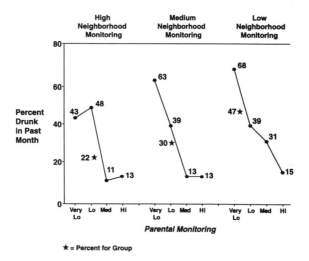

FIG. 12.8. Parental monitoring and binge drinking of ninth graders by levels of neighborhood monitoring.

vigilant of adolescent behavior, having parents who do not monitor closely is less problematic.

Conclusion

The analyses just presented provide strong support for the value of an ecological model, and they demonstrate how developmental processes can vary as a function of the context and the characteristics of the individual. In this particular case, we see that the processes of parental and neighborhood monitoring can play an important role in reducing the likelihood of adolescent binge drinking. We found that both the amount and effectiveness of these two processes varied by the developmental status of the adolescent and the context of the neighborhood.

These findings have important implications for how we conceptualize the forces that shape adolescent development. They also have valuable practical implications for policy and practice. Because both neighborhood and parental monitoring are factors that have a strong relationship to adolescent behavior, demonstrate some variability among individuals, and are concrete behaviors that could conceivably be taught to parents and other adults, they hold promise as factors that could enhance adolescent development.

From a practical perspective, these findings also provide insight into the contexts and developmental periods that would most benefit from programmatic interventions. For example, the data show that parental monitoring was most effective in deterring adolescent binge drinking during the ninth grade. Thus, if communities must target their programs, the data indicate that parents of younger adolescents—especially those with children who are approaching the ninth grade—would benefit most. Similarly, the findings indicate that parental monitoring is most important in neighborhoods where nonparental adults are not vigilant about monitoring teen behavior. Consequently, targeting parents in such neighborhoods could be an efficient strategy. Such knowledge could also be quite empowering to parents from low-quality neighborhoods. *How* parents monitor their children has an effect on the latter's behavior, and its importance for the children's well-being is actually enhanced. When parents know this, they should be both reassured and motivated.

COSTS AND BENEFITS
OF A COLLABORATIVE RESEARCH MODEL

A collaborative approach to studying adolescents in context has a number of benefits. These benefits accrue to citizens and scholars alike. From the community's perspective, collaborative research can be quite empowering and useful. Because the community has some influence over the questions that are asked, the findings are much more likely to be relevant, thus increasing the likelihood that the results will be attended to and acted upon.

A second benefit of the collaborative research model is that local citizens come to see themselves not as recipients of research knowledge, but as partners in the process of acquiring knowledge. In learning how to conduct research, citizens come to better understand the benefits and value of the scientific process. They also learn skills that can be applied to other community issues. Furthermore, understanding the value of research can improve public relations and the university's image, especially at publicly funded institutions.

In addition to these benefits to local citizens and policymakers, community-based action research can also be beneficial to researchers. Because communities that become involved in collaborative research are usually committed to the research and the resulting findings, they are usually willing to provide both financial and human resources to support the project. For example, TAP in Wisconsin is totally self-supporting. Involved communities underwrite all financial costs, and they provide an even greater contribution of human resources. Over the past 5 years, we have received nearly $70,000 in direct funding and approximately an equal amount in matching funds from participating communities. In addition, each county or community that conducts the survey must commit a minimum of 25 volunteer days from steering committee members, in addition to the 40–50 days provided by county extension faculty. It is my experience that communities are willing to provide funding and other types of support for research that they believe will be beneficial to them.

Another benefit of collaborative research for researchers is that it can provide access to subjects who are often difficult to reach. TAP has been invited into communities that are often difficult to access, such as Native-American adolescents living on reservations. In addition, we often get access to students, and are often accommodated by school administrators who recognize how the research will benefit them.

The final benefit of collaborative research is usually overlooked by most researchers who adhere to the traditional top–down approach to knowledge discovery. This is the failure to recognize that social-science research should be a reciprocal process that can be informed by current empirical and theoretical developments, as well as by the insights of parents, educators, and professionals who regularly interact with adolescents and their families. Furthermore, it is from adolescents and those who live and work with them that emerging issues, social problems, and policy concerns usually arise. If scholars want to be at the cutting edge of adolescent life, they should look to each other, as well as to the young people they wish to understand. As Bronfenbrenner (1979) noted in his seminal work on the study of the ecology of human development, "basic science needs public policy even more than public policy needs basic science" (p. 8).

Limitations of Collaborative Research

Although I am a strong believer in the value of collaborative research for understanding and promoting adolescent development in context, such an approach is not without its drawbacks. A primary limitation is that the researcher must give up some control of the project. Unlike traditional approaches to research, the collaborative researcher must share some power with the citizens with whom he or she is working. This involves being sensitive to community needs and norms, and ensuring that the community's as well as the researcher's questions are addressed.

A second limitation is that there is a tendency for nonresearchers to ask questions about *many* issues, rather than a few. In contrast, researchers are more often interested in examining fewer issues, but in greater depth. Thus, tension between the depth versus breadth of a research study is apt to arise in collaborative research with communities.

Finally, when working with any group of people, there will inevitably be differences of opinion and values. For example, when addressing such important and potentially "charged" issues as adolescent sexuality and mental health, these differences can lead to lengthy debates and heated disagreements. The political side of collaborative research is one of its greatest challenges *and* greatest strengths because it is through such debate and dialogue that politics are transformed into community action on behalf of citizens. All of these factors make the collaborative research model more complicated and time-consuming than traditional approaches to social-science research.

CONCLUSION

Although I hope this chapter makes a convincing case for the value of community-based, collaborative research and provides a challenge to how researchers conduct research, I do not advocate that all research on adolescents be collaborative. Rather, I argue for greater balance in our research endeavors. Like the ongoing tensions between quantitative versus qualitative research, and basic versus applied research, I believe there is little to be gained by arguing that one is better than the other. What is needed is a greater balance between traditional and collaborative approaches to research, and an increased sensitivity to the needs and concerns of those we study. If we are interested in understanding how contexts can impact adolescent trajectories, and ultimately the more practical but challenging problem of enhancing the contexts that affect adolescents, we need to give more attention to how research can lead to action, as well as to the value of collaboratively designing research with the citizens who can benefit from it.

REFERENCES

Argyris, C., Putnam, R., & Smith, D. (1985). *Action science*. San Francisco: Jossey-Bass.

Barnes, G., & Welte, J. (1986). Adolescent alcohol abuse: Subgroup differences and relationship to other problem behaviors. *Journal of Adolescent Research, 1*, 79–94.

Boyer, E. (1990). *Scholarship reconsidered: Priorities of the professoriate*. Princeton, NJ: Princeton University Press.

Bronfenbrenner, U. (1979). *The ecology of human development*. Cambridge, MA: Harvard University Press.

Bronfenbrenner, U. (1989). Ecological systems theory. *Annals of Child Development, 6*, 187–249.

Centers for Disease Control. (1991a). Perceptions of sexual behavior: Findings from a national sex knowledge survey, United States, 1989. *Morbidity and Mortality Weekly Report, 39*, 255.

Centers for Disease Control. (1991b). Premarital sexual experience among adolescent women, United States, 1970–1988. *Morbidity and Mortality Weekly Report, 39*, 929.

Centers for Disease Control. (1992). Sexual behavior among high school students. *Morbidity and Mortality Weekly Report, 40*, 885–888.

Comerci, G., & McDonald, D. I. (1990). Prevention of substance abuse in children and adolescents. *Adolescent Medicine: State of the Art Reviews, 1*(1), 127–143.

Galambos, N. L., & Mags, J. L. (1991). Out of school care of young adolescents and self-reported behavior. *Developmental Psychology, 27*, 644–655.

Irwin, C. E., Bundis, C. D., Brodt, S. E., Bennett, J. A., & Rodriguez, R. Q. (1991). *The health of America's youth: Current trends in health status and utilization of health services*. San Francisco: University of California at San Francisco.

Johnston, L. D., O'Malley, P. M., & Bachman, J. G. (1989). *Drug use, drinking and smoking: National Survey results from high school, college and young adult population, 1975–1988*. Rockville, MD: National Institute on Drug Abuse, U.S. Department of Health and Human Services, DHHS Publication No. (ADM) 89-1638.

Newcomb, M., & Bentler, P. (1988). *Consequences of adolescent drug use: Impact on the lives of young adults*. Beverly Hills, CA: Sage.

Office of Substance Abuse Prevention. (1987). *Literature review on alcohol and youth*. Rockville, MD: The National Clearinghouse for Alcohol and Drug Information, Department of Health and Human Services (RPO 703).

Patterson, G., & Strouthamer-Loeber, M. (1984). The correlation of family management practices and delinquency. *Child Development, 36*, 1299–1307.

Price, R., & Polister, P. (1980). *Evaluation and action in the social environment*. New York: Academic Press.

Rapoport, R. N. (1985). Research and action. In R. N. Rapoport (Ed.), *Children, youth and families: The action-research relationship* (pp. 1–25). New York: Cambridge University Press.

Richardson, J. L., Dwyer, K., McGuigan, K., Hansen, W. B., Dent, C., Johnson, C. A., Sussman, S. Y., Brannon, B., & Flay, B. (1989). Substance abuse among eighth grade students who take care of themselves after school. *Pediatrics, 84*, 556–566.

Rosen, D. S. Xiangdon, M., & Blum, R. W. (1990). Adolescent health: Current trends and critical issues. *Adolescent Medicine: State of the Art Reviews, 1*(1), 15–31.

Small, S. A. (1990). *Preventive programs that support families with adolescents*. Washington, DC: Carnegie Council on Adolescent Development.

Small, S. A., & Eastman, G. E. (1991). Rearing adolescents in contemporary society: A conceptual framework for understanding the responsibilities and needs of parents. *Family Relations, 40*, 455–462.

Small, S. A., & Luster, T. (1994). Adolescent sexual activity: An ecological, risk-factor approach. *Journal of Marriage and the Family, 56*, 1–14.

Steinberg, L. (1986). Latchkey children and susceptibility to peer pressure: An ecological analysis. *Developmental Psychology, 22,* 433–439.

Steinberg, L., & Darling N. (1991, May). *The broader context of social influence in adolescence.* Paper presented at an international conference on "The Development of Motivational Systems in Adolescence: Interindividual differences and Contextual Factors in Interaction," German Research Foundation and the University of Geissen, Schloss Rauischholzhausen, Germany.

Steinberg, L., Dornbusch, S., & Brown, B. (1992). Ethnic differences in adolescent achievement: An ecological perspective. *American Psychologist, 47,* 723–729.

Watkins, B. L. (1991). A quite radical idea: The invention and elaboration of collegiate correspondence study. In B. L. Watkins & S. J. Wright (Eds.), *The foundations of American distance education: A century of collegiate correspondence study* (pp. 1–36). Dubuque, IA: Kendall/Hunt.

CHAPTER THIRTEEN

Community-Based Action Research and Adolescent Development: Commentary

Aaron T. Ebata
University of Illinois

The chapter by Small (chap. 12, this volume) describes the Teen Assessment Project (TAP)—a collaborative process that makes citizens, practitioners, and researchers partners in a research effort that attempts to (a) meet the practical concerns of communities, and (b) contribute to the scholarly goals of social science. Small contends that this community-based action-research approach has four positive consequences. Specifically, it can:

- increase the likelihood of community action by increasing the community's interest and investment in the research process;
- contribute to more enlightened policies and program planning;
- provide an opportunity for educating citizens, practitioners, and researchers; and
- contribute to broadening our understanding of adolescents and their contexts of development.

In this chapter, I briefly comment on each of these points by providing additional examples and pointing out some of the strengths and limitations of Small's approach. I also discuss some findings from the TAP, and comment on the opportunities and challenges this approach provides in contributing to our knowledge of communities and their effects on adolescent development.

IMPLICATIONS FOR COMMUNITY INVESTMENT
AND ACTION

What are the needs of youth in a community? Are students worried about violence, acquired immune deficiency syndrome (AIDS), or future employment? Should parents be worried about sex, drugs, or satanism? The answers to these questions might be clear if there were community-based data on the concerns and behaviors of youth. Although public concern might be common, it is rare that communities systematically collect information from youth to guide programs or policies.

Although there are some methods available to communities for conducting needs assessments (e.g., Blyth & Bensen, 1992; Blyth & Roehlkepartain, 1993; Dubow, Lovko, & Kausch, 1990), the TAP described by Small is different. In this approach, the community is required to take a more proactive, collaborative role in "owning" the process as well as the product. The project depends on (and encourages) the mobilization of the community to identify the issues to be studied, and ultimately to use the data gathered through its efforts. The community asks questions that address their concerns, and their youth get an opportunity to make their thoughts, feelings, and concerns known.

It makes intuitive sense that communities would feel greater investment in a process that they initiate and help develop. Small suggests two reasons why this might be so. The first is that local data are more "believable" because they are relevant and meaningful, and thus have greater potential for impact than results derived from studies conducted somewhere else. The second is that communities are more likely to mobilize efforts to address the needs of youth by participating in the TAP process. Although plausible, it would be useful to know whether these claims are justified. We need to know whether local data *are* more effective in changing the perceptions or beliefs of people who may have strong preconceptions and beliefs. For example, are newsletters and programs that use local data more effective than those that use more general sources of data?

Just having information on youth needs may not ensure appropriate community action. For example, Dubow et al. (1990) described a research effort initiated by a request for assistance from a community task force. Data on the kinds of problems adolescents experience, the kinds of help they seek, and the reasons for not seeking help were collected and presented to the task force. According to Dubow (personal communication, March 26, 1993), the only community response was the organization of a 1-day "resource fair" to increase teens' awareness of local agencies that provide resources for youth. The empirical evidence on community response is sparse, and more research on this issue appears warranted.

IMPLICATIONS FOR PROGRAM PLANNING AND POLICY

Small reports that the TAP process has resulted in many communities initiating policy or programs for the welfare of youth. It is clear that this kind of effort can serve as a useful needs-assessment tool for local communities. But what are the effects of the process and resulting programs? For example, Small reports that, in most communities that have conducted the TAP survey, citizens "are more aware of the concerns facing local young people and their families and are more willing to do something about them," and that numerous programs and efforts have resulted. But the empirical questions remain: Does the program raise awareness among local citizens? Is action more likely using this process? How are communities that participate in the process different from those that do not? What are the short- and long-term impacts of such a program on a community and its youth? These questions are difficult to answer, but evaluations are possible.

The TAP sets the stage for follow-up surveys that could prove useful in evaluating community prevention efforts, as well as contributing to knowledge about adolescent development. Small does not report any follow-up studies in communities that have conducted TAP surveys, but clearly such information would be valuable.

IMPLICATIONS FOR EDUCATION

The TAP provides opportunities for the education of community members, practitioners, parents, and researchers. Participation in the process may give community members and parents (or at least those who are involved in the process) a greater knowledge and appreciation of research. It opens the door for discussions about the benefits and limitations of research, and provides a link for understanding how results from research conducted in other locations can be useful and important.

The process also provides opportunities for the continuing education of practitioners. Being part of the research process from the initial stages, and having the responsibility for interpreting and presenting results to the community, provides an "apprenticeship" experience that is crucial in developing knowledge and appreciation of the research process. From our own efforts in Illinois, we find that these experiences are often helpful in reducing the tendency of extension field staff to reject research findings in favor of personal experience, or to accept without question statistics or statements found in secondary sources or the popular media.

Small also uses the process as an opportunity for parent education. A series of newsletters on different topics summarizes findings from studies in each community, compares these findings to those found in the literature, and discusses topics that are of interest to parents. The results also provide parents with information of which they may not have been aware (or chose not to pay attention to). For example, in our own research, we have found that parents greatly underestimate two of the most common sources of difficulties for their children: school pressures/concerns and conflict with siblings.

Finally, the process makes it more likely that researchers are seen as contributors to a school or community's interests, rather than being self-serving academicians "at the university." In my own work, I have found that researchers often do not leave good impressions with schools or with parents. Research participants often feel "used" and see the research process as something that only benefits the researcher. In the TAP process, youth and parents see a return on their investment in terms of newsletters and publicized efforts resulting from the survey. This ethic of "leaving something behind," or returning something of value to research participants, is one that can (and perhaps should) be part of any community-based research effort.

IMPLICATIONS FOR THE STUDY OF ADOLESCENTS AND COMMUNITIES

How can the TAP process contribute to our understanding of adolescents and communities? As Small suggests, it provides the opportunity to use specific conditions in local communities as crucibles for hypothesis testing and refinement—to see if general processes operate similarly under different conditions, to identify conditions under which certain processes and outcomes are most likely to occur, or to generate new hypotheses. The use of local data that might be compared to data from other locations may give us a better understanding of the effects of particular contexts of development, and of the processes within contexts that may explain these effects (Bronfenbrenner, Moen, & Garbarino, 1984).

To do so, however, requires having comparable data on different locations. One approach would be to conduct large, collaborative, multisite studies using comparable measures (e.g., the MacArthur Network on Successful Adolescent Development in High Risk Neighborhoods; Jessor, 1993). The TAP model offers an alternative to large, multisite studies. If comparable sampling procedures and measures are used, data from different community studies might be aggregated and used to study context effects (e.g., Blyth & Bensen, 1992; Blyth & Roehlkepartain, 1993). Although there are some advantages to this model, there are limitations as well. These limitations involve selection factors and the comparability of data gathered at different points in time.

Although TAP has been implemented in various locales, the sample of communities is still primarily midwestern and largely small town or rural (a characteristic shared with work by Blyth and his colleagues). How generalizable are the results of TAP community studies to other communities? One could argue that communities willing to go through the TAP process may be quite different from other communities in important ways. The mobilization of interest and effort may be a result of: (a) perceptions of great need by certain community forces; and/or (b) a certain level of concern, interest, and motivation among a "critical mass" of individuals in a community. We need to get a sense of whether communities that participate in the TAP process are representative of other communities, or whether (and how) they might be different.

Although combining data across communities to make community comparisons may provide an important source of information, care must be taken in combining results of surveys that may have been administered at different times. It is possible that some data types may be susceptible to historical trends or the effects of social change (e.g., patterns of drug use). If data from different communities are not collected during a comparable time period, there may be a confound between location and time—differences in certain indicators (e.g., drug use) might reflect period effects as well as community differences.

What Can the Process Tell Us About Context Effects?

Small illustrates the use of TAP data in understanding what may be neighborhood effects. For example, he shows that, although parental and neighborhood monitoring are significantly related to binge drinking, parental monitoring seems to be particularly important when there are low levels of neighborhood monitoring.

However, the methods and analytic procedures confound possible person effects with neighborhood effects. In aggregating perceptions about neighborhoods across youth from different neighborhoods, it is not clear whether we are seeing the effects of neighborhoods or persons. We assume that people who have similar perceptions occupy similar neighborhoods—that their perceptions accurately reflect some neighborhood conditions or at least some neighborhood boundaries. But the analyses do not differentiate youth from different neighborhoods.

It is likely that there is variation among people within neighborhoods—that there is a "non-shared community environment" (Ebata, 1993). Just as siblings within a family may experience differential treatment (leading to different perceptions of the same family), individuals within communities may experience different communities by the way they select experiences, evoke responses from others, and interpret their experiences (Caspi, chap. 4, this volume). They may also have differential access to risks and resources in the community because of their income or education, location of their residence, availability of transportation, and socially imposed barriers (e.g., discrimination).

A first step in disentangling person effects from context effects would be to see how perceptions of the neighborhood are actually distributed across neighborhoods. How much congruence (or variance) is there among adolescents who live in a certain community or neighborhood? Is there greater variance among neighborhoods than within neighborhoods? Is there something different about adolescents who have different perceptions of their parents and neighborhoods, or are neighborhoods actually different? We might expect variability across individuals in similar circumstances, and this might reflect factors that may contribute to our understanding of risk and resilience, and the interaction between persons and environments.

What Can the Process Tell Us About Development?
Developmental Trends, Context Changes,
or Cohort Differences?

As mentioned earlier, any effort to examine how contexts affect development must consider the possible confounding of age, cohort, and history (Schaie, 1965), as well as community effects. Disentangling, or at least understanding, the effects may be even more important for communities in making programmatic decisions. The TAP process can be fully realized if regular follow-up data on successive cohorts of youth can be collected to examine trends in variables of interest. This would be especially helpful in evaluating programmatic efforts by providing information on historical changes that may be due to community interventions. For small communities, having data on successive cohorts over time, and having access to comparative data (from other communities), can be especially helpful in interpreting findings and making recommendations based on these findings.

In a recent survey of a small rural school (School A), my students and I found a number of significant differences between seventh and eighth graders. For example, eighth graders reported lower grades, lower levels of academic competence, and more negative perceptions of teachers. They were also more likely to cite school work and school pressures as major sources of difficulty in their lives. These differences were not particularly surprising, given the literature on developmental and contextual changes during early adolescence. However, other data from the students, parents, and teachers led us to suspect that these differences reflect cohort differences, rather than the results of developmental or contextual changes. The eighth graders seemed to have had more difficulties in school than their seventh-grade schoolmates in previous years as well, and may be a particularly troubled group of students.

The attribution of differences to developmental changes or the consequences of contextual changes (e.g., teachers having higher expectations and tougher grading practices) might lead to prevention efforts centered around the seventh- to eighth-grade transition. The attribution of differences to preexisting and continuing cohort differences might lead to special attention being paid to that particular eighth-grade cohort across time.

We were about to conclude that this eighth-grade cohort might be at "greater risk" for subsequent difficulties when we completed analyses of data from a neighboring school (School B). The results from School B forced us to temper our conclusions about School A. There were no differences between seventh and eighth graders in School B. Furthermore, the seventh and eighth graders in School B were similar to the eighth graders in School A. The "unusual" eighth graders in School A suddenly seemed "normal" when compared with seventh and eighth graders from another school. In fact, it was now the seventh graders in School A that seemed "unusual," albeit in a more positive way.

Window for Intervention or Evaluation?

Small provides another opportunity to examine how differences in assumptions and interpretations might influence application. In his chapter, he reports that there is a stronger correlation between parental monitoring and binge drinking among ninth graders, compared with seventh and eleventh graders. He suggests that prevention efforts might be more effectively targeted during that period because the effects of parental monitoring seem to be "more effective in deterring adolescent binge drinking."

There may be several explanations for the higher correlation between monitoring and binge drinking in the ninth grade, and our assumptions about these explanations may influence decisions regarding prevention programming. One possibility is that the effects of parental monitoring are greater during the ninth grade than at other times, as Small suggests, and that there is something "special" that happens in ninth grade that is particularly meaningful.

Another possibility is that ninth grade is merely a better "window" on a phenomenon that is the result of processes that have been in place for a number of years. The larger correlations may be due to greater variability in binge drinking (or monitoring) during the ninth grade.

If the interpretation is that "something" is happening in ninth grade that makes parental monitoring provide "more bang for the buck," it might be reasonable to target that time period for prevention efforts. However, if the interpretation is that ninth grade is an especially good window for viewing the results of ongoing developmental processes, one might conclude that ninth grade might be an important time to *evaluate* prevention efforts, rather than to *initiate* them. In either case, one could argue for earlier intervention so that parents will be ready to monitor effectively by the ninth grade—when it might be especially important, or when the effects of monitoring would be most apparent.

Although these two explanations can be explored with further analysis of existing data (e.g., comparing variances in binge drinking and monitoring across grade levels), longitudinal data on several cohorts would be necessary to adequately address issues that may be important for prevention programming and evaluation, as well as for understanding adolescent development.

CONCLUSION

The TAP is an excellent example of how a community-based action-research approach can enhance the community context for youth, as well as our understanding of how community contexts influence adolescent development. In his chapter, Small describes some of the potential benefits to this approach. Although there are some limitations and challenges in using this approach, there are also methods to ensure that it can be a rich and fruitful model for how research can inform and be informed by application.

REFERENCES

Blyth, D. A., & Bensen, P. L. (1992, March). *Communities as contexts for adolescents: Are some healthier than others?* Paper presented at the biennial meeting of the Society for Research on Adolescence, Washington, DC.

Blyth, D. A., & Roehlkepartain, E. C. (1993). *Healthy communities, healthy youth.* Minneapolis, MN: The Search Institute.

Bronfenbrenner, U., Moen, P., & Garbarino, J. (1984). Child, family, and community. In R. Parke (Ed.), *Review of child development research: The family* (Vol. 7, pp. 283–328). Chicago: The University of Chicago Press.

Dubow, E. F., Lovko, K. R., & Kausch, D. F. (1990). Demographic differences in adolescents' health concerns and perceptions of helping agents. *Journal of Clinical Child Psychology, 19,* 44–45.

Ebata, A. T. (1993, November). *Creating contexts for development: Adolescents' and parents' constructions of school and community in rural settings.* Paper presented at the annual meeting of the National Council on Family Relations, Baltimore, MD.

Jessor, R. (1993). Successful adolescent development among youth in high-risk settings. *American Psychologist, 48,* 117–126.

Schaie, K. W. (1965). A general model for the study of development problems. *Psychological Bulletin, 64,* 92–107.

PART FIVE

FUTURE DIRECTIONS

CHAPTER FOURTEEN

Commentary:
On Developmental Pathways and
Social Contexts in Adolescence

Laurence Steinberg
Temple University

The chapters in this volume may be viewed as a collective representation of our thinking about the study of adolescent development in the 1990s. Although the various authors approach the study of adolescence from different theoretical perspectives, and with an eye toward explaining different phenomena, each of the chapters shares two concerns: (a) an interest in studying adolescent development within the broader ecology in which young people come of age (hence the emphasis on *context* throughout the volume); and (b) an interest in looking at adolescence not as a discontinuous period, but as inherently linked to what precedes and follows it developmentally (hence the emphasis on *pathways*). The first theme reflects the profound influence of Bronfenbrenner (1979) and other human ecologists on the study of adolescence. The second theme reflects the important contributions of life-span developmentalists (e.g., Hetherington & Baltes, 1988).

In some regards, the chapters considered together illustrate how much the field of adolescent development has changed in the past several decades. Today, most students of adolescence take for granted the contextualistic, life-span bent represented in this volume. But it is important to remember that, even as recently as 20 years ago, neither the ecological nor the life-span approach was especially influential in the study of adolescence. Until the late 1970s, the dominant paradigms in the study of adolescence were traditional psychological paradigms that deemphasized, if not outright ignored, the social context of the period, and drew firm boundaries around adolescence as a developmental stage best studied in isolation from childhood or adulthood.

Even a cursory skimming of the scientific journals of the 1950s, 1960s, and 1970s reveals that empirical research on adolescence at that time focused mainly on a small number of narrowly defined, decontextualized psychological questions: the development of logical or moral reasoning (almost always investigated from a Piagetian perspective), the development of identity (almost always from an Eriksonian perspective), or changes in youngsters' susceptibility to the social influence of parents versus peers (almost always from a social learning perspective). Rarely did one study change over time *within* the adolescent decade, and almost never did one study the links between adolescence and childhood or adulthood. No one ever asked about the broader context in which young people come to reason abstractly, develop a coherent sense of identity, or balance the demands of elders and agemates. Now, interestingly, one scarcely sees empirical research on formal operations, identity status, or parent–peer cross-pressures in the same scientific journals that gave so much coverage to these topics just a few decades ago. Is it possible that the pendulum has swung too far in the other direction?

The contextual and life-span approaches to the study of adolescence seem here to stay, at least for the time being. Their presence and significance may be temporary, and at some future point some commentator in my position may wonder—as I have here about the disappearance of research on formal operations, identity status, and cross-pressures—what happened to the studies of context and trajectory that so dominated adolescence research in the 1990s. But as long as the contexual and life-span approaches are with us at present, it is important to explore and examine some of the basic assumptions and constructs inherent in them and reflected in the chapters in this collection. That is my purpose in this brief commentary.

THE LOGIC OF ADOLESCENCE

The logic of adolescence is revealed in the origins of the word. Derived from the Latin, *adolescere*—to grow into maturity—adolescence connotes both change and purpose. Fundamentally, we view it as a period of transition, of growing *into,* rather than as a static time in the individual life span. By its very definition, adolescence is a period of preparation, defined less by its own essence and more by what follows it—maturity.

The definition of *adolescence* underscores two fundamental aspects of the period that need to be addressed in any comprehensive view of the era, and that are appropriately highlighted in this volume. First, in many respects, adolescence is about motion and momentum, about growing "into" something, about making a transition, and about getting from one point to another. This is not to say that adolescence is not interesting in its own right. Rather, it is to underscore that we cannot understand adolescence without examining what has come before it in the life span and what will follow it. This idea is captured in the notion of a *pathway*, or *developmental trajectory*. The second part of the definition emphasized here is that it implies an endpoint: maturity. Adolescence is not merely about motion for the sake of motion, or motion without direction. The psychosocial movement we call adolescence has a purpose, and that purpose is readying the individual—biologically, intellectually, emotionally, and socially—for adulthood. This aspect of the definition also underscores the need to look at pathways (rather than just movement) in adolescence. It also forces us to adopt a contextual viewpoint in our research and theorizing. Because the nature of adulthood and the definition of *maturity* vary from context to context, the nature of the preparation process must be contextually variable as well. Any intelligent perspective on adolescence must simultaneously capture both the sense of motion inherent in the period and the importance of recognizing contextual variability in the adolescent experience.

The psychosocial agenda of the period is shaped by a combination of the universal and the particular. The universal features of adolescence, such as biological maturation and cognitive growth, instigate change and impel the young person toward maturity. The particular features of adolescence—the specific circumstances under which a young person or a cohort of young people comes of age—provide a purpose for the period, however. They dictate the definition of psychosocial maturity, structure the pathways through which maturity is pursued, and determine, in large measure, whether the pursuit is successful. No discussion of the logic of adolescence is complete without a consideration of both sets of elements.

ON DEVELOPMENTAL TRAJECTORIES

The idea of the developmental trajectory, or pathway, is a useful heuristic device, but it is imperative that we not lose sight that it is simply heuristic, and not an objective reality. As Kagan (1980) and others have pointed out, Western thinkers are driven to find continuity in individual lives even when such continuity is difficult to document empirically. In our search to map out the developmental pathways into and through adolescence, we may fall prey to the same temptation. Thus, it is important to recognize that, even though adolescents actively structure their own experiences, they do not consciously follow pathways or trajectories as one might follow a map while on a journey. The *pathway* is a useful metaphor because we, as scientists, find it helpful to organize information about individuals' lives in a way that permits us to form the information into a coherent, organized pattern. In reality, individuals' lives probably are far less organized and continuous than we present them to be in the empirical stories we create about them.

As a heuristic, the notion of the developmental trajectory has the potential to integrate familiar aspects of interpersonal, intraindividual, and contextualistic perspectives on development. From the interpersonal perspective on adolescence, heavily influenced by social learning theory, models of the developmental trajectory take seriously the notion that the course of adolescents' lives is shaped by the social influences of those around them, including parents, peers, and other agents of socialization. These models implore us to better understand how adolescents are placed onto certain trajectories, but not others, and how forces in the proximal social environment maintain an individual on a particular course or steer him or her onto a new one.

To these interpersonal models one must add a hefty dose of intraindividual development, however, drawing on cognitive–developmental, psychoanalytic, or neoanalytic theories of adolescence. Adolescents are not passive objects launched on trajectories like projectiles fired from rifles, or buffeted about by the winds of social influence like billiard balls on a pool table. Rather, adolescents are active, changing agents who select and affect the environments in which they participate. In this regard, developmental trajectories are not fixed paths that are charted for the adolescent by others or by society, but routes toward an endpoint that are chosen, or even created, by an active, self-directed organism. Thus, intraindividual models of developmental trajectories demand that we ask how adolescents construct and create their trajectories.

From the contextualistic perspective, we add that the nature of the social influence an adolescent experiences and the opportunities and choices the individual selects are pursued within the constraints of a broader context that is bound by culture and history. The contextualistic perspective fills in certain gaps inherent in the interpersonal and intraindividual views of adolescence. The interpersonal model, with its focus on proximal processes of social influence (mainly parents and peers), fails to address how these proximal forces are shaped by broader social influences. As such, it is likely to overstate the influence of the immediate settings in which the adolescent lives. However, the intraindividual model, with its emphasis on internal processes of developmental change, does not pay sufficient attention to the objective conditions in the adolescent's ecology that genuinely constrain his or her developmental trajectory. Thus, within the intraindividual perspective, there is a tendency to cast the adolescent as an active constructor of his or her own development, with few limits on what he or she constructs. Contextual visions of the developmental trajectory attempt to redress these weaknesses.

What is a developmental trajectory, then, and how does one best incorporate the idea into research on adolescence? In my view, a developmental trajectory is a probabilistic pathway through time and space shaped simultaneously by three sets of factors: (a) characteristics of the developing adolescent, (b) influences of the immediate environment, and (c) opportunities and constraints inherent in the broader context. A comprehensive model of developmental pathways through adolescence must incorporate information about all three sets of influences. My vision of the adolescent's developmental trajectory, then, is not unlike that of a spaceship in flight: Its pathway is determined by the joint interaction of characteristics of the spaceship (e.g., the direction in which it was launched, the power of its thrust), characteristics of the immediate environment through which it travels (e.g., the gravitational pulls of the various objects in space can alter its course), and features of the larger solar system that contain both the ship and the immediate environment.

ON THE SOCIAL CONTEXT OF ADOLESCENCE

The chapters in this volume emphasize the evolving models of context that have come to play an important role in the study of adolescent development in recent decades. How has contextualism evolved in the study of adolescence? I see these models as having developed through five distinct phases.

I noted earlier that, until the late 1970s, studies of context were virtually nonexistent. The underlying assumption in most adolescent research, at least within the discipline of developmental psychology, was that context did not matter, and that the study of adolescence was best informed by a search for universals in development during the second decade of life. This was the first phase in the development of contextual models in the study of adolescence. Little regard was paid to differences among individuals in background characteristics that might affect the development or display of these universals. Thus, research on formal operations, identity development, peer-influence processes, parental socialization, and so on rarely took into account the contexts in which these developmental processes occurred. In general, the study of adolescent development was largely the study of the development of White, middle-class male adolescents, although this was more often than not a matter of convenience than of intentional sample restriction. To draw on an example from the research with which I am most familiar—adolescent socialization in the family—the typical approach would have been to look at the relation between some aspect of parenting (e.g., parental authority) and some aspect of adolescent adjustment (e.g., self-esteem), without any regard for the broader environment in which the adolescent or parent lived.

The second phase, which dominated the early 1980s and still has vestiges in the scientific literature today, was marked by an appreciation of contextual factors, but a misunderstanding of how to incorporate them into research designs. In this era of research, one assessed some aspect of context (typically some aspect of the adolescent's "social address") and controlled for it, either through selective sampling or statistical manipulation. The goal here was to identify and describe developmental universals in the adolescence "net" of contextual nuisance. In the typical design, one might look at the relation between two variables (again, for purposes of illustration, parental authority and adolescent self-esteem) after controlling for a third variable (e.g., parental education). This approach was assumed to provide an estimate of the relation between parental authority and self-esteem "uncontaminated" by potential confounding factors.

The third phase in the development of contextual models, which dominated most of the 1980s, was a focus on the immediate context of adolescent development in an attempt to specify the proximal processes through which significant others influenced adolescent behavior. Typically, a researcher would focus on one context at a time, and analyze the social exchanges taking place within it. During this era, for example, there was increasing popularity of family-interaction research, with an emphasis on the development and use of elaborate, microanalytic coding techniques designed to uncover reciprocal interactional processes. Similar steps were taken in studies of peer relationships and classroom interaction. Thus, one might look at the relation between parental authority and adolescent self-esteem, as well as the interactive process of decision making in the family, and how certain patterns of interpersonal exchanges affected, and were affected by, adolescent self-image.

These models of proximal processes set the stage for the fourth phase in the evolution of contextual models of adolescent development, which broadened the contextual landscape to include settings beyond the proximal environment of the family, peer group, or classroom. In these models, interchanges in the proximal environment were cast as mediating between some aspect of adolescent functioning and a more distal aspect of the broader ecology. Regression models, path models, and, later, structural-equation models dominated the scene in the late 1980s and early 1990s. In such models, an investigator might take a distal environmental variable—such as maternal employment, parental divorce, ethnicity, or socioeconomic status (SES)—and examine whether and how one or more proximal processes mediated the link between the distal variable and the adolescent outcome of interest. For instance, one might find that adolescents from divorced and nondivorced homes report different levels of self-esteem; one might then ask whether differences in patterns of parental authority in divorced versus nondivorced households mediate the relation between parental divorce and adolescent self-esteem. Such mediational models remain extremely popular in the study of adolescence today.

In the early 1990s, contextual research in adolescence entered a new phase, which is reflected in many of the chapters in this volume. This phase was characterized by two shifts. The first was the emergence of moderational models, in which contextual factors were assumed to moderate social-influence processes. Instead of asking whether certain proximal processes accounted for observed differences among adolescents from divorced and nondivorced families, or between minority and nonminority youngsters, for example, researchers began asking whether the operative processes of influence were different in divorced versus nondivorced families, or minority versus nonminority families. This strategy necessitates separating one's sample according to a contextual variable of interest and looking within these groups at the relevant proximal process. Thus, one might partition one's sample into divorced and nondivorced families and examine whether the correlation between parental authority and adolescent self-esteem differs in the two groups.

The second development in the evolution of contextual models of adolescence that took place in the early 1990s (and also reflected in this volume) involved the simultaneous investigation of adolescent development in multiple contexts. Researchers began to combine models of familial influence with those of peer influence, for example, and examined how proximal processes in these two settings interacted to influence the young person's development or behavior, either in an additive or multiplicative fashion. Thus, a researcher might ask how patterns of parental authority interact with some aspect of peer relationships (e.g., an adolescent's status in the peer group) to ultimately influence the young person's self-esteem.

Based on the chapters in this volume, it seems safe to say that, in the years to come, the field will continue to employ mediational, moderational, and multisetting models of contextual influence in the study of adolescent development. In the next decade, we can anticipate the integration of these three approaches into more comprehensive models of context that examine multiple interacting settings and different levels of analysis.

THE LIMITS OF "EMPTY" CONTEXTUALISM

If there is a common shortcoming in the chapters in this volume, it is the passion with which the authors have embraced contextualism and ignored the important contributions of the interpersonal and intraindividual approaches to the study of adolescence. In their race to understand the environment in which the adolescent comes of age, it seems to me that the chapter authors have, at times, overlooked what we have learned about (a) proximal processes of social influence in adolescence and (b) intraindividual development during the second decade. It is important to rediscover these bodies of work.

Although an important and heretofore neglected endeavor, mapping the social ecology of adolescence is not a substitute for understanding the interpersonal processes that link context and individual development over time. It is not sufficient to simply specify aspects of the proximal or distal environments in which adolescents live and link these features to aspects of adolescent functioning without examining the social and psychological processes that mediate these links. Yet there is a surprising absence of this level of analysis in current research on adolescence. The field needs more systematic discussion of basic social–psychological processes, such as imitation, social influence, social comparison, and social referencing. We need to keep in mind that any contextual influence must be mediated through some sort of interpersonal process, and we need to work toward the development of models that specify what these processes are and how they operate in adolescence.

The relative lack of consideration of intrapersonal processes in contemporary contextual models of adolescence is equally problematic. In our quest to better understand the context in which young people come of age, do we truly want to leave behind such basic concepts as identification, individuation, and attachment? What has happened to the study of cognitive dissonance, attribution, or expectation? Can we truly hope to have a comprehensive theory of adolescent development that ignores motivation, emotional expression, and cognitive development? I think not.

This is not a call for a return to the adolescence research of the 1970s—to decontextualized studies of formal operations or identity foreclosure. However, these bodies of work are necessary to include even within a largely contextualistic perspective on adolescence. Twenty years ago, we studied psychological processes in adolescence without regard for the context in which they occur. Today, all too often, we study the context of adolescence without considering the psychological processes that occur within it. There is a need to study developmental processes within context.

FUTURE DIRECTIONS

The chapters in this volume represent a giant step toward the integration of contextual models of development into the study of developmental trajectories in adolescence. Ultimately, however, I believe we must articulate a vision of the developmental trajectory that incorporates elements from the interpersonal and intraindividual traditions, as well as the contextual approach. From the interpersonal theorists, let us accept that the adolescent's pathway toward adulthood is not fixed in childhood, but continuously shaped by the social agents he or she encounters along the way. From the intraindividual theorists, let us embrace the idea that social influence in adolescence is not simply received, but selected, constructed, and shaped by an active, changing organism. Accordingly, developmental trajectories are not simply followed; to a large extent, they are created. From the contextualists, let us agree that both the content of the socialization encountered and the opportunities to forge one's own trajectory are context bound. These three notions suggest a number of basic implications for the design of policies and practices affecting young adolescents. First, the adolescent's pathway into adulthood is not fixed prior to adolescence, but subject to change depending on the nature of the adolescent's social interactions. This recognition indicates the need for policies that assist the individual adolescent, as well as help the social agents and institutions that touch young people's lives—perhaps most importantly, the family and the school. Second, adolescents actively shape their own developmental trajectories. This notion suggests that any policies designed to facilitate adolescent competence or well-being should take advantage of the young person's need for agency and self-direction; policies aimed at helping young people should empower them to make healthy choices and wise decisions, rather than make such choices and decisions for them. Finally, developmental trajectories are context bound. This implies that any interventions designed for young people should be sensitive to the diversity of the youth population and the circumstances under which young people come of age. Rather than insist that all policies for young people be forged in the universalistic tradition, a contextually sensitive approach begins from the premise that particular policies and practices are likely to have different effects (and different degrees of success) in different environments.

In conclusion, we need to recognize that developmental trajectories or pathways in adolescence are: (a) socially influenced by others in the adolescent's proximal environment, (b) actively pursued by the individual adolescent, and (c) contextually limited by the broader ecology. From a research perspective, one might reasonably ask what the potent processes of social influences are during adolescence and how these influences change over time, how the developing adolescent views and constructs experiences in the social world, and how the broader context moderates these processes of social influence and social construction. These are the questions for future research that emerge from the chapters in this collection. Their investigation will require a new integration of intrapersonal, interpersonal, and contextual perspectives on the period.

REFERENCES

Bronfenbrenner, U. (1979). *The ecology of human development: Experiments by nature and design.* Cambridge, MA: Harvard University Press.
Hetherington, E., & Baltes, P. (1988). Child psychology and life-span development. In E. Hetherington, R. Lerner, & M. Perlmutter (Eds.), *Child development in life-span perspective* (pp. 1–20). Hillsdale, NJ: Lawrence Erlbaum Associates.
Kagan, J. (1980). Perspectives on continuity. In O. Brim & J. Kagan (Eds.), *Constancy and change in human development* (pp. 1–42). Cambridge, MA: Harvard University Press.

Author Index

255

Blum, R. W., 223, 232
Blyth, D., 7, 12, 63, 68, 74, 236, 238, 239, 242
Bolger, N., 54
Boorman, S. A., 47, 56
Bourdieu, P., 178, 195
Boyer, E., 213, 232
Boykin, W., 90, 114
Braddock, J. H., 88, 96, 99, 112, 114
Brannon, B., 223, 232
Breiger, R. L., 47, 56
Brener, L., 136
Brim, O. G., 73
Brittain, C. V., 151, 173
Broderick, P., 109, 114
Brodt, S. E., 212, 232
Brody, G., 147
Bronfenbrenner, U., 6, 8, 10, 11, 46, 54, 79, 89, 114, 120, 124, 151, 173, 202, 205, 207, 214, 222, 224, 230, 232, 238, 242, 245, 253
Brookins, G. K., 89, 117, 137
Brookover, W. B., 109, 114
Brooks-Gunn, J., 3, 11, 121, 136
Brown, B. B., 7, 10, 11, 40, 54, 81, 105, 117, 151–154, 159, 170–173, 197, 198, 200, 201, 203, 205–207, 222, 233
Brown, D. R., 108, 109, 114
Brown, W., 115, 117
Bryk, A. S., 57, 73, 88, 116
Buchanan, L., 7, 11, 51, 54, 81, 198, 207
Buhrmester, D., 172, 174
Bundis, C. D., 212, 232
Burchard, J., 115, 118
Burchard, N., 115, 118
Burgeson, R., 7, 12
Burt, R. S., 47, 54
Burton, L. M., 10, 120–127, 134, 136, 138, 139–141, 144–146
Busch-Rossnagel, N. A., 3, 12
Bush, D. M., 121, 136
Bushwall, P. L., 159, 173
Butler, M., 34

C

Cairns, R. B., 9, 17, 33, 35, 42–45, 48–54, 69, 73, 75, 80
Cairns, B. D., 9, 17, 33, 35, 42, 45, 48, 50–54, 75, 80
Campbell, E. Q., 109, 114
Carlsmith, J. M., 159, 173
Carlton-Ford, S., 7, 12
Carnegie Council on Adolescent Development, 2, 3, 11
Carter, R. L., 17, 33
Caspi, A., 4, 9, 11, 36, 54, 63, 72, 73, 75, 77, 79, 80, 81, 83, 140, 141, 146, 147, 239
Castro, J. J., 64, 74
Cattell, R. B., 32, 33, 69, 73
Ceci, S. J., 202, 205, 207
Centers for Disease Control, 212, 232
Cernkovich, S. A., 48, 55
Cichetti, D., 117
Clark, M. L., 105, 106, 114
Clark, R. M., 87, 89, 100, 107, 108, 114, 122, 136
Clasen, D. R., 81, 154, 173
Clausen, J. S., 4, 11, 90, 114
Coelho, G. V., 136
Cohen, A. K., 35, 55
Cohen, J. M., 42, 55
Coie, J. D., 48, 53, 55
Coleman, J. S., 57, 73, 109, 114, 119, 136, 151, 173, 181, 195
Coles, R. B., 121, 125, 136
Colfer, P., 87, 117
Comerci, G., 223, 232
Conger, K. J., 120, 136
Conger, R. D., 120, 136, 153, 174
Coppotelli, H. A., 48–49, 55
Coutts, L. M., 64, 74
Crockett, L. J., 1–3, 10, 11, 75, 76, 146, 147
Crouter, A. C., 1, 7, 11, 76, 144, 147

D

Dale, R. R., 57, 73
Danziger, S. K., 95, 114
Darling, N., 152, 158, 174, 200, 207, 222, 233
Davis, A., 122, 136
Delugach, J. D., 49, 55
Dent, C., 223, 232
Dilworth-Anderson, P., 123, 135, 136
Dishion, T. J., 43, 56, 159, 172, 173, 205, 207
Dodge, K. A., 48, 49, 53, 55
Dollard, J., 122, 136
Domhoff, G. W., 91, 114
Dornbusch, S. M., 105, 117, 119, 120, 136, 137, 152, 158, 159, 173, 200, 207, 222, 233

Dorr, A., 114
Downey, G., 54
Dubow, E. F., 236, 242
Dubrow, N., 120, 126, 136
Duncan, G., 136
Dunn, J., 82
Dunphy, D., 38
Dwyer, K., 223, 232

E

Eastman, G. E., 223, 232
Ebata, A., 10, 235, 239, 242
Eccles, J. S., 7, 11, 81, 172, 174, 198, 207
Eckert, P., 10, 82, 152–154, 170, 174, 179, 195, 197–199, 207
Eder, D., 41, 55, 153, 174
Edwards, C. A., 50, 51, 55
Edwards, O., 88, 114
Eicher, S. A., 154, 173
Eichorn, D. H., 110, 114
Elder, G. H., 4, 8, 11, 77, 81, 83, 88, 102, 109, 114, 120, 136
Elley, W. B., 61, 73
Elliott, D. S., 2, 3, 11, 15, 22, 23, 33, 35, 48, 55
Elliott, G. R., 11, 119, 121, 135–138, 173, 174, 207
Entwistle, D. R., 152, 174
Epps, E. G., 88, 94, 114
Erikson, E., 38
Esbensen, F., 15, 16, 22, 33
Eyferth, K., 120, 137
Eysenck, H. J., 32, 33
Eysenck, S. B. G., 32, 33

F

Farber, N. B., 95, 114
Farley, R., 88, 113, 125, 136
Farmer, T. W., 50, 55
Farrington, D. P., 15, 33
Feather, N. T., 57, 73
Feiring, C., 48, 55
Feldman, S. S., 11, 119, 121, 135–138, 153, 172–174, 207
Festinger, L., 46, 55
Fine, M., 102, 107, 108, 114, 115
Flanagan, C., 7, 11, 81, 198, 207
Flay, B., 223, 232
Freud, A., 151, 174

Foch, T. T., 12
Fordham, S., 105, 115, 141, 147
Freeman, R. B., 108, 115
Fuligni, A. J., 172, 174
Furman, W., 154, 174
Furstenberg, F. F., 92, 115

G

Galambos, N. L., 223, 232
Garbarino, J., 120, 126, 136, 238, 242
Garibaldi, A. M., 100, 106, 111, 115
Gariépy, J.-L., 51, 54
Garmezy, N., 5, 11, 12, 87, 90, 104, 108, 115, 116
Gary, L. E., 108, 109, 114
Geary, P. A., 100, 115
Gest, S., 51, 54
George, L., 123, 124, 135
Gibbs, J. T., 119, 125, 136
Gibson, K. R., 136
Ginsburg, A. L., 100, 108, 115
Giordano, P. C., 48, 55, 63, 73
Giroux, B., 15, 16, 34
Glaser, B., 127, 136
Glor-Scheib, S., 89, 116
Goodlad, J. I., 117
Gordon, E., 88, 115
Gottlieb, G., 9, 11
Graber, J. H., 121, 136
Graham, S., 88, 109, 112, 115
Grasmiek, H., 20, 33
Gray, G., 83
Gross, R. T, 159, 173
Gullotta, T. P., 173
Gurin, P., 94, 115

H

Haan, N., 114
Hallinan, M. T., 40, 41, 55
Halverson, C. F., 41, 56
Hamburg, B. A., 121, 136
Hamburg, D. A., 2, 3, 11, 136
Hannan, M. T., 34
Hansen, W. B., 223, 232
Hanson, S. L., 100, 108, 115
Hare, B., 112, 115
Harter, S., 3, 11, 142, 147
Hartup, W. W., 35, 55
Hastorf, A. H., 159, 173

Subject Index

impulsive, 62
inattentive, 62
juvenile delinquency, *see Delinquent behavior*
misconduct/misbehavior, 80, 81, 99, 171, 223
norm-violations, 64, 65, 68
stealing/theft, 21, 22, 24, 26–31, 160
temper tantrums, 76
vandalism, 22
Behavioral changes, 78, 82
Behavioral dispositions, 3, 78, 81, 82, 90, 140–141, 153
Behavioral genetics, 8
Beliefs, 37, 53, 113, 128, 152, 176, 178, 185, 197–199, 206, 216, *see also Religious beliefs; Family, beliefs*
Biological
changes, 97, 247
predisposition, 5
Black, *see African-American*

C

"Chance encounters," 4, 78, 79
Changes experienced by adolescents
in family structure, 78
cumulative, 78
death, 78, 130
illness, 78
geographic location, 78
establishment of own household, 78
college, 78
work force participation, 78
marriage, 78
unemployment, 78, 130
Child care, 92, 95, 108, 177
Church, 87, 93, 94, 104, 108–109, 129, 221
Classism, 131
Classroom
activities, 50, 51, 92, 94, 97, 98, 112, 113, 198
as a context for development, 40, 97, 100, 111, 250
disruptions in, 92
structure of, 92, 97, 112, 113, 198
Cluster analysis, 16, 18, 19
Co-development, 198
Cognitive developmental perspective, 248
Cohort, 240, 241, 242, 247
Collaboration, 235, 236, 238

College, 1, 40, 87, 95, 99–103, 181–186, 194, *see also Transition, to college*
Community(-ies), 10, 51, 89, 91, 95, 105, 109, 155, 176, 180, 181, 182, 191, 198–199, 211, 213–218, 222, 229, 230, 237–239
activities, 23, 29, 31
African-American, 103, 105, 108, 124, 128, 132
as a context for development, 10, 87, 90, 103, 120–121, 175, 198, 212, 215, 224, 235, 240, 242
impoverished, 93, 120, 133, 198, 199, *see also Inner-city; Ghetto*
leaders, 90, 103, 127, 128, 133, 216–218, 220, 221, 239
organizations, 90, 103, 239, 108, 217, 218, 220
needs and concerns, 216, 231, 235, 236
"non-shared community environment," 239
profiles of, 127
resources, *see Resources, community*
Communities of practice, 175–180, 182–185, 189, 192–194, 197, 198, 205
Community-based action research, 10, 211, 214, 222, 230, 235, 238, 242
Community psychologists, 214
Competence, 41, 88, 94, 102, 104, 108, 109, 253
Competition, 180, 181, 187, 188, 192
Context, 2, 6, 7, 8, 77, 80, 120, 235, 238, 240, 247, 249–253, *see also Classroom; Community; Environment; Family; School; Neighborhood*
cultural, 6, 89–90, 104, 110, 141, 142, 215, 248
economic, 88, 119, 120, 122, 140, 146, 215
historical, 6, 121, 140, 239, 240, 248
interactions among, 6, 7, 38–40, 151, 198–207, 224, 227, 229, 251
social, 3, 5, 9, 10, 52, 75, 79, 81, 110, 119–122, 124, 133–135, 140, 146, 152–155, 170–172, 211, 215, 245, 246, 248, 249
societal, 105, 107, 110
Continuity, *see Development, continuity in*
Contraceptives, 192, 193
Cooperation, 90, 190
Cooperative Extension, 212, 216, 218, 220, 221, 230

O

Outreach, 211
Opportunities, *see Adolescent opportunities*

P

Parenting, 37, 38, 40, 78, 91, 104–105, 107,
124, 151–154, 158–172, 203, 204,
249, 250, 251
  discipline, 124, 144, 159, 172
  education, 237
  style, 10, 152, 158, 160, 197, 200–203,
  205, 206, 222
Parents, 93, 122, 212, 213, 215, 217, 218,
221, 230, 237, 238, 240
  choices for adolescents, 38–40, 79, 80,
  158–159
  communication with adolescents, 217, 221
  concern by, 100, 218, 223
  divorce of, *see Divorce*
  employment situation, 7, 61
  encouragement by, 100, 152, 158, 159
  expectations, 45, 59–60, 97, 184, 200, 223
  influence on adolescents, 7, 36, 38–40,
  151, 153, 155, 162, 164, 168–172,
  192, 198, 199, 201, 206, 217, 246,
  248, 249, 251, 253
  involvement with adolescents, 158, 221
  involvement with schools, 90, 152, 159
  monitoring by, 23, 29, 31, 32, 40, 98, 107,
  152, 159, 204, 220, 223–229, 239,
  241, 242
  peer networks of, 124
  remarriage of, *see Remarriage*
  supervision by, 98, 104, 199, 223
Pattern-analytic approach, *see Cluster
  analysis; Personological approach;
  Typological approach*
Patterns of behavior, 2, 3, 100
Peer group(s), 177, 250, *see also
  Relationships, friendships*
  age heterogeneity of, 36, 181, 184, 192
  as a context for development, 6, 7, 10,
  23, 36, 37, 40, 48, 51–53, 79–82, 87,
  96, 97, 99, 101, 104–106, 108, 121,
  151–154, 160, 162, 164, 171, 172,
  201, 202, 246, 248–251
  assessment of, 37, 46–51
  attitudes of, 37, 43, 48, 100, 152, 153
  cliques, 197

crowds, 40, 151–157, 160–166, 168–172,
197–206
  delinquency of, 23, 28, 30, 31, 33, 35, 36,
  45, 48, 52, 63–65, 81, 152, 153
  development of, 37, 38, 41, 44–46, 51–53
  filtering function of, 154, 170, 198–201,
  206
  homophily within, 42, 43, 46, 52, 102
  membership in, 35, 38, 46, 51, 52, 81,
  153, 251
  niche-picking, *see Niche-picking*
  older, 36, 68
  processes, 42, 44, 51–53
  reinforcement of initial dispositions, 48,
  81, 82, 170
  selection of, 1, 9, 52, 80, 82, 103, 153
  sexual pressures from, 63, 68, 72
  social pressures from, 36–37, 44, 45, 63,
  68, 72, 96, 98, 151, 153, 154, 172, 246
  structure of, 37, 38, 41, 42, 44–48, 51, 52
"Perfectibility," 142, 143
Person characteristics, 2, 5–6, 8–9, 17, 77,
79, 80–82, 90, 96, 99, 104, 106, 112,
152, 207, 224, 229, 248–249
Person-environment fit, 10, 36–37, 43, 45,
80–82, 153, 199, 206
Person-environment interactions, 6, 8, 9, 17,
90, 96–97, 99, 109, 110, 111, 199,
203–206, 225–229, 248, 253
  conceptualizations of, 8, 96–97
  methodological difficulties, 8, 239–240
Personality, 5, 6, 76, 77, 140–142, 95
  individual differences in, 141
  coherence in, 108, 109
"Personological" approach, 16, 17, 76, 77,
143, 144, 198
Piagetian perspective, 246
"Planful competence," 90
Plasticity, 3
Policy, 2, 10, 58, 72, 87, 90, 95, 109–113,
212–215, 217, 219, 220, 222,
229–231, 235–237
Poverty, 8, 10, 89, 90, 93, 95, 97, 110, 121,
125, 128
Prejudice, 90, 105, *see also Racism*
Prenatal care, 92
Prevention, 46, 218, 220, 237, 241, *see also
  Intervention*
Problem behaviors, *see Behavior problems*
Prosocial behavior, 34, 151, 154, 155, 158,
160, 164–166, 168, 170–172
Prospective study, 15